C Boyer

Experiential Organizational Behavior

C Boyer

Theodore T. Herbert
University of North Carolina

Peter Lorenzi
University of Kansas

Experiential Organizational Behavior

Macmillan Publishing Co., Inc.
New York

Collier Macmillan Publishers
London

Copyright © 1981, Theodore T. Herbert

Printed in the United States of America

All rights reserved. No part of this book may be reproduced or transmitted in any form or by any means, electronic or mechanical, including photocopying, recording, or any information storage and retrieval system, without permission in writing from the Publisher.

Macmillan Publishing Co., Inc.
866 Third Avenue, New York, New York 10022

Collier Macmillan Canada, Ltd.

Library of Congress Cataloging in Publication Data
Main entry under title:

Experiential organizational behavior.

1. Organizational behavior—Addresses, essays, lectures. I. Herbert, Theodore T. II. Lorenzi, Peter.
HD58.7.E96 1981   302.3′5   80-22327
ISBN 0-02-353620-9

Printing: 1 2 3 4 5 6 7 8   Year: 1 2 3 4 5 6 7 8

iv

Foreword

This book is based on the premise that the study of organizational behavior (OB) requires an experiential perspective. The authors believe that an experiential approach to the study of organizational behavior provides students with tangible, personal examples of the abstract (to them at least!) theories of OB which will allow them to identify and analyze behavior and to assimilate and integrate theoretical approaches.

Experiential exercises complement theories and models; they do not replace one another. The role of the professor shifts from one of a lecturer or provider of information to a facilitator and resource person. In a sense, the professor spends less time on what we traditionally call *teaching* and now focuses her efforts on student *learning*. But we also caution against *over-reliance* on experiential modes of learning; exercises are not the whole story. The exercises provide a focal starting point, a concrete base for departure for traveling through what can often be viewed by students as a complex, pedantic, and tortuous path from one fuzzy theory to the next. Exercises are reality checks, review sessions, or digestive tracts in the very difficult process of introducing students to the nature of the organizational animal.

We emphasize three interrelated modes of experiential learning:

Group problem-solving allows each student to solve problems by sharing his or her knowledge, opinions, and interpretations of theories in a process that emphasizes the role of interpersonal communication and persuasion. An excellent example of group problem solving entails a "survival" exercise where students jointly struggle to determine the "best" answer to a demanding problem.

Case analysis in a group setting allows for a greater exchange of information and individual perceptions, we believe, than a full class discussion allows. Typically, each group must produce a decision or recommendation that can be (1) defended in a full class forum or (2) written up for subsequent evaluation by the professor.

Role playing allows each student to better understand the behavior of others by "walking in their shoes" and seeing the problem from the viewpoint of another person.

In addition to "experiential" materials, the text includes articles, essays, editorials, and the like, included as food for thought. Intended to provoke discussion and additional perspectives on the nature of managerial work, this resource material is intended to represent both the philosophy and behaviors of managerial life.

The book you are about to read is the product of a lengthy managerial process. *Experiential Organizational Behavior* commenced with a magnanimous expression of faith by Ken MacLeod of Macmillan. Janet Ward assisted in the preliminary compilation of materials, collected from a diverse group of cooperative authors, each of whom is identified within the text. Larry Pate and Frank Pinet offered excellent professional input and Connie Brooks Swayze provided great typing services, often at unreasonable hours. Bobby Freidmann, Sue Lammers Richeson, and many other students added insights to the whole process.

David Forgione and Edward Neve, our editor and production supervisor, respectively, at Macmillan kept a steady hand on the entire process and they helped an uninitiated junior author through some demanding periods.

Finally, the entire project could never have occurred without the skill, dedication, cooperation, and good humor of Hank Sims. He has been with us since Day One. This is the second time the junior author has been able to thank Hank formally; it will probably not be the last time either.

Peter Lorenzi
Lawrence KS

Contents

FOREWORD — v

SECTION I
Introduction

1. BELL & PAPER — 2

2. PERFORMANCE, OR ELSE — 3
Wall Street Journal

3. OVERDRIVEN EXECS — 5
Wall Street Journal

4. THE MANAGER'S JOB — 10
Henry Mintzberg

5. WORKING WOMAN — 31
Niki Scott

6. MANAGER'S JOURNAL — 33
Wall Street Journal

SECTION II
The Formal Organizational System:
Technology and Structure

7. CHANGE-OF-WORK PROCEDURES — 38
Norman F. Maier

8. THE LAB TECHNICIAN'S LAMENT — 42
Peter Lorenzi

9. JOB DESIGN PREFERENCES   44
Peter Lorenzi

10. DRAWING AN ORGANIZATIONAL CHART   46
Henry P. Sims, Jr.

11. THE TECHNOLOGICAL IMPERATIVE   48
Peter Lorenzi

12. STRUCTURE IS NOT ORGANIZATION   49
Robert H. Waterman, Jr., Thomas J. Peters, Julien R. Phillips

13. JOB ANALYSIS AND DESIGN   64
Antone F. Alber, Henry P. Sims, Jr., Andrew D. Szilagyi, Jr.

SECTION III
The Individual As a System

14. PARABLE   72
Anonymous

15. TEACHING HOW TO COPE WITH WORKPLACE CONFLICT   73
Business Week

16. PYGMALION IN MANAGEMENT   77
J. Sterling Livingston

17. SETTING INDIVIDUAL OBJECTIVES   92
E. Allen Slusher & Henry P. Sims, Jr.

18. PERFORMANCE APPRAISAL AND THE DESIGN OF WORK   97
Peter Lorenzi

19. VALUE SYSTEMS: MANAGERIAL ATTITUDES AND BEHAVIOR   98
Patrick Suessmuth & Marit Steger

20. HOW TO MAKE A POINT LOGICALLY AND CLEARLY   105
Elizabeth Brenner

21. ANALYSIS OF JOB-RELATED STRESS   107
James E. Gibson, John Ivancevich & James Donnelly

SECTION IV
The Social System

22. GROUP RANKING TASK: SUBARCTIC SURVIVAL   112
Experiential Learning Methods

23. UNION OFFICIAL   119
Robert Schrank

24. FURNITURE FACTORY   124
Robert Schrank

25. MACHINIST   126
Robert Schrank

26. FALSE PROMISES   129
Stanley Aronowitz

27. SPEEDIER CHICKENS   134
Wall Street Journal

28. A NEW LOOK AT MANAGERIAL DECISION MAKING   138
Victor H. Vroom

29. LEADERSHIP: AN OPERANT APPROACH   151
Henry P. Sims, Jr.

30. LEADERSHIP: SAD FACTS AND SILVER LININGS   156
Thomas J. Peters

SECTION V
Modification and Integration Processes

31. ANNUAL SALARY EVALUATION   170
Edward E. Lawler III

32. INFLUENCE SYSTEMS IN ORGANIZATIONS: 174
LEADERSHIP STYLES
Fremont Kast & James Rosensweig

33. ORGANIZATIONAL CHANGE: MUNICIPAL LIGHT   182
Fremont Kast & James Rosensweig

Contents

34. THE MOVING DILEMMA 192
Peter Lorenzi

35. ON THE FOLLY OF REWARDING A 193
WHILE HOPING FOR B
Steven Kerr

36. THE PROMOTION DECISION 209
Peter Lorenzi

37. A NEW LEADERSHIP POSITION 212
James E. Gibson, John Ivancevich & James Donnelly

SECTION VI
Organizational Behavior: Perspective for Tomorrow

38. THE SWING TO PRACTICALITY IN THE B-SCHOOLS 216
Business Week

39. CAPITALIZING ON SOCIAL CHANGE 220
Business Week

40. SOCIOLOGIST 225
Robert Schrank

41. NEW BENEFITS FOR NEW LIFESTYLES 236
Business Week

42. RULES OF THUMB 240
Peter Lorenzi

43. 1995: THE YEAR IN REVIEW 241
Peter Lorenzi

Experiential Organizational Behavior

Introduction

1

Bell & Paper

1. BELL ONE

2. BELL TWO

3. PAPER ONE

<table>
<tr><td rowspan="2" colspan="2"></td><td colspan="2" align="center">Worker's Behavior</td></tr>
<tr><td align="center">Performance</td><td align="center">Nonperformance</td></tr>
<tr><td rowspan="2">Managerial
Strategy</td><td>Apply</td><td></td><td></td></tr>
<tr><td>Withdraw</td><td></td><td></td></tr>
</table>

2

Performance, or Else

Every now and then, we hear someone assert that there is no reason why a government entity cannot perform some task as well or better than a private entity. Indeed it is sometimes true. Both are merely groups of people; the government group might be highly skilled and motivated; the private one dull and sloppy.

But in the real world there are a number of reasons why private organizations typically outperform public organizations. The reasons deserve exploration at a time of rising disenchantment with the performance of government; if we are to change government it would be good to know what about it really needs to be changed.

The fundamental difference, without a doubt, is competition. The private organizations that perform best are those that are under some form of external pressure, usually competition from some other private organization. The managers face a real risk of failure, of loss, of reduced status. That risk, plus potential rewards, motivates them to push themselves and their employes towards higher performance and greater efficiency.

Public entities, by and large, function as monopolies. Their managers and their employes usually have the normal human desire to be useful members of society. But there are few external pressures for efficiency and discipline.

Now the effects of this can be fairly benign as long as the public sector is a relatively small part of the work-performing economy. But when its relative size expands—as has happened dramatically in recent years—and as it is asked to take on more and more tasks and as its work force becomes increasingly unionized and demanding of rewards unrelated to performance, the public sector's inefficiency takes on real importance. At some point there is a day of reckoning, such as the one New York City now faces, where there is no longer a ghost of a chance of raising the kind of money needed to keep the ponderous enterprise going.

The question then boils down to two parts: Can government be taken out of tasks it performs badly; or, in the absence of that, can it be subjected to

Reprinted by permission of *The Wall Street Journal.* © Dow Jones & Company, Inc. (1975). All Rights Reserved.

competition or other types of external pressures that compel better performance? The answer, quite simply, is yes—but only when Congressmen, state legislatures and city councils come to realize that their fundamental obligation is to the taxpayers and the citizenry rather than to the government entities they are supposed to be supervising.

We can cite any number of examples of how public entities can be put under greater pressure: The Postal Service could be shorn of its monopoly on first-class mail delivery; Amtrak could be relieved of its federal subsidy and thus forced to shape up or sell out; federal, state and local services could often be put on a voucher basis so that market competition could select the best methods of supply.

In other words, the public sector, its managers and its employes can be subjected, to a marked degree, to competitive pressures similar to those of the private sector. The notion that this would result in breaches of propriety or ethical standards or in organizational chaos, is largely a myth.

Ultimately, however, this becomes not a problem of analysis or logic, but of political forces. There are really few people who doubt that competition encourages performance and efficiency. But there are plenty of pressures on Congress, state legislatures, and city councils to coddle government entities. New York is a perfect example of a city where those pressures have overwhelmed the interests of the ordinary taxpayer.

A proper public perception of the political problem must begin with the recognition that government has fundamental incapacities for performing economic tasks well. It must then recognize that a continued slump into mass economic inefficiency will thwart the nation's expectations of rising living standards. With that recognition it is then time to tell the politicians to get better performance, or get out.

Issues

1. Define (1) public organization and (2) private organization. Are there other types of organizations in our society?
2. Describe the different purposes of public and private organizations.
3. How do public organizations' goals differ from private organizations' goals?
4. How are public and private organizations similar?
5. How does competition affect behavior?

George Getschow

Staff Reporter of THE WALL STREET JOURNAL

3

Overdriven Execs

Some Middle Managers Cut Corners to Achieve High Corporate Goals

Pressure to Keep Output Up Led to a Secret Speedup In a GM Assembly Line

How Heinz Got Into a Pickle

To hear some middle managers there tell it, the "pressure-cooker" atmosphere at Pittsburgh's H.J. Heinz Co. wasn't confined to the concern's steamy food-processing plants.

"When we didn't meet our growth targets, the top brass really came down on us," recalls a former marketing official at the company's huge Heinz U.S.A. division. "And everybody knew that if you missed the targets enough, you were out on your ear."

In this environment, some harried managers apparently resorted to deceptive bookkeeping when they couldn't otherwise meet profit goals set by the company's top executives. Invoices were misdated and payments to suppliers were made in advance—sometimes to be returned later in cash—all with the aim, insiders say, of showing the sort of smooth profit growth that would please top management and impress securities analysts.

Annual Meeting Delayed

Today, Heinz officials won't comment on the profit-juggling practices or on what led to them until an investigation is completed by the board of directors' audit committee. However, what began as an attempt to satisfy de-

Reprinted by permission of *The Wall Street Journal*, © Dow Jones & Company, Inc. (1979). All Rights Reserved.

manding superiors undoubtedly has tarnished the image of one of the country's corporate stalwarts: The Heinz annual meeting has been delayed and the outside auditors' opinion of the company's fiscal-1979 report has been withheld until the juggling scheme's precise effect—currently estimated at a cumulative $8.5 million—on previously reported Heinz earnings is determined.

Whether at Heinz or at any of thousands of other U.S. companies, pressure to achieve goals is, of course, an everyday fact of life. Properly applied—through threat of punishment or promise of reward—such pressure can motivate employes to turn in their maximum performance. Sometimes, though, corporate goals are set too high or are simply unreasonable. Then, an employe often confronts a hard choice—to risk being branded incompetent by telling superiors that they ask too much, or to begin taking unethical or illegal shortcuts.

A certain amount of tension is desirable," explains Paul Lawrence, professor of organizational behavior at the Harvard Business School. "But at many companies the pressures to perform are so intense and the goals so unreasonable that some middle managers feel the only way out is to bend the rules, even if it means compromising personal ethics."

Painful Results

Bent rules or broken laws, in turn, can lead to painful problems for companies. At some, as in the case of Heinz, the result is public embarrassment. But at others, pressure-induced managerial misconduct has brought product-liability and shareholder lawsuits, union troubles, government investigations and even criminal charges. Still other companies, worried that they might become involved in such problems, are devising codes of conduct for employes.

Middle managers, experts say, are the most likely members of the corporate hierarchy to confront the ethical dilemmas that can arise when the dictum goes out to meet company objectives. Unlike top executives, these managers often have little say in how such goals are set; yet unlike production-line workers, whose unions protect them from retribution for occasional shortcomings, a middle manager's future rides almost solely on his ability to serve up whatever the boss demands.

What's more, many experts predict that if the economy slides into a recession, the pressure on middle managers to meet increasingly tough goals will intensify, as will the probability of legal and ethical conflicts. "When a manager feels his job or his division's survival is at stake," Harvard's Prof. Lawrence observes, "the corporation's standards of business conduct are apt to be sacrificed."

Consider the incident at Dorsey Corp.'s glass-container plant in Gulfport, Miss. Manager William Tate, aware that the aging facility's output was falling behind that of other company plants, began to fear that Dorsey would close his plant and throw him and 300 other employes out of work. According to the company, Mr. Tate secretly started altering records and eventually inflated the value of the plant's production by about 33%.

Janitor Blows Whistle

The overreporting was discovered when a janitor, ignoring Mr. Tate's order to burn the actual records, instead hid the documents behind a chicken coop and showed them to company auditors visiting on an inspection tour. Mr. Tate was fired, and Dorsey Corp. was forced to restate downward its 1977 and 1978 earnings to reflect the production discrepancy.

Mr. Tate refuses to discuss the matter. But his wife, Gayle, says her husband was under "constant pressure" to raise the plant's production. "Bill knew that as long as he kept production up, he and his men had a job. But when it fell, that was it," she says.

John Pollock, Dorsey's president and chairman, doesn't disagree that managers such as Mr. Tate are under pressure to turn in a better performance each year "because our stockholders expect and deserve continuing improvement." But he does deny that the company routinely fires managers who don't meet production goals. Ironically, Mr. Pollock adds that Dorsey never had any intention of closing the plant or of dismissing Mr. Tate.

"He was a hard-working guy, and his production was good," Mr. Pollock says of his former plant manager. "There's really no logical explanation for his behavior. Perhaps he felt he was the only guy who could save the plant and the jobs of his workers. But if that's the case, he was a false messiah, because he was under no more pressure than other managers except in his own mind."

While pressure to increase profit is as old as the business world itself, that pressure nowadays is often intensified by government regulations. Sometimes, in fact, middle managers discover that compliance with new laws means falling short of other corporate goals. What can happen next is illustrated by a Ford Motor Co. incident that, although it occurred more than seven years ago, is still a textbook example of a manager's dilemma.

Then, certain Ford managers, worried that many of the company's 1973-model cars would flunk the government's emission standards that year, performed unauthorized "maintenance" on engines undergoing federal certification tests. The tinkering was discovered after a computer analyst noticed that some unscheduled maintenance had been jotted down in company records submitted to the Environmental Protection Agency. Although Ford maintained that its top management wasn't aware of the test tampering, the company did agree to pay $7 million in criminal and civil penalties to settle the matter.

Harvey Copp, a former Ford official who was then in charge of emission testing and who brought the tampering incident to the company's attention, today contends that senior Ford officers were pressuring middle managers to get the engines certified. "If they failed," Mr. Copp explains, "it would have been impossible for Ford to meet its ambitious production and earnings goals that year."

While Mr. Copp emphasizes that top Ford executives didn't condone the test tampering, he does think that they "created the environment" for it to occur. "When senior management puts the squeeze on, it encourages short-cuts," he says.

Not Enough Questions?

Others agree that top executives must share some of the blame for middle managers' illegal or unethical behavior. "There's a tendency for top management at many companies to keep pushing for the numbers without bothering to ask their managers how they got them," says Harry Levinson, a management consultant in Cambridge, Mass. "And when top management doesn't ask, lower management figures anything goes as long as they're meeting their targets."

Such thinking apparently sparked discord at a big Chevrolet truck plant in Flint, Mich., where three plant managers installed a secret control box in a supervisor's office last year to override the control panel that governs the speed of the assembly line. With the secret box, they were able to speed up the assembly line—a serious violation of the General Motors Corp. contract with the United Auto Workers—and thus increase production. One of the managers explains how the hidden box originated:

"At Chevrolet, we're given a production goal each week that's predicated on the assumption that everything will go perfectly. The problem is that on an assembly line, nothing ever does. There's always a conveyor breakdown or high absenteeism or something. As a result, we were constantly missing our targets, and the bosses were putting pressure on us to do something about it.

"We tried to explain our problems to higher-ups in the company, but we were told, 'I don't care how you do it—just do it.' Given our predicament, we felt the control panel was the only way we could make up for the excessive downtime we were experiencing."

Downtime Disappeared

With the aid of the hidden controls, the managers soon began meeting their production goals—and winning praise from their superiors. Says the manager: "They had to know we were speeding up the line, because they could see in their reports that we suddenly didn't have any downtime. But they never asked questions, so while we knew what we were doing was wrong ethically, we figured it must have been okay in the eyes of the company."

GM denies this and says its top management wasn't aware of the secret box. Beyond that, the company declines comment. However, the UAW workers who discovered the secret speedup and later won $1 million in back pay from GM say they won't soon forget the matter. "It created considerable ill will toward GM managers that will probably linger for years," says Samuel Duncan, a local UAW official in Flint. The three supervisors were temporarily suspended and later transferred to other GM production plants.

Reacting to publicity given corporate payoffs here and abroad and the stricter laws that followed, many companies have introduced in the past decade detailed codes of conduct for employes. Though aimed mostly at proscribing illegal payments to politicians or insider-trading violations of securities laws, many of these codes also spell out what is and isn't ethical in the normal course of business. Thus, middle managers presumably have less reason to step over the line.

But some companies, stung by the consequences of middle managers' wrongdoing, now are going further. They are trying to make sure that in motivating people, they don't create an atmosphere conducive to unethical behavior.

One such company is Mead Corp., which in 1976 found itself among 23 folding-box companies indicted on charges of price fixing. The charges, to which Mead pleaded no contest, stemmed from activities among some of the company's middle managers and came as "a shocker" to top management, a spokesman says.

Since then, Mead has reevaluated the way it motivates its managers. Among other things, it has begun involving middle managers in developing corporate goals. Moreover, Mead's senior executives, in reviewing middle managers' performance, now are asking how results are obtained, not just what they were. Two years ago, an official says, "we didn't bother to ask the 'how' part of the question."

Issues

1. Who sets the goals for middle managers in an organization?
2. Describe the sources of pressure for a middle manager.
3. What are the middle manager's obligations to her subordinates?
4. What alternative choices would you have recommended to Mr. Tate?

Henry Mintzberg

The Manager's Job: Folklore and Fact

The classical view says that the manager organizes, coordinates, plans, and controls; the facts suggest otherwise

If you ask a manager what he does, he will most likely tell you that he plans, organizes, coordinates, and controls. Then watch what he does. Don't be surprised if you can't relate what you see to these four words.

When he is called and told that one of his factories has just burned down, and he advises the caller to see whether temporary arrangements can be made to supply customers through a foreign subsidiary, is he planning, organizing, coordinating, or controlling? How about when he presents a gold watch to a retiring employee? Or when he attends a conference to meet people in the trade? Or on returning from that conference, when he tells one of his employees about an interesting product idea he picked up there?

The fact is that these four words, which have dominated management vocabulary since the French industrialist Henri Fayol first introduced them in 1916, tell us little about what managers actually do. At best, they indicate some vague objectives managers have when they work.

The field of management, so devoted to progress and change, has for more than half a century not seriously addressed *the* basic question: What do managers do? Without a proper answer, how can we teach management? How can we design planning or information systems for managers? How can we improve the practice of management at all?

Our ignorance of the nature of managerial work shows up in various ways in the modern organization—in the boast by the successful manager that he never spent a single day in a management training program; in the turnover of corporate planners who never quite understood what it was the manager wanted; in the computer consoles gathering dust in the back room because the managers never used the fancy on-line MIS some analyst thought they

Reprinted by permission of the Harvard Business Review. "The Manager's Job: Folklore and Fact" by Henry Mintzberg (July–August 1975). Copyright © 1975 by The President and fellows of Harvard College, all rights reserved.

needed. Perhaps most important, our ignorance shows up in the inability of our large public organizations to come to grips with some of their most serious policy problems.

Somehow, in the rush to automate production, to use management science in the functional areas of marketing and finance, and to apply the skills of the behavioral scientist to the problem of worker motivation, the manager— that person in charge of the organization or one of its subunits—has been forgotten.

My intention in this article is simple: to break the reader away from Fayol's words and introduce him to a more supportable, and what I believe to be a more useful, description of managerial work. This descriptive derives from my review and synthesis of the available research on how various managers have spent their time.

In some studies, managers were observed intensively ("shadowed" is the term some of them used); in a number of others, they kept detailed diaries of their activities; in a few studies, their records were analyzed. All kinds of managers were studied—foremen, factory supervisors, staff managers, field sales managers, hospital administrators, presidents of companies and nations, and even street gang leaders. These "managers" worked in the United States, Canada, Sweden, and Great Britain. In the ruled insert on page 16 is a brief review of the major studies that I found most useful in developing this description, including my own study of five American chief executives officers.

A synthesis of these findings paints an interesting picture, one as different from Fayol's classical view as a cubist abstract is from a Renaissance painting. In a sense, this picture will be obvious to anyone who has ever spent a day in a manager's office, either in front of the desk or behind it. Yet, at the same time, this picture may turn out to be revolutionary, in that it throws into doubt so much of the folklore that we have accepted about the manager's work.

I first discuss some of this folklore and contrast it with some of the discoveries of systematic research—the hard facts about how managers spend their time. Then I synthesize these research findings in a description of ten roles that seem to describe the essential content of all managers' jobs. In a concluding section, I discuss a number of implications of this synthesis for those trying to achieve more effective management, both in classrooms and in the business world.

Some Folklore and Facts about Managerial Work

There are four myths about the manager's job that do not bear up under careful scrutiny of the facts.

1 Folklore

The manager is a reflective, systematic planner. The evidence on this issue is overwhelming, but not a shred of it supports this statement.

Fact

Study after study has shown that managers work at an unrelenting pace, that their activities are characterized by brevity, variety, and discontinuity, and that they are strongly oriented to action and dislike reflexive activities. Consider this evidence:

Half the activities engaged in by the five chief executives of my study lasted less than nine minutes, and only 10% exceeded one hour.[1] A study of 56 U.S. foremen found that they averaged 583 activities per eight-hour shift, an average of 1 every 48 seconds.[2] The work pace for both chief executives and foremen was unrelenting. The chief executives met a steady stream of callers and mail from the moment they arrived in the morning until they left in the evening. Coffee breaks and lunches were inevitably work related, and ever-present subordinates seemed to usurp any free moment.

A diary study of 160 British middle and top managers found that they worked for a half hour or more without interruption only about once every two days.[3]

Of the verbal contacts of the chief executives in my study, 93% were arranged on an ad hoc basis. Only 1% of the executives' time was spent in open-ended observational tours. Only 1 out of 368 verbal contacts was unrelated to a specific issue and could be called general planning. Another researcher finds that "in *not one single case* did a manager report the obtaining of important external information from a general conversation or other undirected personal communication"[4]

No study has found important patterns in the way managers schedule their time. They seem to jump from issue to issue, continually responding to the needs of the moment.

Is this the planner that the classical view describes? Hardly. How, then, can we explain this behavior? The manager is simply responding to the pressures of his job. I found that my chief executives terminated many of their own activities, often leaving meetings before the end, and interrupted their desk work to call in subordinates. One president not only placed his desk so that he could look down a long hallway but also left his door open when he was alone—an invitation for subordinates to come in and interrupt him.

---

[1]All the data from my study can be found in Henry Mintzberg, *The Nature of Managerial Work* (New York: Harper & Row, 1973).

[2]Robert H. Guest, "Of Time and the Foreman," *Personnel,* May 1956, p. 478.

[3]Rosemary Stewart, *Managers and Their Jobs* (London: Macmillan, 1967); see also Sune Carlson, *Executive Behaviour* (Stockholm: Strömbergs, 1951), the first of the diary studies.

[4]Francis J. Anguilar, *Scanning the Business Environment* (New York: Macmillan, 1967), p. 102.

Experiential Organizational Behavior

Clearly, these managers wanted to encourage the flow of current information. But more significantly, they seemed to be conditioned by their own work loads. They appreciated the opportunity cost of their own time, and they were continually aware of their ever-present obligations—mail to be answered, callers to attend to, and so on. It seems that no matter what he is doing, the manager is plagued by the possibilities of what he might do and what he must do.

When the manager must plan, he seems to do so implicitly in the context of daily actions, not in some abstract process reserved for two weeks in the organization's mountain retreat. The plans of the chief executives I studied seemed to exist only in their heads—as flexible, but often specific, intentions. The traditional literature notwithstanding, the job of managing does not breed reflective planners; the manager is a real-time responder to stimuli, an individual who is conditioned by his job to prefer live to delayed action.

2 Folklore

The effective manager has no regular duties to perform. Managers are constantly being told to spend more time planning and delegating, and less time seeing customers and engaging in negotiations. These are not, after all, the true tasks of the manager. To use the popular analogy, the good manager, like the good conductor, carefully orchestrates everything in advance, then sits back to enjoy the fruits of his labor, responding occasionally to an unforeseeable exception.

But here again the pleasant abstraction just does not seem to hold up. We had better take a closer look at those activities managers feel compelled to engage in before we arbitrarily define them away.

Fact

In addition to handling exceptions, managerial work involves performing a number of regular duties, including ritual and ceremony, negotiations, and processing of soft information that links the organization with its environment. Consider some evidence from the research studies:

A study of the work of the presidents of small companies found that they engaged in routine activities because their companies could not afford staff specialists and were so thin on operating personnel that a single absence often required the president to substitute.[5]

One study of field sales managers and another of chief executives suggest that it is a natural part of both jobs to see important customers, assuming the managers wish to keep those customers.[6]

---

[5]Unpublished study by Irving Choran, reported in Mintzberg, *The Nature of Managerial Work.*

[6]Robert T. Davis, *Performance and Development of Field Sales Managers* (Boston: Division of Research, Harvard Business School, 1957); George H. Copeman, *The Role of the Managing Director* (London: Business Publications, 1963).

Someone, only half in jest, once described the manager as that person who sees visitors so that everyone else can get his work done. In my study, I found that certain ceremonial duties—meeting visiting dignitaries, giving out gold watches, presiding at Christmas dinners—were an intrinsic part of the chief executive's job.

Studies of managers' information flow suggest that managers play a key role in securing "soft" external information (much of it available only to them because of their status) and in passing it along it along to their subordinates.

3 Folklore

The senior manager needs aggregated information, which a formal management information system best provides. Not too long ago, the words *total information system* were everywhere in the management literature. In keeping with the classical view of the manager as that individual perched on the apex of a regulated, hierarchical system, the literature's manager was to receive all his important information from a giant, comprehensive MIS.

But lately, as it has become increasingly evident that these giant MIS systems are not working—that managers are simply not using them—the enthusiasm has waned. A look at how managers actually process information makes the reason quite clear. Managers have five media at their command—documents, telephone calls, scheduled and unscheduled meetings, and observational tours.

Fact

Managers strongly favor the verbal media—namely, telephone calls and meetings. The evidence comes from every single study of managerial work. Consider the following:

In two British studies, managers spent an average of 66% and 80% of their time in verbal (oral) communication.[7] In my study of five American chief executives, the figure was 78%.

These five chief executives treated mail processing as a burden to be dispensed with. One came in Saturday morning to process 142 pieces of mail in just over three hours, to "get rid of all the stuff." This same manager looked at the first piece of "hard" mail he had received all week, a standard cost report, and put it aside with the comment, "I never look at this."

These same five chief executives responded immediately to 2 of the 40 routine reports they received during the five weeks of my study and to four items in the 104 periodicals. They skimmed most of these periodicals in seconds, almost ritualistically. In all, these chief executives of good-sized organizations initiated on their own—that is, not in response to something else—a grand total of 25 pieces of mail during the 25 days I observed them.

An analysis of the mail the executives received reveals an interesting

---

[7]Stewart, *Managers and Their Jobs*; Tom Burns, "The Directions of Activity and Communication in a Departmental Executive Group," *Human Relations* 7, no. 1 (1954): 73.

picture—only 13% was of specific and immediate use. So now we have another piece in the puzzle: not much of the mail provides live, current information—the action of a competitor, the mood of a government legislator, or the rating of last night's television show. Yet this is the information that drove the managers, interrupting their meetings and rescheduling their workdays.

Consider another interesting finding. Managers seem to cherish "soft" information, especially gossip, hearsay, and speculation. Why? The reason is its timeliness; today's gossip may be tomorrow's fact. The manager who is not accessible for the telephone call informing him that his biggest customer was seen golfing with his main competitor may read about a dramatic drop in sales in the next quarterly report. But then it's too late.

To assess the value of historical, aggregated, "hard" MIS information, consider two of the manager's prime uses for his information—to identify problems and opportunities[8] and to build his own mental models of the things around him (e.g., how his organization's budget system works, how his customers buy his product, how changes in the economy affect his organization, and so on). Every bit of evidence suggests that the manager identifies decision situations and builds models not with the aggregated abstractions an MIS provides, but with specific tidbits of data.

Consider the words of Richard Neustadt, who studied the information-collecting habits of Presidents Roosevelt, Truman, and Eisenhower:

It is not information of a general sort that helps a President see personal stakes; not summaries, not surveys, not the *bland analgams*. Rather . . . it is the odds and ends of *tangible detail* that pieced together in his mind illuminate the underside of issues put before him. To help himself he must reach out as widely as he can for every scrap of fact, opinion, gossip, bearing on his interests and relationships as President. He must become his own director of his own central intelligence.[9]

The manager's emphasis on the verbal media raises two important points:

First, verbal information is stored in the brains of people. Only when people write this information down can it be stored in the files of the organization—whether in metal cabinets or on magnetic tape—and managers apparently do not write down much of what they hear. Thus the strategic data bank of the organization is not in the memory of its computers but in the minds of its managers.

Second, the manager's extensive use of verbal media helps to explain why he is reluctant to delegate tasks. When we note that most of the manager's important information comes in verbal form and is stored in his head, we can

---

[8]H. Edward Wrapp, "Good Managers Don't Make Policy Decisions," HBR September-October 1967, p. 91; Wrapp refers to this as spotting opportunities and relationships in the stream of operating problems and decisions; in his article Wrapp raises a number of excellent points related to this analysis.

[9]Richard E. Neustadt, *Presidential Power* (New York: John Wiley, 1960), pp. 153–154; italics added.

Research on Managerial Work

Considering its central importance to every aspect of management, there has been surprisingly little research on the manager's work, and virtually no systematic building of knowledge from one group of studies to another. In seeking to describe managerial work, I conducted my own research and also scanned the literature widely to integrate the findings of studies from many diverse sources with my own. These studies focused on two very different aspects of managerial work. Some were concerned with the characteristics of the work—how long managers work, where, at what pace and with what interruptions, with whom they work, and through what media they communicate. Other studies were more concerned with the essential content of the work—what activities the managers actually carry out, and why. Thus, after a meeting, one researcher might note that the manager spent 45 minutes with three government officials in their Washington office, while another might record that he presented his company's stand on some proposed legislation in order to change a regulation.

A few of the studies of managerial work are widely known, but most have remained buried as single journal articles or isolated books. Among the more important ones I cite (with full references in the footnotes) are the following:

Sune Carlson developed the diary method to study the work characteristics of nine Swedish managing directors. Each kept a detailed log of his activities. Carlson's results are reported in his book <u>Executive Behavior</u>. A number of British researchers, notably Rosemary Stewart, have subsequently used Carlson's method. <u>In Managers and Their Jobs</u>, she describes the study of 160 top and middle managers of British companies during four weeks, with particular attention to the differences in their work.

Leonard Sayles's book <u>Managerial Behavior</u> is another important reference. Using a method he refers to as "anthropological," Sayles studied the work content of middle- and lower-level managers in a large U.S. corporation. Sayles moved freely in the company, collecting whatever information struck him as important.

Perhaps the best-known source is <u>Presidential Power</u>, in which Richard Neustadt analyzes the power and managerial behavior of Presidents Roosevelt, Truman, and Eisenhower. Neustadt used secondary sources—documents and interviews with other parties—to generate his data.

Robert H. Guest, in <u>Personnel</u>, reports on a study of the foreman's working day. Fifty-six U.S. foremen were observed and each of their activities recorded during one eight-hour shift.

Richard C. Hodgson, Daniel J. Levinson, and Abraham Zaleznik studied a team of three top executives of a U.S. hospital. From that study they wrote <u>The Executive Role Constellation</u>. These researchers addressed in particular the way in which work and socioemotional roles were divided among the three managers.

William F. Whyte, from his study of a street gang during the Depression, wrote <u>Street Corner Society</u>. His findings about the gang's leadership, which George C. Homans analyzed in <u>The Human Group</u>, suggest some interesting similarities of job content between street gang leaders and corporate managers.

My own study involved five American CEOs of middle- to large-sized organizations—a consulting firm, a technology company, a hospital, a consumer goods company, and a school system. Using a method called "structural observation," during one intensive week of observation for each executive I recorded various aspects of every piece of mail and every verbal contact. My method was designed to capture data on both work characteristics and job content. In all, I analyzed 890 pieces of incoming and outgoing mail and 368 verbal contacts.

well appreciate his reluctance. It is not as if he can hand a dossier over to someone; he must take the time to "dump memory"—to tell that someone all he knows about the subject. But this could take so long that the manager may find it easier to do the task himself. Thus the manager is damned by his own information system to a "dilemma of delegation"—to do too much himself or to delegate to his subordinates with inadequate briefing.

4 Folklore

Management is, or at least is quickly becoming, a science and a profession. By almost any definitions of *science* and *profession*, this statement is false. Brief observation of any manager will quickly lay to rest the notion that managers practice a science. A science involves the enaction of systematic, analytically determined procedures or programs. If we do not even know what procedures managers use, how can be prescribe them by scientific analysis? And how can we call management a profession if we cannot specify what managers are to learn? For after all, a profession involves "knowledge of some department of learning or science" (*Random House Dictionary*).[10]

Fact

The managers' programs—to schedule time, process information, make decisions, and so on—remain locked deep inside their brains. Thus, to describe these programs, we rely on words like *judgment* and *intuition*, seldom stopping to realize that they are merely labels for our ignorance.

I was struck during my study by the fact that the executives I was observing—all very competent by any standard—are fundamentally indistinguishable from their counterparts of a hundred years ago (or a thousand years ago, for that matter). The information they need differs, but they seek it in the same way—by word of mouth. Their decisions concern modern technology, but the procedures they use to make them are the same as the procedures of the nineteenth-century manager. Even the computer, so important for the specialized work of the organization, has apparently had no influence on the work procedures of general managers. In fact, the manager is in a kind of loop, with increasingly heavy work pressures but no aid forthcoming from management science.

Considering the facts about managerial work, we can see that the manager's job is enormously complicated and difficult. The manager is overburdened with obligations; yet he cannot easily delegate his tasks. As a result, he is driven to overwork and is forced to do many tasks superficially. Brevity, fragmentation, and verbal communication characterize his work. Yet these are the very characteristics of managerial work that have impeded scientific attempts to improve it. As a result, the management scientist has concentrated his efforts on the specialized functions of the organization, where he

---

[10] For a more thorough, though rather different, discussion of this issue, see Kenneth R. Andrews, "Toward Professionalism in Business Management," HBR March-April 1969, p. 49.

---

could more easily analyze the procedures and quantify the relevant information.[11]

But the pressures of the manager's job are becoming worse. Where before he needed only to respond to owners and directors, now he finds that subordinates with democratic norms continually reduce his freedom to issue unexplained orders, and a growing number of outside influences (consumer groups, government agencies, and so on) expect his attention. And the manager has had nowhere to turn for help. The first step in providing the manager with some help is to find out what his job really is.

Back to a Basic Description of Managerial Work

Now let us try to put some of the pieces of this puzzle together. Earlier, I defined the manager as that person in charge of an organization or one of its subunits. Besides chief executive officers, this definition would include vice presidents, bishops, foremen, hockey coaches, and prime ministers. Can all of these people have anything in common? Indeed they can. For an important starting point, all are vested with formal authority over an organizational unit. From formal authority comes status, which leads to various interpersonal relations, and from these comes access to information. Information, in turn, enables the manager to make decisions and strategies for his unit.

The manager's job can be described in terms of various "roles," or organized sets of behaviors identified with a position. My description, shown in *Exhibit I*, comprises ten roles. As we shall see, formal authority gives rise to the three interpersonal roles, which in turn give rise to the three informational roles; these two sets of roles enable the manager to play the four decisional roles.

Interpersonal Roles

Three of the manager's roles arise directly from his formal authority and involve basic interpersonal relationships.

1. First is the *figurehead* role. By virtue of his position as head of an organizational unit, every manager must perform some duties of a ceremonial nature. The president greets the touring dignitaries, the foreman attends the wedding of a lathe operator, and the sales manager takes an important customer to lunch.

The chief executives of my study spent 12% of their contact time on cere-

---

[11]C. Jackson Grayson, Jr., in "Management Science and Business Practice," HBR July-August 1973, p. 41, explains in similar terms why, as chairman of the Price Commission, he did not use those very techniques that he himself promoted in his earlier career as a management scientist.

monial duties; 17% of their incoming mail dealt with acknowledgments and requests related to their status. For example, a letter to a company president requested free merchandise for a crippled schoolchild; diplomas were put on the desk of the school superintendent for his signature.

Duties that involve interpersonal roles may sometimes be routine, involving little serious communication and no important decision making. Nevertheless, they are important to the smooth functioning of an organization and cannot be ignored by the manager.

2. Because he is in charge of an organizational unit, the manager is responsible for the work of the people of that unit. His actions in this regard constitute the *leader* role. Some of these actions involve leadership directly—for example, in most organizations the manager is normally responsible for hiring and training his own staff.

In addition, there is the indirect exercise of the leader role. Every manager must motivate and encourage his employees, somehow reconciling their individual needs with the goals of the organization. In virtually every contact the manager has with his employees, subordinates seeking leadership clues probe his actions: "Does he approve?" "How would he like the report to turn out?" "Is he more interested in market share than high profits?"

The influence of the manager is most clearly seen in the leader role. For-

EXHIBIT I. The Manager's Roles

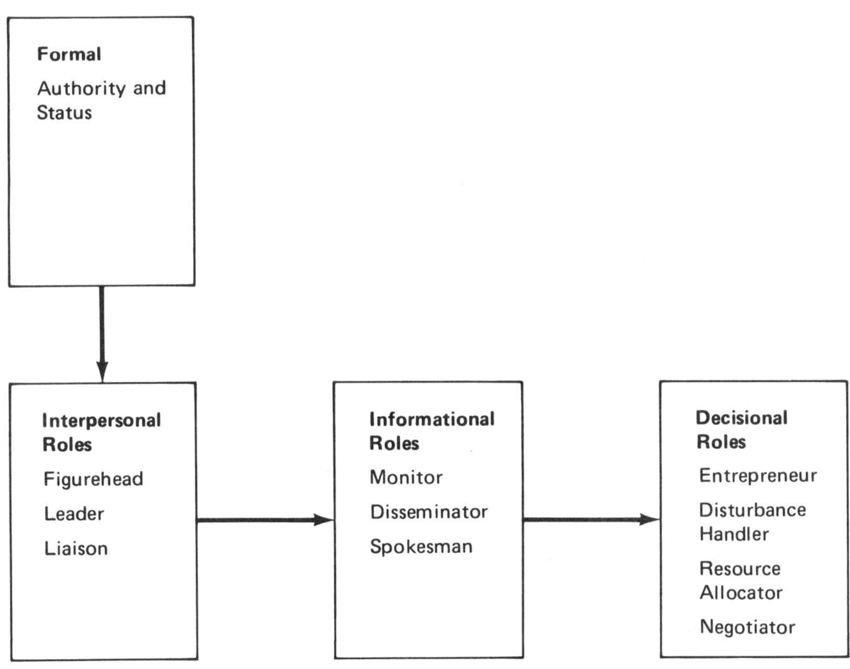

mal authority vests him with great potential power; leadership determines in large part how much of it he will realize.

3. The literature of management has always recognized the leader role, particularly those aspects of it related to motivation. In comparison, until recently it has hardly mentioned the *liaison* role, in which the manager makes contacts outside his vertical chain of command. This is remarkable in light of the finding of virtually every study of managerial work that managers spend as much time with peers and other people outside their units as they do with their own subordinates—and, surprisingly, very little time with their own superiors.

In Rosemary Stewart's diary study, the 160 British middle and top managers spent 47% of their time with peers, 41% of their time with people outside their unit, and only 12% of their time with their superiors. For Robert H. Guest's study of U.S. foremen, the figures were 44%, 46%, and 10%. The chief executives of my study averaged 44% of their contact time with people outside their organizations, 48% with subordinates, and 7% with directors and trustees.

The contacts the five CEOs made were with an incredible wide range of people: subordinates; clients, business associates, and suppliers; and peers— managers of similar organizations, government and trade organization officials, fellow directors on outside boards, and independents with no relevant organizational affiliations. The chief executives' time with and mail from these groups is shown in *Exhibit II* on page 23. Guest's study of foremen shows, likewise, that their contacts were numerous and wide ranging, seldom involving fewer than 25 individuals, and often more than 50.

As we shall see shortly, the manager cultivates such contacts largely to find information. In effect, the liaison role is devoted to building up the manager's own external information system—informal, private, verbal, but, nevertheless, effective.

Informational Roles

By virtue of his interpersonal contacts, both with his subordinates and with his network of contacts, the manager emerges as the nerve center of his organizational unit. He may not know everything, but he typically knows more than any member of his staff.

Studies have shown this relationship to hold for all managers, from street gang leaders to U.S. presidents. In *The Human Group*, George C. Homans explains how, because they were at the center of the information flow in their own gangs and were also in close touch with other gang leaders, street gang leaders were better informed than any of their followers.[12] And Richard

---

[12] George C. Homans, *The Human Group* (New York: Harcourt, Brace & World, 1950), based on the study by William F. Whyte entitled *Street Corner Society*, rev. ed. (Chicago: University of Chicago Press, 1955).

Neustadt describes the following account from his study of Franklin D. Roosevelt:

The essence of Roosevelt's technique for information-gathering was competition. 'He would call you in,' one of his aids once told me, 'and he'd ask you to get the story on some complicated business, and you'd come back after a couple of days of hard labor and present the juicy morsel you'd uncovered under a stone somewhere, and *then* you'd find out he knew all about it, along with something else you *didn't* know. Where he got this information from he wouldn't mention, usually, but after he had done this to you once or twice you got damn careful about *your* information.'[13]

We can see where Roosevelt "got this information" when we consider the relationship between the interpersonal and informational roles. As leader, the manager has formal and easy access to every member of his staff. Hence, as noted earlier, he tends to know more about his own unit than anyone else does. In addition, his liaison contacts expose the manager to external information to which his subordinates often lack access. Many of these contacts are with other managers of equal status, who are themselves nerve centers in their own organization. In this way, the manager develops a powerful data base of information.

The processing of information is a key part of the manager's job. In my study, the chief executives spent 40% of their contact time on activities devoted exclusively to the transmission of information; 70% of their incoming mail was purely informational (as opposed to requests for action). The manager does not leave meetings or hang up the telephone in order to get back to work. In large part, communication *is* his work. Three roles describe these informational aspects of managerial work.

1. As *monitor*, the manager perpetually scans his environment for information, interrogates his liaison contacts and his subordinates, and receives unsolicited information, much of it as a result of the network of personal contacts he has developed. Remember that a good part of the information the manager collects in his monitor role arrives in verbal form, often as gossip, hearsay, and speculation. By virtue of his contacts, the manager has a natural advantage in collecting this soft information for his organization.

2. He must share and distribute much of this information. Information he gleans from outside personal contacts may be needed within his organization. In his *disseminator* role, the manager passes some of his privileged information directly to his subordinates, who would otherwise have no access to it. When his subordinates lack easy contact with one another, the manager will sometimes pass information from one to another.

3. In his *spokesman* role, the manager sends some of his information to people outside his unit—a president makes a speech to lobby for an organization cause, or a foreman suggests a product modification to a supplier. In addition, as part of his role as spokesman, every manager must inform and

[13]Neustadt, *Presidential Power*, p. 157.

---

satisfy the influential people who control his organizational unit. For the foreman, this may simply involve keeping the plant manager informed about the flow of work through the shop.

The president of a large corporation, however, may spend a great amount of his time dealing with a host of influences. Directors and shareholders must be advised about financial performance; consumer groups must be assured that the organization is fulfilling its social responsibilities; and government officials must be satisfied that the organization is abiding by the law.

Decisional Roles

Information is not, of course, an end in itself; it is the basic input to decision making. One thing is clear in the study of managerial work: the manager plays the major role in his unit's decision-making system. As its formal authority, only he can commit the unit to important new courses of action; and as its nerve center, only he has full and current information to make the set of decisions that determines the unit's strategy. Four roles describe the manager as decision-maker.

1. As *entrepreneur*, the manager seeks to improve his unit, to adapt it to changing conditions in the environment. In his monitor role, the president is constantly on the lookout for new ideas. When a good one appears, he initiates a development project that he may supervise himself or delegate to an employee (perhaps with the stipulation that he must approve the final proposal).

There are two interesting features about these development projects at the chief executive level. First, these projects do not involve single decisions or even unified clusters of decisions. Rather, they emerge as a series of small decisions and actions sequenced over time. Apparently, the chief executive prolongs each project so that he can fit it bit by bit into his busy, disjointed schedule and so that he can gradually come to comprehend the issue, if it is a complex one.

Second, the chief executives I studied supervised as many as 50 of these projects at the same time. Some projects entailed new products or processes; others involved public relations campaigns, improvement of the cash position, reorganization of a weak department, resolution of a morale problem in a foreign division, integration of computer operations, various acquisitions at different stages of development, and so on.

The chief executive appears to maintain a kind of inventory of the development projects that he himself supervises—projects that are at various stages of development, some active and some in limbo. Like a juggler, he keeps a number of projects in the air; periodically, one comes down, is given a new burst of energy, and is sent back into orbit. At various intervals, he put new projects on-stream and discards old ones.

2. While the entrepreneur role describes the manager as the voluntary initiator of change, the *disturbance handler* role depicts the manager invol-

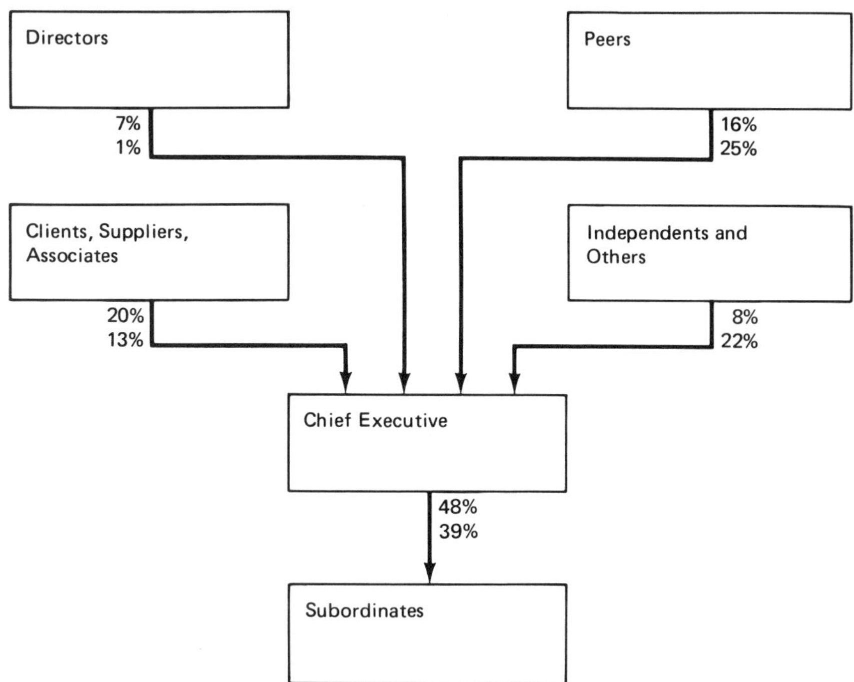

Note: The top figure indicates the proportion of total contact time spent with each group and the bottom figure, the proportion of mail from each group.

EXHIBIT II.   The Chief Executives' Contacts

untarily responding to pressures. Here change is beyond the manager's control. He must act because the pressures of the situation are too severe to be ignored: strike looms, a major customer has gone bankrupt, or a supplier reneges on his contract.

It has been fashionable, I noted earlier, to compare the manager to an orchestra conductor, just as Peter F. Drucker wrote in *The Practice of Management:*

The manager has the task of creating a true whole that is larger than the sum of its parts, a productive entity that turns out more than the sum of the resources put into it. One analogy is the conductor of a symphony orchestra, through whose effort, vision and leadership individual instrumental parts that are so much noise by themselves become the living whole of music. But the conductor has the composer's score; he is only interpreter. The manager is both composer and conductor.[14]

Now consider the words of Leonard R. Sayles, who has carried out systematic research on the manager's job:

[14]Peter F. Drucker, *The Practice of Management* (New York: Harper & Row, 1954), pp. 341–342.

[The manager] is like a symphony orchestra conductor, endeavouring to maintain a melodious performance in which the contributions of the various instruments are coordinated and sequenced, patterned and paced, while the orchestra members are having various personal difficulties, stage hands are moving music stands, alternating excessive heat and cold are creating audience and instrument problems, and the sponsor of the concert is insisting on irrational changes in the program.[15]

In effect, every manager must spend a good part of his time responding to high-pressure disturbances. No organization can be so well run, so standardized, that it has considered every contingency in the uncertain environment in advance. Disturbances arise not only because poor managers ignore situations until they reach crisis proportions, but also because good managers cannot possibly anticipate all the consequences of the actions they take.

3. The third decisional role is that of *resource allocator*. To the manager falls the responsibility of deciding who will get what in his organizational unit. Perhaps the most important resource the manager allocates is his own time. Access to the manager constitutes exposure to the unit's nerve center and decision-maker. The manager is also charged with designing his unit's structure, that pattern of formal relationships that determines how work is to be divided and coordinated.

Also, in his role as resource allocator, the manager authorizes the important decisions of his unit before they are implemented. By retaining this power, the manager can ensure that decisions are interrelated; all must pass through a single brain. To fragment this power is to encourage discontinuous decision making and a disjointed strategy.

There are a number of interesting features about the manager's authorizing others' decisions. First, despite the widespread use of capital budgeting procedures—a means of authorizing various capital expenditures at one time—executives in my study made a great many authorization decisions on an ad hoc basis. Apparently, many projects cannot wait or simply do not have the quantifiable costs and benefits that capital budgeting requires.

Second, I found that the chief executives faced incredibly complex choices. They had to consider the impact of each decision on other decisions and on the organization's strategy. They had to ensure that the decision would be acceptable to those who influence the organization, as well as ensure that resources would not be overextended. They had to understand the various costs and benefits as well as the feasibility of the proposal. They also had to consider questions of timing. All this was necessary for the simple approval of someone else's proposal. At the same time, however, delay could lose time, while quick approval could be ill considered and quick rejection might discourage the subordinate who had spent months developing a pet project.

One common solution to approving projects is to pick the man instead of the proposal. That is, the manager authorizes those projects presented to

---

[15]Leonard R. Sayles, *Managerial Behavior* (New York: McGraw-Hill, 1964), p. 162.

Where do I get my information, and how? Can I make greater use of my contacts to get information? Can other people do some of my scanning for me? In what areas is my knowledge weakest, and how can I get others to provide me with the information I need? Do I have powerful enough mental models of those things I must understand within the organization and in its environment?

What information do I disseminate in my organization? How important is it that my subordinates get my information? Do I keep too much information to myself because dissemination of it is time-consuming or inconvenient? How can I get more information to others so they can make better decisions?

Do I balance information collecting with action taking? Do I tend to act before information is in? Or do I wait so long for all the information that opportunities pass me by and I become a bottleneck in my organization?

What pace of change am I asking my organization to tolerate? Is this change balanced so that our operations are neither excessively static nor overly disrupted? Have we sufficiently analyzed the impact of this change on the future of our organization?

Am I sufficiently well informed to pass judgment on the proposals that my subordinates make? Is it possible to leave final authorization for more of the proposals with subordinates? Do we have problems of coordination because subordinates in fact now make too many of these decisions independently?

What is my vision of direction for this organization? Are these plans primarily in my own mind in loose form? Should I make them explicit in order to guide the decisions of others in the organization better? Or do I need flexibility to change them at will?

How do my subordinates react to my managerial style? Am I sufficiently sensitive to the powerful influence my actions have on them? Do I fully understand their reactions to my actions? Do I find an appropriate balance between encouragement and pressure? Do I stifle their initiative?

What kind of external relationships do I maintain, and how? Do I spend too much of my time maintaining these relationships? Are there certain types of people whom I should get to know better?

Is there any system to my time scheduling, or am I just reacting to the pressures of the moment? Do I find the appropriate mix of activities, or do I tend to concentrate on one particular function or one type of problem just because I find it interesting? Am I more efficient with particular kinds of work at special times of the day or week? Does my schedule reflect this? Can someone else (in addition to my secretary) take responsibility for much of my scheduling and do it more systematically?

Do I overwork? What effect does my work load have on my efficiency? Should I force myself to take breaks or to reduce the pace of my activity?

Am I too superficial in what I do? Can I really shift moods as quickly and frequently as my work patterns require? Should I attempt to decrease the amount of fragmentation and interruption in my work?

Do I orient myself too much toward current, tangible activities? Am I a slave to the action and excitement of my work, so that I am no longer able to concentrate on issues? Do key problems receive the attention they deserve? Should I spend more time reading and probing deeply into certain issues? Could I be more reflective? Should I be?

Do I use the different media appropriately? Do I know how to make the most of written communication? Do I rely excessively on face-to-face communication, thereby putting all but a few of my subordinates at an informational disadvantage? Do I schedule enough of my meetings on a regular basis? Do I spend enough time touring my organization to observe activity at first hand? Am I too detached from the heart of my organization's activities, seeing things only in an abstract way?

How do I blend my personal rights and duties? Do my obligations consume all my time? How can I free myself sufficiently from obligations to ensure that I am taking this organization where I want it to go? How can I turn my obligations to my advantage?

---

him by people whose judgment he trusts. But he cannot always use this simple dodge.

4. The final decisional role is that of *negotiator*. Studies of managerial work at all levels indicate that managers spend considerable time in negotiations: the president of the football team is called in to work out a contract with the holdout superstar; the corporation president leads his company's contingent to negotiate a new strike issue; the foreman argues a grievance problem to its conclusion with the shop steward. As Leonard Sayles puts it, negotiations are a "way of life" for the sophisticated manager.

These negotiations are duties of the manager's job; perhaps routine, they are not to be shirked. They are an integral part of his job, for only he has the authority to commit organizational resources in "real time," and only he has the nerve center information that important negotiations require.

The Integrated Job

It should be clear by now that the ten roles I have been describing are not easily separable. In the terminology of the psychologist, they form a gestalt, an integrated whole. No role can be pulled out of the framework and the job be left intact. For example, a manager without liaison contacts lacks external information. As a result, he can neither disseminate the information his employees need nor make decisions that adequately reflect external conditions. (In fact, this is a problem for the new person in a managerial position, since he cannot make effective decisions until he has built up his network of contacts.)

Here lies a clue to the problems of team management.[16] Two or three people cannot share a single managerial position unless they can act as one entity. This means that they cannot divide up the ten roles unless they can very carefully reintegrate them. The real difficulty lies with the informational roles. Unless there can be full sharing of managerial information—and, as I pointed out earlier, it is primarily verbal—team management breaks down. A single managerial job cannot be arbitrarily split, for example, into internal and external roles, for information from both sources must be brought to bear on the same decisions.

---

[16]See Richard C. Hodgson, Daniel J. Levinson, and Abraham Zaleznik, *The Executive Role Constellation* (Boston: Division of Research, Harvard Business School, 1965), for a discussion of the sharing of roles.

To say that the ten roles form a gestalt is not to say that all managers give equal attention to each role. In fact, I found in my review of the various research studies that

. . . sales managers seem to spend relatively more of their time in the interpersonal roles, presumably a reflection of the extrovert nature of the marketing activity;

. . . production managers give relatively more attention to the decisional roles, presumably a reflection of their concern with efficient work flow;

. . . staff managers spend the most time in the informational roles, since they are experts who manage departments that advise other parts of the organization.

Nevertheless, in all cases the interpersonal, informational and decisional roles remain inseparable.

Toward More Effective Management

What are the messages for management in this description? I believe, first and foremost, that this description of managerial work should prove more important to managers than any prescription they might derive from it. That is to say, *the manager's effectiveness is significantly influenced by his insight into his own work.* His performance depends on how well he understands and responds to the pressures and dilemmas of the job. Thus managers who can be introspective about their work are likely to be effective at their jobs. The ruled insert on page 25 offers 14 groups of self-study questions for managers. Some may sound rhetorical; none is meant to be. Even though the questions cannot be answered simply, the manager should address them.

Let us take a look at three specific areas of concern. For the most part, the managerial logjams—the dilemma of delegation, the data base centralized in one brain, the problems of working with the management scientist—revolve around the verbal nature of the manager's information. There are great dangers in centralizing the organization's data bank in the minds of its managers. When they leave, they take their memory with them. And when subordinates are out of convenient verbal reach of the manager, they are at an informational disadvantage.

1. *The manager is challenged to find systematic ways to share his privileged information.* A regular debriefing session with key subordinates, a weekly memory dump on the dictating machine, the maintaining of a diary of important information for limited circulation, or other similar methods may ease the logjam of work considerably. Time spent disseminating this information will be more than regained when decisions must be made. Of course, some will raise the question of confidentiality. But managers would do well to weigh the risks of exposing privileged information against having subordinates who can make effective decisions.

If there is a single theme that runs through this article, it is that the pressures of his job drive the manager to be superficial in his actions—to overload himself with work, encourage interruption, respond quickly to every stimulus, seek the tangible and avoid the abstract, make decisions in small increments, and do everything abruptly.

2. *Here again, the manager is challenged to deal consciously with the pressures of superficiality by giving serious attention to the issues that require it, by stepping back from his tangible bits of information in order to see a broad picture, and by making use of analytical inputs.* Although effective managers have to be adept at responding quickly to numerous and varying problems, the danger in managerial work is that they will respond to every issue equally (and that means abruptly) and that they will never work the tangible bits and pieces of informational input into a comprehensive picture of their world.

As I noted earlier, the manager uses these bits of information to build models of his world. But the manager can also avail himself of the models of the specialists. Economists describe the functioning of markets, operations researchers simulate financial flow processes, and behavioral scientists explain the needs and goals of people. The best of these models can be searched out and learned.

In dealing with complex issues, the senior manager has much to gain from a close relationship with the management scientists of his own organization. They have something important that he lacks—time to probe complex issues. An effective working relationship hinges on the resolution of what a colleague and I have called "the planning dilemma."[17] Managers have the information and the authority; analysts have the time and the technology. A successful working relationship between the two will be effected when the manager learns to share his information and the analyst learns to adapt to the manager's needs. For the analyst, adaptation means worrying less about the elegance of the method and more about its speed and flexibility.

It seems to me that analysts can help the top manager especially to schedule his time, feed in analytical information, monitor projects under his supervision, develop models to aid in making choices, design contingency plans for disturbances that can be anticipated, and conduct "quick-and-dirty" analysis for those that cannot. But there can be no cooperation if the analysts are out of the mainstream of the manager's information flow.

3. *The manager is challenged to gain control of his own time by turning obligations to his advantage and by turning those things he wishes to do into obligations.* The chief executives of my study initiated only 32% of their own contacts (and another 5% by mutual agreement). And yet to a considerable extent they seemed to control their time. There were two key factors that enabled them to do so.

First, the manager has to spend so much time discharging obligations that

[17]James S. Hekimian and Henry Mintzberg, "The Planning Dilemma," *The Management Review,* May 1968, p. 4.

if he were to view them as just that, he would leave no mark on his organization. The unsuccessful manager blames failure on the obligations; the effective manager turns his obligations to his own advantage. A speech is a chance to lobby for a cause; a meeting is a chance to reorganize a weak department; a visit to an important customer is a chance to extract trade information.

Second, the manager frees some of his time to do those things that he—perhaps no one else—thinks important by turning them into obligations. Free time is made, not found, in the manager's job; it is forced into the schedule. Hoping to leave some time open for contemplation or general planning is tantamount to hoping that the pressures of the job will go away. The manager who wants to innovate initiates a project and obligates others to report back to him; the manager who needs certain environmental information establishes channels that will automatically keep him informed; the manager who has to tour facilities commits himself publicly.

The Educator's Job

Finally, a word about the training of managers. Our management schools have done an admirable job of training the organization's specialists—management scientists, marketing researchers, accountants, and organizational development specialists. But for the most part they have not trained managers.[18]

Management schools will begin the serious training of managers when skill training takes a serious place next to cognitive learning. Cognitive learning is detached and informational, like reading a book or listening to a lecture. No doubt much important cognitive material must be assimilated by the manager-to-be. But cognitive learning no more makes a manager than it does a swimmer. The latter will drown the first time he jumps into the water if his coach never takes him out of the lecture hall, gets him wet, and gives him feedback on his performance.

In other words, we are taught a skill through practice plus feedback, whether in a real or a simulated situation. Our management schools need to identify the skills managers use, select students who show potential in these skills, put the students into situations where these skills can be practiced, and then give them systematic feedback on their performance.

My description of managerial work suggests a number of important managerial skills—developing peer relationships, carrying out negotiations, motivating subordinates, resolving conflicts, establishing information networks and subsequently disseminating information, making decisions in conditions of extreme ambiguity, and allocating resources. Above all, the manager needs to be introspective about his work so that he may continue to learn on the job.

[18] See J. Sterling Livingston, "Myth of the Well-Educated Manager," HBR January-February 1971, p. 79.

Many of the manager's skills can, in fact, be practiced, using techniques that range from role playing to videotaping real meetings. And our management schools can enhance the entrepreneurial skills by designing programs that encourage sensible risk taking and innovation.

No job is more vital to our society than that of the manager. It is the manager who determines whether our social institutions serve us well or whether they squander our talents and resources. It is time to strip away the folklore about managerial work, and time to study it realistically so that we can begin the difficult task of making significant improvements in its performance.

Issues

1. Discuss the difference between normative and descriptive theories of managerial behavior. Which of these types describes Mintzberg's approach?
2. What are the limits to Mintzberg's case studies? What alternative methods can be used to evaluate managers' behavior?
3. Can students of organizational behavior assist the practicing manager? How?

5

Niki Scott

Working Woman

They are female managers, employed by the same Baltimore company. They are approximately the same age, earn the same income and supervise the same number of people.

Yet they approach their jobs in entirely different ways, says one woman who has worked for both of them.

Janice was her boss for nearly a year. Lynn has been her boss for the past six months. "And the way I feel about my job has changed completely because of the difference in those two people," she said.

"Janice gave out responsibility, but didn't let me really assume it. She would say she wanted me to handle something, but then would tell me exactly what to do and say—and checked every day to be sure I was on top of things.

"Lynn, on the other hand, gives me a certain area of responsibility and assumes I have it under control unless I tell her otherwise. If you ask her, she's willing to help. But she still lets me have the final say.

"Janice made it clear she wanted to be responsible for everything—that she, alone, was important.

"She couldn't delegate authority because she was afraid it would make her less important to the company. She allowed herself to be harassed by petty details and overlooked broad concepts.

"She even typed all her own memos!

"But when I transferred to Lynn's department, she said, 'Let me tell you what I'm looking for. I want a business partner, here; I want us to work together.'

"She said, 'I want someone who will tell me when an idea is no good—someone who can think for herself. I want someone who can take over here when I move on—and I do plan to move on.'

"Lynn isn't threatened by me because she plans to move up too. She wants me to learn her job so she can do something else. You can't imagine how important that is to me.

"There's another major difference," said this working woman. "With Jan-

Nicki Scott's article copyrighted, 1978, Universal Press Syndicate. All rights reserved.

ice, I never knew what kind of a day I would have. That depended entirely on what sort of a day Janice had—she was ruled completely by her own emotions.

"If she was in a good mood, the whole department was relaxed and productive. But if she had a bad day, all of us had a bad one. She was tense and irritable and took it out on us.

"She was inconsistent, too. She might like an idea ond day and hate it the next—depending upon her mood. She would overreact completely (over a trifle) one day, then ignore real cause for annoyance on the next.

"Lynn, on the other hand, is solid and consistent. I'm not even aware of her moods, because they never come into play. Her emotions simply do not enter the picture.

So at the end of the day, we haven't dealt on a personal level—only on a professional one. And if she says something one day, I can be sure she'll mean it the next.

"There's no favoritism, either, because she's concerned only with performance—not with personalities," she said.

"I've learned a lot from working for these two women. They seem to represent the best and the worst as far as bosses are concerned. When I'm in management, I'm sure I'll remember them, too.

"One taught me what to do, and one taught me what not to do."

Issues

1. Summarize the differences between the two supervisors, Lynn and Janice.
2. How do the managerial philosophies of the two supervisors differ?
3. What type of employees would prefer to work for Janice? For Lynn?

Bernard Wysocki Jr.

Manager's Journal

New Supervisors

CHICAGO—The way Peter Schmidt tells it, his first 18 months as a boss have been pretty traumatic. "Sometimes I feel like I'm being drawn and quartered" on the job, he says.

As chief accountant at a medium-sized gear company here, Mr. Schmidt supervises a handful of bookkeepers who previously worked without supervision. One underling has frequently chastised him "for not picking up the in-house system quickly enough," he says. Another tries to boss him around. "She's old enough to be my mother—and she acts like it," he maintains.

So, like many a troubled manager these days, Mr. Schmidt has turned to consultants for help. . . . He and 170 other new supervisors are jammed into a ballroom at the O'Hare Motor Inn, waiting for . . . enlightenment.

Promptly at 9 a.m., seminar leader Jay Terry strides to the podium. He's a fast-talking former teacher and corporate personnel man who promises six hours of practical advice.

"You probably know all the technical information you need to do your job," he begins. On the other hand, most new supervisors need to learn a lot about dealing with people on the job.

One of the best ways to motivate employes, Mr. Terry says, is to tell them exactly what you are trying to accomplish as boss. But few supervisors communicate this "big picture" effectively, he adds. To prove it, he gives a quick test. "How many of you know the five most important things that measure the success of your immediate boss?" Mr. Terry asks. Only a few hands go up. "That's the first thing you should ask your boss when you go back to work tomorrow."

But it probably isn't a good idea for a new boss to ask employes about *their* individual goals right away. Probing too early, he says, can make a subordinate suspicious. Until boss and subordinate have begun to trust each other,

Reprinted by permission of *The Wall Street Journal*, © Dow Jones & Company, Inc. (1979). All Rights Reserved.

the employe is apt to wonder, "are we setting goals to catch me or to help me grow and develop?"

One way to help a subordinate grow is to learn the proper way to praise him, Mr. Terry says. The wrong way is to give the employe a quick slap on the back and say, "good job" or "attaboy." Better to say, "I'm happy about the way you processed those invoices so quickly. You really saved us a lot of bucks. Thanks." Taking the latter approach, the boss has told the subordinate how he feels ("I'm happy") and told him exactly what he's happy about, so the employe knows how to repeat the praise-worthy behavior.

Mr. Terry also suggests that there's a right way and a wrong way to interrupt a subordinate while he's working. The wrong way is to stroll over to his desk and say, "are you busy right now?" "That's a hard question to field," Mr. Terry says. If the employe says, "No, I'm not busy," he sounds like he's goofing off. If he says, "yes, I'm busy," he sounds a little rude. Better to ask, "is this a good time to interrupt?"

Mr. Terry isn't just a corporate Amy Vanderbilt, however. He's all for being the tough guy on certain occasions. Consider how he recommends dealing with chronically tardy subordinates:

Tell the employe, "we have a problem and it has to be resolved. I'm upset that you keep coming in late because it really screws up the invoice processing," or the telephone load, or whatever. The key thing is to let the employe know how you feel and to let him know that his tardiness messes up the offfice and makes life difficult for the people around him.

The latecomer is likely to offer some kind of excuse. The boss, Mr. Terry says, should brush aside all excuses until the employe admits he's creating a problem. Only then is the employe likely to vow to get beter. About 5% of the time, however, the latecomer simply won't admit he's causing a problem. In that case, the boss should say that the latecomer is passing up any chance of being promoted and might be fired.

What's more, the boss must be willing to back up his threat, or he loses credibility and authority. That's a particular problem for new supervisors, who frequently find their authority put to the test right away.

Al Sporny, manager of a tire store in downtown Chicago, is one seminar participant who remembers facing such a test his first day as a manager. On the same day that Mr. Sporny was promoted from mechanic to service manager, the tire store decided to extend hours until 9 p.m. on certain evenings. But despite Mr. Sporny's orders, none of the mechanics would agree to take a night shift.

"So I fired the ringleader," the 33-year-old Mr. Sporny recalls, and he told the other mechanics, "if I have to fire all of you, I will." Mr. Sporny said the blowup prevented him from sleeping for two nights. The ringleader "had a family; he had a girl six months old," Mr. Sporny recalls. "But it was his career or my career." Fortunately, he adds, the remaining mechanics agreed to work nights, and the ringleader humbly asked for his job back. He agreed to work nights and was reinstated.

Power plays should be a last resort, or course. By frequently barking commands at subordinates, Mr. Terry says, a boss separates himself from the people who work for him. "Power erodes relationships," he says, and dries up sources of information that the boss needs to do his job.

Most of the time, Mr. Terry says, the best way to run the show is by suggestion. The boss sells his idea, and the source of his power is competence rather than his position as boss.

Issues

1. As a manager, what are useful antecedents of good performance by an employee/subordinate?
2. As a manager, what are useful consequences of good (or bad) performance by an employee/subordinate?
3. Why do employees "test" their new supervisor? How can a supervisor succeed in passing this test?

The Formal Organizational System: Technology and Structure

7

Change-of-Work Procedures

PURPOSE: (1) To diagnose and practice overcoming resistance to change. (2) To illustrate the distinction between the quality of a decision and its acceptability. (3) To provide a practice in participative decision making.

ADVANCE PREPARATION: None.

GROUP SIZE: Subgroups of five. Total class can be any size. Works best with groups of from four to six.

TIME REQUIRED: 50 minutes.

SPECIAL MATERIALS: None.

SPECIAL PHYSICAL REQUIREMENTS: None.

RELATED TOPICS: Applied motivation and job design. Group decision making and problem solving, Leadership, Power, Interpersonal communication.

Introduction

Most changes in organizations are seldom confined to the technical aspects of production; they may also require alterations in the *work* and *social* satisfactions of the employees. New methods must be not only of high *quality* (i.e., workable and efficient from an objective standpoint), but they must also be *acceptable* to the employees who will be using them.

This added factor of acceptance makes the problem of introducing changes different from purely technical problems of evaluating new equipment or procedures. For one thing, the quality of a solution and its acceptability are different characteristics and do not necessarily go together. A second complication is that while management can control solution quality by reserving decision making to itself, acceptance is inherently voluntary with the employees and is not subject to the will of management. At the same time, failure to obtain employee acceptance of changes that affect them aggravates

Developed by N. R. F. Maier. Adapted for the present volume by D. T. Hall. Used by permission of the author.

many of the problems of management. In some instances resistance is expressed directly in the form of grievances about rates and earnings, quits, work stoppages and open hostility toward management. In other instances, the resistance may be shown in such indirect ways as restriction of output, waste, low-quality workmanship, slow learning of the new methods, excessive absenteeism, and the like.

One might think of two general approaches to introducing change: *selling* and *mutual problem solving*. In selling, facts and arguments are presented to employees showing the advantages of change. In mutual problem solving, the manager and his subordinates discuss the need for change and arrive jointly at a plan for change. In between these two approaches is *consultation,* in which the manager discusses the need for change with subordinates, solicits their ideas, and then makes the decision alone.

In order to deal with problems of change, the first step is to learn the nature of the resistance to change. In the present case there are a variety of forces operating. Some of these are in the direction of change, some opposed or resisting. The supervisor in charge will want to identify the resistance forces and try to reduce them, while trying to constructively use the positive forces.

The kind of discussion the new supervisor stimulates may introduce new negative or new positive forces so that the outcome may, in part, be determined by the discussion he initiates.

Procedure

Step 1: 5 Minutes

The group is divided into subgroups of five. If the total group size is not a multiple of five, some subgroups of four or six can be used. All groups are to select one of their members to act as the foreman, "Thompson." After the foremen have been chosen, they should raise their hands to indicate that the group has a leader.

The other members in each group will be crew members and observer(s). Beginning with the foreman and going in clockwise order, their names will be "Jackson," "Stevenson," and "Walters." The fifth member (and sixth, if present) will be observers.

Step 2: 5 Minutes

When all members have received their roles, the group leader will read aloud the section entitled "General Information," below.

General Information

In a company manufacturing subassemblies for the automobile industry, the assembly work is done by small groups of employees. Several of these groups are under the supervision of a foreman, Thompson. In one of these groups, Jackson, Stevenson, and Walters work together assembling fuel pumps.

This operation is divided into three jobs or positions, called position 1, position 2, and position 3. Supplies for each position are located next to the bench where the man works. The men work side by side and can help each other out if they wish. Since all the jobs are simple and fairly similar, these three employees exchange positions on the line every now and then. This trading of positions was developed by the men themselves. It creates no financial problem because the crew is paid by a group piece rate. In this way the three members share the production pay equally.

Presently each of you will be asked to be one of the following: Thompson, Jackson, Walters, or Stevenson. Today, Thompson, the foreman, has asked Jackson, Walters, and Stevenson to meet with him in his office. He said he wanted to talk about "something."

Next, the role players should then study (only) their individual roles in preparation for the small group discussions. The roles for Thompson, Jackson, Stevenson, and Walters are found in the Appendix to [the Instructor's Manual], as are the instructions for observers.

The Thompsons should stand up beside their groups when they have finished studying their roles, thus giving the group leader a signal that they are ready to begin.

When all foremen are standing, the group leader will set the stage for the role-playing by commenting that the foreman has asked the crew members to meet with him to discuss a problem before starting work. He will explain that when the foreman is asked to sit down, this will be the signal that Thompson has entered his office. He hopes that the employees will speak to him as he enters.

Step 3: 25 Minutes

The leader will ask if anyone has any questions. When everyone understands his function, the leader will ask the foremen to sit down. All groups should role-play simultaneously. Approximately 25 minutes are needed by the average group to reach a decision.

Step 4: 15 Minutes

Collect results.

Issues

1. What conclusions can be drawn from the table of results? Is there any relationship between the method used and the degree of acceptance or resistance? What method was used most often?
2. Construct a problem analysis diagram of this situation. What were the *resistance*

forces (i.e., the members' objections to the change)? What were the *change* forces (i.e., possible gains or advantages to the crew under the new method)?
3. Which of the forces in the diagram are based on emotions (fear, hostility, etc.)? Which are based on actual information about the changes?
4. As a strategy for change, is it generally better to try to reduce the resistance forces or to increase the change forces?

8

The Lab Technician's Lament

Sharon Spender is a lab technician for IBM in Colorado Springs. She started two months ago after moving from where she had worked since graduation. Susan received an associate degree in chemistry in 1974 and had worked in two laboratory jobs since graduation before deciding to move west at the age of 25.

Sharon works in the product development area of the Office Products Division. In particular, she works on a project that is attempting to improve the IBM III photocopy machine. Her work involves the rubber roller that is used to set the ink used in photocopying; Sharon and her colleague, Tom, are trying variations in the composition of the roller that would decrease the copying costs. The actual task requires Sharon to mix formulas involving liquid rubber, to prepare the rollers for the production process where the rollers are produced (baked and finished), and to test the finished products for certain specified heat and chemical properties. The liquid rubber is messy to work with, but the goal of the project is challenging to Sharon. The job allows Sharon a degree of autonomy in her work day, but her specific day-to-day responsibilities are determined by Bob, the head chemist in her group. Bob has a B.S. in chemistry and four years of experience in his job. Although only 26, Bob aspires to head his own department. Currently, Bob's group is under the responsibility of Harold, who manages another group of chemists as well. Bob believes that the groups will be split soon, and that he will be named the new head.

In a two month performance review with Harold, Sharon expressed a degree of boredom and frustration with her job. "I feel like I'm not (or IBM is not) using abilities to the fullest—my previous experience is going to waste." She believes that Bob delegates the lower level of preliminary tasks to her and Tom, only to have Bob take who did not complete his degree and was originally hired as temporary lab technician and was only recently assigned permanent status, accepts Bob's explanation that Tom and Sharon are "only technicians" and that Bob is responsible for carrying experiments through to completion. Tom sees his job as "getting paid by the hour," so he tolerates the conditions. But, as Sharon notes, "he's not too thrilled with the situation either." IBM rewards suggestions or improvements from the employees and Sharon feels that Bob is occasionally too eager to "step in when the experiment may result in concrete results."

In their meeting, Harold attributed most of Sharon's feeling to her newness on the job and that more experience will clear up her problem. But Harold expressed appreciation that Sharon was willing to share her problems with him and that she was interested in doing a good job.

Issues

1. Summarize the problems and actions you would recommend to Sharon. Compare Tom and Sharon's approaches to the job—does this have an influence on your analysis?
2. How does perception affect behavior here? Contrast the different individual's perceptions of their situation.

9

Job Design Preferences

Job design is concerned with a number of attributes of a job. Among these attributes are the job itself, the requirements of the job, the interpersonal interaction opportunities on the job, and performance outcomes. There are certain attributes that are preferred by individuals. Some prefer job autonomy while others prefer to be challenged by different tasks. It is obvious that individual differences in preferences would be an important consideration for managers. An exciting job for one person may be seen as too demanding for another individual. Managers could use this type of information in attempting to create job design conditions that match organizational and individual goals and preferences.

The Job Attribute Preference Form is presented below. Please read it carefully and complete it after considering each characteristic listed. Not all job design characteristics are included for your consideration. Just use those that are included on the form.

Job Attribute Preferences

A. Your Preferences

Decide which of the following is most important to you. Place a 1 in front of the most important characteristic. Continue numbering the items in order of importance until the least important is ranked 10. There are no right answers since individuals differ in their job design preferences. Do not discuss your individual rankings until the instructor forms groups.

_______ Variety in tasks required to do
_______ Seeing the completed product
_______ Freedom from supervision
_______ Working with people
_______ Responsibility for getting the job done
_______ Developing friendships at work
_______ Clear job requirements or specifications
_______ Importance of my work to society

_______ Having the resources to do the job well
_______ Feedback on performance from the manager

B. Other's Preferences

In the A section you have provided your preferences, now number the items as you think others would rank them. Consider others who are in your course, class, or program. That is, those who are also completing this exercise. Rank the factors from 1 (most important) to 10 (least important).

_______ Variety in tasks required to do
_______ Seeing the completed product
_______ Freedom from supervision
_______ Working with people
_______ Responsibility for getting the job done
_______ Developing friendships at work
_______ Clear job requirements or specifications
_______ Importance of my work to society
_______ Having the resources to do the job well
_______ Feedback on performance from the manager

Procedure

Stage I

1. Individually complete the A and B portions of the Job Attribute Preference form.

Stage II

1. The instructor will form groups of 4 to 6 students.
2. Discuss the differences in the rankings individuals made on the A and B parts of the form.

Issues

1. How would managers' preferences be expected to differ from those of blue collar workers?
2. How could information concerning job preferences of employees help the manager? Give examples.
3. What aspects of the job design are the manager most likely to be able to control? least likely to control?

10

Drawing an Organizational Chart

Filmore National Bank has been a leading financial institution in Metropolis since its founding in 1882 by a grandnephew of President Millard Filmore. When the law permitting bank holding companies was enacted five years ago, Filmore National instituted an aggressive acquisition plan. To date 23 subsidiary banks have been added to the Filmore Corporation. Although each subsidiary bank is encouraged to make full use of the numerous staff services at the parent bank, top management is firmly committed to a policy of decentralization. Even though such specialized departments as Gold Exchange are located only at the headquarters bank in Metropolis, each subsidiary bank offers a full range of services through its own professional staff. In keeping with the policy of decentralization, each subsidiary is operated as an autonomous profit center.

For the purposes of this exercise *you* will assume the role of President of the Lawrence Security Bank. Lawrence Security was acquired by Filmore National last year. Lawrence Security was previously owned by nine small businessmen and you have served as president for over seven years. Bob Evans is the executive vice president.

Lawrence Security employs 62 people organized into four major departments: Operations, Loans, Accounting, and the newest department, Marketing. Each department is headed by a Vice President of the Security Bank. Operations includes main bank tellers, motor banking, and maintenance. The loans department is divided into Mortgage, Auto and Personal, and Commercial. Accounting involves Bookkeeping, Data Processing, and the new Filmore Management Information System (MIS). Marketing encompasses Customer Relations, New Accounts, and Advertising.

Joan Nolan is Vice President of Marketing, Ken Baker is Vice President of Operations, Jim Stevens is Vice President of Accounting Services, and Larry Pate is Vice President of Loans.

Used by permission of Henry P. Sims.

In the past, your organization has been small enough so that you believed formal organization charts were unnecessary. However, your supervisor at Filmore has asked you to formulate a chart for him. This is your immediate task: Draw the organization chart for Lawrence Security Bank.

(Hints: Use only the information given—no other information is available. When available, use both personal names and titles on your chart.)

11

The Technological Imperative

Lou Grant, editor of the Los Angeles Tribune, has come to you to assist him in adapting new technology to his organization. Economic pressures have forced the paper's owner to replace the reporter's traditional typewriter with computerized word-processing equipment. Not only does this affect the reporters, but also the typesetters—workers who compose each page of the paper by hand and set the printing presses with "hot" lead plates—are facing computerized page composing and "cold" photo off-set printing techniques. Mr. Grant is concerned about potential impacts on the work process at the paper, and he seeks your educated assistance in anticipating and solving problems.

Issues

1. Describe a theoretical model or basis for your analysis of this situation. How do the concepts of technology, job design, and organizational change affect people?
2. Contrast the alternative perspectives of the reporters, the typesetters, and the owner.

Robert H. Waterman, Jr., Thomas J. Peters, and Julien R. Phillips

12

Structure Is Not Organization

Diagnosing and solving organizational problems means looking not merely to structural reorganization for answers but to a framework that includes structure and several related factors.

The Belgian surrealist René Magritte painted a series of pipes and titled the series *Ceci n'est pas une pipe:* this is not a pipe. The picture of the thing is not the thing. In the same way, a structure is not an organization. We all know that, but like as not, when we reorganize what we do is to restructure. Intellectually all managers and consultants know that much more goes on in the process of organizing than the charts, boxes, dotted lines, position descriptions, and matrices can possibly depict. But all too often we behave as though we didn't know it; if we want change we change the structure.

Early in 1977, a general concern with the problems of organization effectiveness, and a particular concern about the nature of the relationship between structure and organization, led us to assemble an internal task force to review our client work. The natural first step was to talk extensively to consultants and client executives around the world who were known for their skill and experience in organization design. We found that they too were dissatisfied with conventional approaches. All were disillusioned about the usual structural solutions, but they were also skeptical about anyone's ability to do better. In their experience, the techniques of the behavioral sciences were not providing useful alternatives to structural design. True, the notion that structure follows strategy (get the strategy right and the structure follows) looked like an important addition to the organizational tool kit; yet strategy rarely seemed to dictate unique structural solutions. Moreover, the

The authors want to offer special acknowledgement and thanks to Anthony G. Athos of Harvard University, who was instrumental in the development of the 7-S framework and who, in his capacity as our consultant, helped generally to advance our thinking on organization effectiveness.

By Robert H. Waterman, Jr., Thomas J. Peters, and Julien R. Phillips in *Business Horizons*, June 1980. Copyright, 1980, by the Foundation for the School of Business at Indiana University. Reprinted by permission.

main problem in strategy had turned out to be execution: getting it done. And that, to a very large extent, meant *organization.* So the problem of organization effectiveness threatened to prove circular. The dearth of practical additions to old ways of thought was painfully apparent.

Outside Explorations

Our next step was to look outside for help. We visited a dozen business schools in the United States and Europe and about as many superbly performing companies. Both academic theorists and business leaders, we found, were wrestling with the same concerns.

Our timing in looking at the academic environment was good. The state of theory is in great turmoil but moving toward a new consensus. Some researchers continue to write about structure, particularly its latest and most modish variant, the matrix organization. But primarily the ferment is around another stream of ideas that follow from some startling premises about the limited capacity of decision makers to process information and reach what we usually think of as "rational" decisions.

The stream that today's researchers are tapping is an old one, started in the late 1930s by Fritz Roethlisberger and Chester Barnard, then both at Harvard (Barnard had been president of New Jersey Bell). They challenged rationalist theory, first—in Roethlisberger's case—on the shop floors of Western Electric's Hawthorne plant. Roethlisberger found that simply *paying attention* provided a stimulus to productivity that far exceeded that induced by formal rewards. In a study of workplace hygiene, they turned the lights up and got an expected productivity increase. Then to validate their results they turned the lights down. But something surprising was wrong: productivity went up again. Attention, they concluded, not working conditions per se, made the difference.

Barnard, speaking from the chief executive's perspective, asserted that the CEO's role is to harness the social forces in the organization, to shape and guide values. He described good value-shapers as *effective* managers, contrasting them with the mere manipulators of formal rewards who dealt only with the narrower concept of *efficiency.*

Barnard's words, though quickly picked up by Herbert Simon (whom we'll come back to later), lay dormant for thirty years while the primary management issues focused on decentralization and structure—the appropriate and burning issue of the time.

But then, as the decentralized structure proved to be less than a panacea for all time, and its substitute, the matrix, ran into worse trouble, Barnard's and Simon's ideas triggered a new wave of thinking. On the theory side, it is exemplified by the work of James March and Karl Weick, who attacked the rational model with a vengeance. Weick suggests that organizations learn—

and adapt—very slowly. They pay obsessive attention to internal cues long after their practical value has ceased. Important business assumptions are buried deep in the minutiae of organizational systems and other habitual routines whose origins have been long obscured by time. March goes further. He introduced, only slightly facetiously, the garbage can as an organizational metaphor. March pictures organizational learning and decision making as a stream of choices, solutions, decision makers, and opportunities interacting almost randomly to make decisions that carry the organization toward the future. His observations about large organizations parallel Truman's about the presidency: "You issue orders from this office and if you can find out what happens to them after that, you're a better man than I am."

Other researchers have accumulated data which support this unconventional view. Henry Mintzberg made one of the few rigorous studies of how senior managers actually use time. They don't block out large chunks of time for planning, organizing, motivating, and controlling as some suggest they should. Their time, in fact, is appallingly but perhaps necessarily fragmented. Andrew Pettigrew studied the politics of strategic decision and was fascinated by the inertial properties of organizations. He showed that organizations frequently hold onto faulty assumptions about their world for as long as a decade, despite overwhelming evidence that it has changed and they probably should too.

In sum, what the researchers tell us is. "We can explain why you have problems." In the face of complexity and multiple competing demands, organizations simply can't handle decision making in a totally rational way. Not surprisingly, then, a single blunt instrument—like structure—is unlikely to prove the master tool that can change organizations with best effect.

Somewhat to our surprise, senior executives in the top-performing companies that we interviewed proved to be speaking very much the same language. They were concerned that the inherent limitations of structural approaches could render their companies insensitive to an unstable business environment marked by rapidly changing threats and opportunities from every quarter—competitors, governments, and unions at home and overseas. Their organizations, they said, had to learn how to build capabilities for rapid and flexible response. Their favored tactic was to choose a temporary focus, facing perhaps one major issue this year and another next year or the year after. Yet at the same time, they were acutely aware of their peoples' need for a stable, unifying value system—a foundation for long-term continuity. Their task, as they saw it, was largely one of preserving internal stability while adroitly guiding the organization's responses to fast-paced external change.

Companies such as IBM, Kodak, Hewlett-Packard, GM, Du Pont, and P&G, then, seem obsessive in their attention to maintaining a stable culture. At the same time, these giants are more responsive than their competitors. Typically, they do not seek responsiveness through major structural shifts.

Instead, they seem to rely on a series of temporary devices to focus the attention of the entire organization for a limited time on a single priority goal or environmental threat.

Simon As Exemplar

Thirty years ago, in *Administrative Behavior*, Herbert Simon (a 1977 Nobel laureate) anticipated several themes that dominate much of today's thinking about organization. Simon's concepts of "satisficing" (settling for adequate instead of optimal solutions) and "the limits of rationality" were, in effect, nails in the coffin of economic man. His ideas, if correct, are crucial. The economic man paradigm has not only influenced the economists but has also influenced thought about the proper organization and administration of most business enterprises—and, by extension, public administration. Traditional thought has it that economic man is basically seeking to maximize against a set of fairly clear objectives. For organization planners the implications of this are that one can specify objectives, determine their appropriate hierarchy, and then logically determine the "best" organization.

Simon labeled this the "rational" view of the administrative world and said, in effect, that it was all right as far as it went but that it had decided limits. For one, most organizations cannot maximize—the goals are really not that clear. Even if they were, most business managers do not have access to complete information, as the economic model requires, but in reality operate with a set of relatively simple decision rules in order to *limit* the information they really need to process to make most decisions. In other words, the rules we use in order to get on with it in big organizations limit our ability to optimize anything.

Suppose the goal is profit maximization. The definition of profit and its maximization varies widely even within a single organization. Is it earnings growth, quality of earnings, maximum return on equity, or the discounted value of the future earnings stream—and if so, at what discount rate? Moreover, business organizations are basically large social structures with diffuse power. Most of the individuals who make them up have different ideas of what the business ought to be. The few at the top seldom agree entirely on the goals of their enterprise, let alone on maximization against one goal. Typically, they will not push their views so hard as to destroy the social structure of their enterprise and, in turn, their own power base.

All this leaves the manager in great difficulty. While the research seems valid and the message of complexity rings true, the most innovative work in the field is descriptive. The challenge to the manager is how to organize better. His goal is organization effectiveness. What the researchers are saying is that the subject is much more complex than any of our past prescriptive models have allowed for. What none has been able to usefully say is, "OK, here's what to do about it."

The 7-S Framework

After a little over a year and a half of pondering this dilemma, we began to formulate a new framework for organizational thought. As we and others have developed it and tested it in teaching, in workshops, and in direct problem solving over the past year, we have found it enormously helpful. It has repeatedly demonstrated its usefulness both in diagnosing the causes of organizational malaise and in formulating programs for improvement. In brief, it seems to work.

Our assertion is that productive organization change is not simply a matter of structure, although structure is important. It is not so simple as the interaction between strategy and structure, although strategy is critical too. Our claim is that effective organizational change is really the relationship between structure, strategy, systems, style, skills, staff, and something we call superordinate goals. (The alliteration is intentional: it serves as an aid to memory.)

Our central idea is that organization effectiveness stems from the interaction of several factors—some not especially obvious and some underanalyzed. Our framework for organization change, graphically depicted in the exhibit above, suggests several important ideas:

First is the idea of a multiplicity of factors that influence an organization's ability to change and its proper mode of change. Why pay attention to only one or two, ignoring the others? Beyond structure and strategy, there are at least five other identifiable elements. The division is to some extent arbitrary, but it has the merit of acknowledging the complexity identified in the research and segmenting it into manageable parts.

Second, the diagram [on page 56] is intended to convey the notion of the interconnectedness of the variables—the idea is that it's difficult, perhaps impossible, to make significant progress in one area without making progress in the others as well. Notions of organization change that ignore its many aspects of their interconnectedness are dangerous.

In a recent article on strategy, *Fortune* commented that perhaps as many as 90 percent of carefully planned stretegies don't work. If that is so, our guess would be that the failure is a failure in execution, resulting from inattention to the other S's. Just as a logistics bottleneck can cripple a military strategy, inadequate systems or staff can make paper tigers of the best-laid plans for clobbering competitors.

Finally, the shape of the diagram is significant. It has no starting point or implied hierarchy. A priori, it isn't obvious which of the seven factors will be the driving force in changing a particular organization at a particular point in time. In some cases, the critical variable might be strategy. In others, it could be systems or structure.

Structure

To understand this model of organization change better, let us look at each of its elements, beginning—as most organization discussions do—with structure. What will the new organization of the 1980s be like? If decentralization was the trend of the past, what is next? Is it matrix organization? What will "Son of Matrix" look like? Our answer is that those questions miss the point.

To see why, let's take a quick look at the history of structural thought and development. The basic theory underlying structure is simple. Structure divides tasks and then provides coordination. It trades off specialization and integration. It decentralizes and then recentralizes.

The old structural division was between production and sales. The chart showing this was called a functional organization. Certain principles of organization, such as one-man/one-boss, limited span of control, grouping of like activities, and commensurate authority and responsibility, seemed universal truths.

What happened to this simple idea? Size—and complexity. A company like General Electric has grown over a thousandfold in both sales and earnings in the past eighty years. Much of its growth has come through entry into new and diverse business. At a certain level of size and complexity, a functional organization, which is dependent on frequent interaction among all activities, breaks down. As the number of people or businesses increases arithmetically, the number of interactions required to make things work increases geometrically. A company passing a certain size and complexity threshold must decentralize to cope.

Among the first to recognize the problem and explicitly act on it was Du Pont in 1921. The increasing administrative burden brought about by its diversification into several new product lines ultimately led the company to transform its highly centralized, functionally departmental structure into a decentralized, multidivisional one. Meanwhile, General Motors, which has been decentralized from the outset, was learning how to make a decentralized structure work as more than just a holding company.

However, real decentralization in world industry did not take place until much later. In 1950, for example, only about 20 percent of the *Fortune 500* companies were decentralized. By 1970, 80 percent were decentralized. A similar shift was taking place throughout the industrialized world.

Today three things are happening. First, because of the portfolio concept of managing a business, spun off from General Electric research (which has now become PIMS), companies are saying, "We can do more with our decentralized structure than control complexity. We can shift resources, act flexibly—that is, manage strategically."

Second, the dimensions along which companies want to divide tasks have multiplied. Early on, there were functional divisions. Then came product divisions. Now we have possibilities for division by function, product, market, geography, nation, strategic business unit, and probably more. The rub is that as the new dimensions are added, the old ones don't go away. An insurance company, for example, can organize around market segments, but it still needs functional control over underwriting decisions. The trade-offs are staggering if we try to juggle them all at once.

Third, new centralist forces have eclipsed clean, decentralized divisions of responsibility. In Europe, for example, a company needs a coherent union strategy. In Japan, especially, companies need a centralized approach to the government interface. In the United States, regulation and technology force centralization in the interest of uniformity.

This mess has produced a new organization form: the matrix, which purports, at least in concept, to reconcile the realities of organizational complexity with the imperatives of managerial control. Unfortunately, the two-dimensional matrix model is intrinsically too simple to capture the real situation. Any spatial model that really did capture it would be incomprehensible.

Matrix does, however, have one well-disguised virtue: it calls attention to the central problem in structuring today. That problem is not the one on which most organization designers spend their time—that is, how to divide up tasks. It is one of emphasis and coordination—how to make the whole thing work. The challenge lies not so much in trying to comprehend all the possible dimensions of organization structure as in developing the ability to focus on those dimensions which are currently important to the organization's evolution—and to be ready to refocus as the crucial dimensions shift. General Motors' restless use of structural change—most recently the project center, which led to their effective downsizing effort—is a case in point.

The General Motors solution has a critical attribute—the use of a temporary overlay to accomplish a strategic task. IBM, Texas Instruments, and others have used similar temporary structural weapons. In the process, they have meticulously preserved the shape and spirit of the underlying structure (e.g., the GM division or the TI Product Customer Center). We regularly observe those two attributes among our sample of top performers: the use of the temporary and the maintenance of the simple underlying form.

We speculate that the effective "structure of the eighties" will more likely be described as "flexible" or "temporary"; this matrix-like property will be preserved even as the current affair with the formal matrix structure cools.

Strategy

If structure is not enough, what is? Obviously, there is strategy. It was Alfred Chandler who first pointed out that structure follows strategy, or

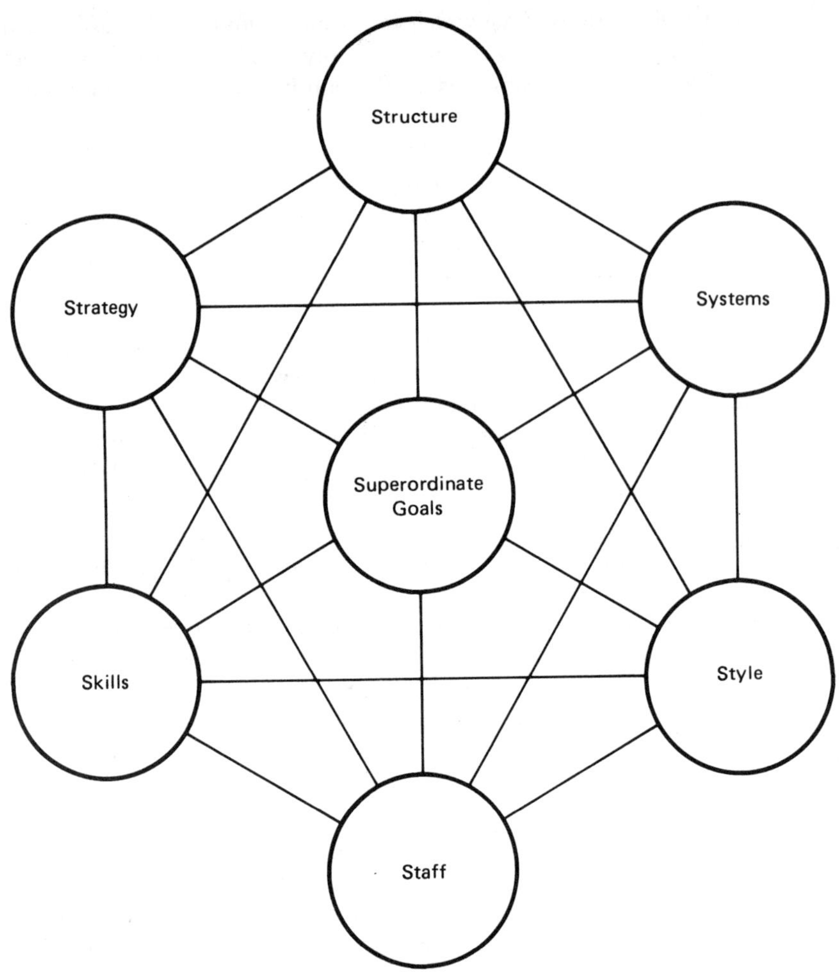

A New View of Organization

more precisely, that a strategy of diversity forces a decentralized structure.[1] Throughout the past decade, the corporate world has given close attention to the interplay between strategy and structure. Certainly, clear ideas about strategy make the job of structural design more rational.

By "strategy" we mean those actions that a company plans in response to or anticipation of changes in its external environment—its customers, its competitors. Strategy is the way a company aims to improve its position vis-a-vis competition—perhaps through low-cost production or delivery,

[1] Alfred D. Chandler, Jr., *Strategy and Structure: Chapters in the History of the American Industrial Enterprise* (Cambridge, Mass.: MIT Press, 1962).

                                          Experiential Organizational Behavior

perhaps by providing better value to the customer, perhaps by achieving sales and service dominance. It is, or ought to be, an organization's way of saying: "Here is how we will create unique value."

As the company's chosen route to competitive success, strategy is obviously a central concern in many business situations—especially in highly competitive industries where the game is won or lost on share points. But "structure follows strategy" is by no means the be-all and end-all of organization wisdom. We find too many examples of large, prestigious companies around the world that are replete with strategy and cannot execute any of it. There is little if anything wrong with their structures; the causes of their inability to execute lie in other dimensions of our framework. When we turn to nonprofit and public-sector organizations, moreover, we find that the whole meaning of "strategy" is tenuous—but the problem of organizational effectiveness looms as large as ever.

Strategy, then, is clearly a critical variable in organization design—but much more is at work.

Systems

By systems we mean all the procedures, formal and informal, that make the organization go, day by day and year by year: capital budgeting systems, training systems, cost accounting procedures, budgeting systems. If there is a variable in our model that threatens to dominate the others, it could well be systems. Do you want to understand how an organization really does (or doesn't) get things done? Look at the systems. Do you want to change an organization without disruptive restructuring? Try changing the systems.

A large consumer goods manufacturer was recently trying to come up with an overall corporate strategy. Textbook portfolio theory seemed to apply: Find a good way to segment the business, decide which segments in the total business portfolio are most attractive, invest most heavily in those. The only catch: Reliable cost data by segment were not to be had. The company's management information system was not adequate to support the segmentation.

Again, consider how a bank might go about developing a strategy. A natural first step, it would seem, would be to segment the business by customer and product to discover where the money is made and lost and why. But in trying to do this, most banks almost immediately come up against an intractable costing problem. Because borrowers are also depositors, because transaction volumes vary, because the balance sheet turns fast, and because interest costs are half or more of total costs and unpredictable over the long term, costs for various market segments won't stay put. A strategy based on today's costs could be obsolete tomorrow.

One bank we know has rather successfully sidestepped the problem. Its key to future improvement is not strategy but the systems infrastructure that will allow account officers to negotiate deals favorable to the bank. For them the system *is* the strategy. Development and implementation of a superior account profitability system, based on a return-on-equity tree, has improved their results dramatically. "Catch a fish for a man and he is fed for a day; teach him to fish and he is fed for life": The proverb applies to organizations in general and to systems in particular.

Another intriguing aspect of systems is the way they mirror the state of an organization. Consider a certain company we'll call International Wickets. For years management has talked about the need to become more market oriented. Yet astonishingly little time is spent in their planning meetings on customers, marketing share, or other issues having to do with market orientation. One of their key systems, in other words, remains *very* internally oriented. Without a change in this key system, the market orientation goal will remain unattainable no matter how much change takes place in structure and strategy.

To many business managers the word "systems" has a dull, plodding, middle-management sound. Yet it is astonishing how powerfully systems changes can enhance organizational effectiveness—without the disruptive side effects that so often ensue from tinkering with structure.

Style

It is remarkable how often writers, in characterizing a corporate management for the business press, fall back on the word "style." Tony O'Reilly's style at Heinz is certainly not AT&T's, yet both are successful. The trouble we have with style is not in recognizing its importance, but in doing much about it. Personalities don't change, or so the conventional wisdom goes.

We think it important to distinguish between the basic personality of a top-management team and the way that team comes across to the organization. Organizations may listen to what managers say, but they believe what managers do. Not words, but patterns of actions are decisive. The power of style, then, is essentially manageable.

One element of a manager's style is how he or she chooses to spend time. As Henry Mintzberg has pointed out, managers don't spend their time in the neatly compartmentalized planning, organizing, motivating, and controlling modes of classical management theory.[2] Their days are a mess—or so it seems. There's a seeming infinity of things they might devote attention to. No top executive attends to all of the demands on his time; the median time spent on any one issue is nine minutes.

What can a top manager do in nine minutes? Actually, a good deal. He can signal what's on his mind; he can reinforce a message; he can nudge people's thinking in a desired direction. Skillful management of his inevitably fragmented time is, in fact, an immensely powerful change lever.

[2] Henry Mintzberg, "The Manager's Job: Folklore and Fact," *Harvard Business Review*, July/August 1975: 49–61.

                                    Experiential Organizational Behavior

By way of example, we have found differences beyond anything attributable to luck among different companies' success ratios in finding oil or mineral deposits. A few years ago, we surveyed a fairly large group of the finders and nonfinders in mineral exploration to discover what they were doing differently. The finders almost always said their secret was "top-management attention." Our reaction was skeptical: "Sure, that's the solution to most problems." But subsequent hard analysis showed that their executives *were* spending more time in the field, *were* blocking out more time for exploration discussions at board meetings, and *were* making more room on their own calendars for exploration-related activities.

Another aspect of style is symbolic behavior. Taking the same example, the successful finders typically have more people on the board who understand exploration or have headed exploration departments. Typically they fund exploration more consistently (that is, their year-to-year spending patterns are less volatile). They define fewer and more consistent exploration targets. Their exploration activities typically report at a higher organizational level. And they typically articulate better reasons for exploring in the first place.

A chief executive of our acquaintance is fond of saying that the way you recognize a marketing-oriented company is that "everyone talks marketing." He doesn't mean simply that an observable preoccupation with marketing is the end result, the final indication of the company's evaluation toward the marketplace. He means that it can be the lead. Change in orientation often starts when enough people talk about it before they really know what "it" is. Strategic management is not yet a crisply defined concept, but many companies are taking it seriously. If they talk about it enough, it will begin to take on specific meaning for their organizations—and those organizations will change as a result.

This suggests a second attribute of style that is by no means confined to those at the top. Our proposition is that a corporation's style, as a reflection of its culture, has more to do with its ability to change organization or performance than is generally recognized. One company, for example, was considering a certain business opportunity. From a strategic standpoint, analysis showed it to be a winner. The experience of others in the field confirmed that. Management went ahead with the acquisition. Two years later it backed out of the business, at a loss. The acquisition had failed because it simply wasn't consistent with the established corporate culture of the parent organization. It didn't fit their view of themselves. The will to make it work was absent.

Time and again strategic possibilities are blocked—or slowed down—by cultural constraints. One of today's more dramatic examples is the Bell System, where management has undertaken to move a service-oriented culture toward a new and different kind of marketing. The service idea, and its meaning to AT&T, is so deeply embedded in the Bell System's culture that the shift to a new kind of marketing will take years.

The phenomenon at its most dramatic comes to the fore in mergers. In almost every merger, no matter how closely related the businesses, the task of integrating and achieving eventual synergy is a problem no less difficult than combining two cultures. At some level of detail, almost everything done by two parties to a merger will be done differently. This helps explain why the management of acquisitions is so hard. If the two cultures are not integrated, the planned synergies will not accrue. On the other hand, to change too much too soon is to risk uprooting more tradition than can be replanted before the vital skills of the acquiree wither and die.

Staff

Staff (in the sense of people, not line/staff) is often treated in one of two ways. At the hard end of the spectrum, we talk of appraisal systems, pay scales, formal training programs, and the like. At the soft end, we talk about morale, attitude, motivation, and behavior.

Top management is often, and justifiably, turned off by both these approaches. The first seems too trivial for their immediate concern ("Leave it to the personnel department"), the second too intractable ("We don't want a bunch of shrinks running around, stirring up the place with more attitude surveys").

Our predilection is to broaden and redefine the nature of the people issue. What do the top-performing companies do to foster the process of developing managers? How, for example, do they shape the basic values of their management candre? Our reason for asking the question at all is simply that no serious discussion of organization can afford to ignore it (although many do). Our reason for framing the question around the development of managers is our observation that the superbly performing companies pay extraordinary attention to managing what might be called the socialization process in their companies. This applies especially to the way they introduce young recruits into the mainstream of their organizations and to the way they manage their careers as the recruits develop into tomorrow's managers.

The process for orchestrating the early careers of incoming managers, for instance, at IBM, Texas Instruments, P&G, Hewlett-Packard, or Citibank is quite different from its counterpart in many other companies we know around the world. Unlike other companies, which often seem prone to sidetrack young but expensive talent into staff positions or other jobs out of the mainstream of the company's business, these leaders take extraordinary care to turn young managers' first jobs into first opportunities for contributing in practical ways to the nuts-and-bolts of what the business is all about. If the mainstream of the business is innovation, for example, the first job might be in new-products introduction. If the mainstream of the business is marketing, the MBA's first job could be sales or product management.

The companies who use people best rapidly move their managers into positions of real responsibility, often by the early- to mid-thirties. Various active support devices like assigned mentors, fast-track programs, and carefully orchestrated opportunities for exposure to top management are hallmarks of their management of people.

In addition, these companies are all particularly adept at managing, in a special and focused way, their central cadre of key managers. At Texas Instruments, Exxon, GM, and GE, for instance, a number of the very most senior executives are said to devote several weeks of each year to planning the progress of the top few hundred.

These, then, are a few examples of practical programs through which the superior companies manage people as aggressively and concretely as others manage organization structure. Considering people as a pool of resources to be nurtured, developed, guarded, and allocated is one of the many ways to turn the "staff" dimension of our 7-S framework into something not only amenable to, but worthy of practical control by senior management.

We are often told, "Get the structure 'right' and the people will fit" or "Don't compromise the 'optimum' organization for people considerations." At the other end of the spectrum we are earnestly advised, "The right people can make any organization work." Neither view is correct. People do count, but staff is only one of our seven variables.

Skills

We added the notion of skills for a highly practical reason: It enables us to capture a company's crucial attributes as no other concept can do. A strategic description of a company, for example, might typically cover markets to be penetrated or types of products to be sold. But how do most of us characterize companies? Not by their strategies or their structures. We tend to characterize them by what they do best. We talk of IBM's orientation to the marketplace, its prodigious customer service capabilities, or its sheer market power. We talk of Du Pont's research prowess, Procter & Gamble's product management capability, ITT's financial controls, Hewlett-Packard's innovation and quality, and Texas Instruments' project management. These dominating attributes, or capabilities, are what we mean by skills.

Now why is this distinction important? Because we regularly observe that organizations facing big discontinuities in business conditions must do more than shift strategic focus. Frequently they need to add a new capability, that is to say, a new skill. The Bell System, for example, is currently striving to add a formidable new array of marketing skills. Small copier companies, upon growing larger, find that they must radically enhance their service capabilities to compete with Xerox. Meanwhile Xerox needs to enhance its response capability in order to fend off a host of new competition. These dominating capability needs, unless explicitly labeled as such, often get lost as the company "attacks a new market" (strategy shift) or "decentralizes to give managers autonomy" (structure shift).

Additionally, we frequently find it helpful to *label* current skills, for the addition of a new skill may come only when the old one is dismantled. Adopting a newly "flexible and adaptive marketing thrust," for example, may be possible only if increases are accepted in certain marketing or distribution costs. Dismantling some of the distracting attributes of an old "manufacturing mentality" (that is, a skill that was perhaps crucial in the past) may be the only way to insure the success of an important change program. Possibly the most difficult problem in trying to organize effectively is that of weeding out old skills—and their supporting systems, structures, etc.—to ensure that important new skills can take root and grow.

Superordinate Goals

The word "superordinate" literally means "of higher order." By superordinate goals, we mean guiding concepts—a set of values and aspirations, often unwritten, that goes beyond the conventional formal statement of corporate objectives.

Superordinate goals are the fundamental ideas around which a business is built. They are its main values. But they are more as well. They are the broad notions of future direction that the top management team wants to infuse throughout the organization. They are the way in which the team wants to express itself, to leave its own mark. Examples would include Theodore Vail's "universal service" objective, which has so dominated AT&T; the strong drive to "customer service" which guides IBM's marketing; GE's slogan, "Progress is our most important product," which encourages engineers to tinker and innovate throughout the organization; Hewlett-Packard's "innovative people at all levels in the organization"; Dana's obsession with productivity, as a total organization, not just a few at the top; and 3M's dominating culture of "new products."

In a sense, superordinate goals are like the basic postulates in a mathematical system. They are the starting points on which the system is logically built, but in themselves are not logically derived. The ultimate test of their value is not their logic but the usefulness of the system that ensues. Everyone seems to know the importance of compelling superordinate goals. The drive for their accomplishment pulls an organization together. They provide stability in what would otherwise be a shifting set of organization dynamics.

Unlike the other six S's, superordinate goals don't seem to be present in all, or even most, organizations. They are, however, evident in most of the superior performers.

To be readily communicated, superordinate goals need to be succinct. Typically, therefore, they are expressed at high levels of abstraction and may mean very little to outsiders who don't know the organization well. But for those inside, they are rich with significance. Within an organization, superordinate goals, if well articulated, make meanings for people. And making meanings is one of the main functions of leadership.

We have passed rapidly through the variables in our framework. What should the reader have gained from the exercise?

We started with the premise that solutions to today's thorny organizing problems that invoke only structure—or even strategy and structure—are seldom adequate. The inadequacy stems in part from the inability of the two-variable model to explain why organizations are so slow to adapt to change. The reasons often lie among our other variables: systems that embody outdated assumptions, a management style that is at odds with the stated strategy, the absence of a superordinate goal that binds the organization together in pursuit of a common purpose, the refusal to deal concretely with "people problems" and opportunities.

At its most trivial, when we merely use the framework as a checklist, we find that it leads into new terrain in our efforts to understand how organizations really operate or to design a truly comprehensive change program. At a minimum, it gives us a deeper bag in which to collect our experiences.

More importantly, it suggests the wisdom of taking seriously the variables in organizing that have been considered soft, informal, or beneath the purview of top management interest. We believe that style, systems, skills, superordinate goals can be observed directly, even measured—if only they are taken seriously. We think that these variables can be at least as important as strategy and structure in orchestrating major change; indeed, that they are almost critical for achieving necessary, or desirable, change. A shift in systems, a major retraining program for staff, or the generation of top-to-bottom enthusiasm around a new superordinate goal could take years. Changes in strategy and structure, on the surface, may happen more quickly. But the pace of real change is geared to all seven S's.

At its most powerful and complex, the framework forces us to concentrate on interactions and fit. The real energy required to redirect an institution comes when all the variables in the model are aligned. One of our associates looks at our diagram as a set of compasses. "When all seven needles are all pointed the same way," he comments, "you're looking at an *organized* company."

1. Describe the relationship between "structure" and "organization".
2. What is meant by the expression "structure follows strategy"?
3. What is the difference between "structure" and "process"?

13

Henry P. Sims, Jr. and Andrew D. Szilzgyi

Job Analysis and Design

Jerry Taylor has been involved with the administrative functions of the National Insurance Company for almost twenty years. About three months ago, Jerry was appointed group manager of the Policyholder Service and Accounting Departments at the home office. Before he actually assumed the job, Jerry was able to get away for a three week management development program at the State University College of Business. One of the topics covered in the program was the concept of job enrichment, or, job redesign. Jerry had read about job enrichment in several of his trade journals, but the program was his first opportunity to think about the concept in some detail. In addition, several of the program participants had had some experience (both positive and negative) with job redesign projects.

Jerry was intrigued with the idea. He knew how boring routine administrative tasks could become, and he knew from his previous supervisory work that turnover of clerical personnel was a real problem. In addition, his conversations with the Administrative Vice-President and Joe Bellows, the Personnel Manager, led him to believe that some trials with redesigning the work would be supported and favorably regarded.

Description of the Work

Group Policyholder Service Department

The principal activities undertaken in this department are the sorting and opening of incoming mail and then matching to accounting files; reviewing of Group Insurance Bills from policy holders; and coding required changes to policies (e.g., new employees and terminations). These activities are carried out by approximately 28 people; 53 percent of whom were over age 35, 82

This case and the analysis are adapted (with permission) from Alber, Antone F., *An Exploratory Study of the Benefits and Costs of Job Enrichment*, Ph.D. dissertation, The Pennsylvania State University, 1977. Several figures are reproduced directly, and major portions of the text are quoted directly. Reprinted by permission.

percent female, 89 percent high school graduates, and 53 percent with less than two years experience in their current job.

Organizationally, the department is headed by a manager. The employees are grouped into the four functional categories of clerical support, senior technician, change coder, and special clerk. The general work flow and a more specific list of the tasks carried out within each functional category are shown in Figure 1.

The Group Policyholder Service Department shares the same physical working area as the Accounting Department. The people within Policyholder Service who work in the different functional categories are in very close proximity to one another, frequently just one desk away. The files for

FIGURE 1. Policyholder Service Department Work Flow and Tasks

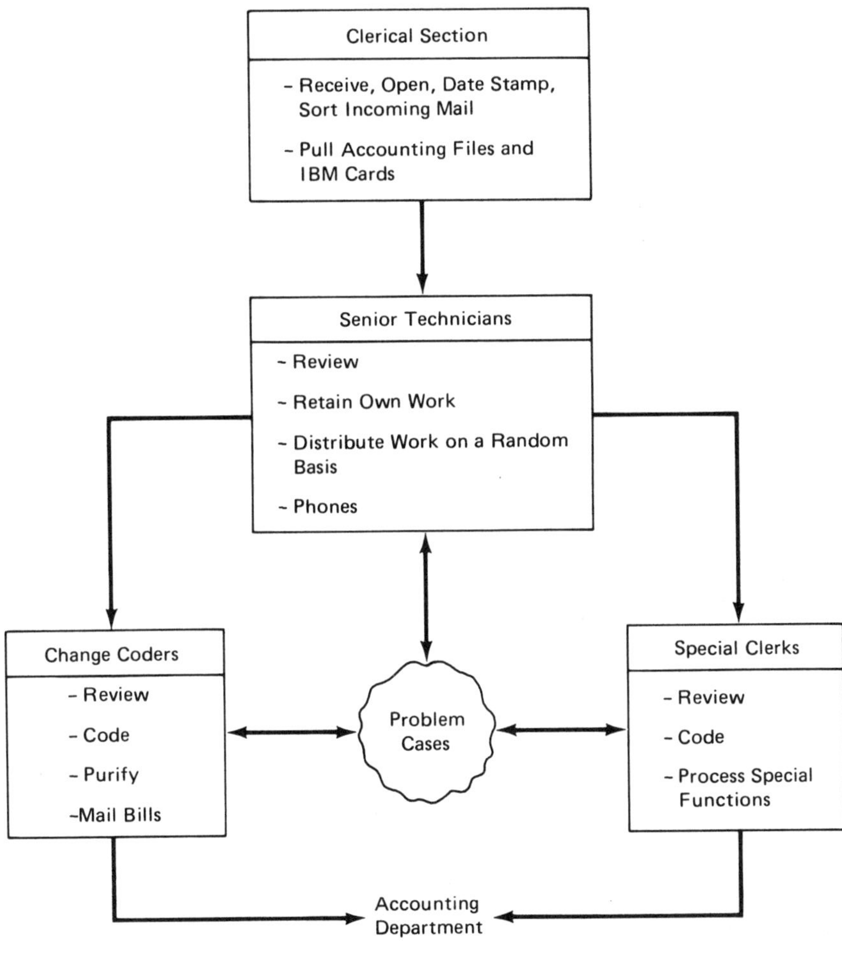

the department are located at one corner of the work area and the supervisors had offices along one side (see Figure 2).

In the last few months, Jerry has observed that the functional breakdown and the accompanying physical arrangement of people and files leads to a number of problems. Since work is assigned or selected on a random basis, there is no personal accountability for it. Files are at one corner of the work area where they can be retrieved by the clerical group and distributed to a senior technician who randomly distributes them to be processed. After a file is coded, it is placed in a holding area for processing by the Accounting Department. Here, assignment of work is also done on a random basis. It was difficult to respond to phone calls or written requests for information promptly, because it is frequently difficult to find a file. In fact, several people are kept busy doing nothing but looking for files.

The typical employee performs a job which consisted of two tasks on approximately an eleven-minute cycle. All work is cross checked. The training for the job is minimal and there are a number of individuals performing the same set of tasks on files randomly issued. A clerk occasionally corresponds with a policyholder, but all correspondence goes out with the manager's signature on it. The manager thus receives all phone calls and correspondence from policyholders.

Because of the random distribution of work, individual performance is difficult to measure. There are spot checks on some completed work by someone other than the doer, but it is difficult or impossible to determine the specific individual who was responsible. Consequently, it is not possible to provide specific information to individuals at regular intervals about their work performance.

Accounting Department

The Accounting Department processes the files, bills, and checks received from the Group Policyholder Service. Premiums are posted on IBM cards and worksheets. Necessary adjustments are made to accounts and the checks, cards, and worksheets are balanced. Approximately 28 people are employed at any one time performing these tasks. Seventy-seven percent of the work force are under 35 years of age. Everyone has at least a high school degree and 54 percent had less than two years experience in the job they were performing.

The department has both a manager and a supervisor. The employees are divided into senior technicians, premium posters, and special clerks. The general work flow and tasks carried out in each of these functional areas is shown in Figure 3. As shown in Figure 2, the Accounting Department shares its work and files with Policyholder Service.

Work is selected on a random basis. Clerks go to a bookcase file and choose the cases they wished to do. Occasionally, correspondence with a policyholder is necessary, and is signed by the manager.

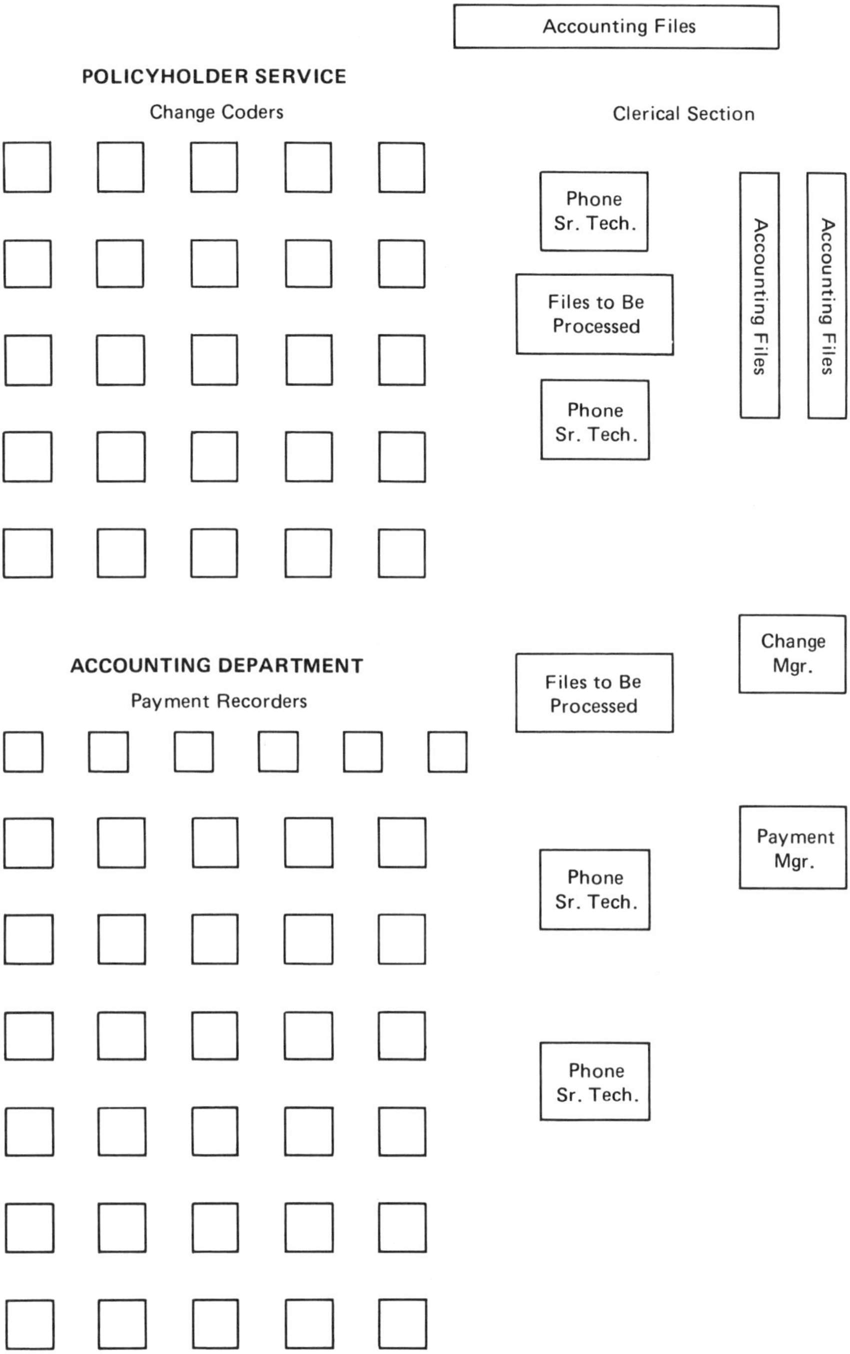

[a]Indicates relative positions and not actual number of employees
or floor space occupied.

FIGURE 2. Policyholder Service Department and Accounting Department Physical Layout[a]

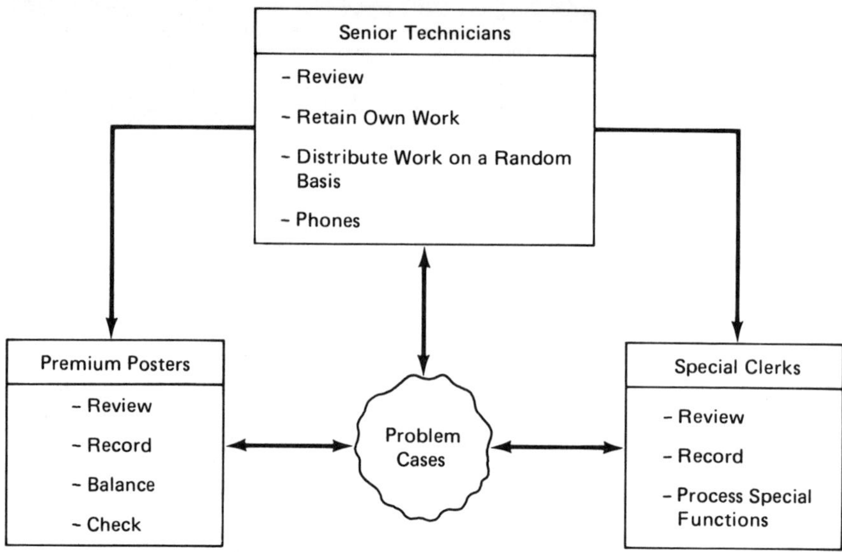

FIGURE 3. Accounting Department Work Flow and Tasks

The Problem of Change

Jerry believes that if the work in his department can be *properly* redesigned, then departmental effectiveness can be improved. In addition, he believes that substantial improvements can be made in terms of individual employee work satisfaction.

In thinking about redesigning the work, Jerry has separated the problem into two parts. First, he is concerned about the *process* of change. How can he best accomplish a job redesign project? Second, Jerry has been concerned with the *arrangement* of the tasks themselves. Before he begins such a project, Jerry hopes to have at least some preliminary ideas about the feasibility of such a change.

First, *as an individual,* write down your thoughts about how Jerry should implement the process of change.

Then, as a group, can you agree on the *process* that Jerry should use to bring about the change?

Next, still *as an individual*, how would you actually redesign the work in Jerry's department?

Finally, *as a group*, how would you redesign the work in Jerry's department?

The Individual As a System

14

Parable

In a *shtetl* in Poland, a rabbi was called upon to settle a dispute between two men. The first man told his story. The rabbi thought and finally said, "I think you are right." The second man said in disbelief, "But rabbi, you have not heard my side yet!" He then proceeded to tell it. The rabbi thought a few moments and said, "I think you are right." At this point a spectator said, "But rabbi, they both can't be right." The rabbi replied, "You're right, too."

15

Teaching How to Cope with Workplace Conflicts

It is nothing if not comical: Sixteen middle-aged executives, divided into teams, race against the clock—and each other—to build a device out of assorted junk that will catch raw eggs gently enough to keep them from breaking. They get the junk from an auctioneer who "sells" such things as metal strips and pieces of string, for which each team can bid up to $55,000. In the background a videotape machine quietly records the sights and sounds of the competition.

Later, the executives watch themselves in action. To their distress, they see themselves mocking their teammates, throwing out authoritarian orders, and showing impatience. Although their goal was to beat the other teams, they discover that most of their conflicts were with persons on their side.

The egg drop exercise, developed by Vector Management Systems Inc., of New York, to open a three-day course on managing conflict, is one of a growing number of techniques offered by consultants who teach managers to recognize and deal with on-the-job conflicts. The techniques may be as simple as self-administered and self-scored questionnaires, such as those offered by Houston-based Teleometrics International Inc. to let managers analyze their own styles of dealing with conflicts. But they also include psychologist-scored surveys that allow subordinates and peers to rate managers on their ability to handle conflicts, as well as courses that run as long as nine days. The disparate methods have one thing in common—a belief that conflict, when properly recognized, is not debilitating to job effectiveness and can actually enhance it.

"There's a lot of energy wasted because many people work toward eliminating conflict," says Kenneth Sole, a psychologist who runs conflict seminars at NTL Institute for Applied Behavioral Science in Bethel, Me. "My goal is not to have fewer conflicts, but to make conflicts productive."

Charles Reiner, Vector's president, notes that there are five ways to deal

Reprinted from the February 18, 1980 issue of *Business Week* by special permission, © 1980 by McGraw-Hill, Inc., New York, N.Y. 19020. All rights reserved.

with conflicts: compromise, competition, avoidance, collaboration, and accommodation. "As psychologists we've worked studiously to suspend value judgments about the five styles," he says. "We try to give course participants an ability to use all of them, and by the end of our seminar their bias against or for any one style is considerably reduced."

Increasing Tension

The proliferation of conflict seminars comes at a time of increasing tension in the workplace. The influx of women and minorities into the work force has caused problems that can rarely be resolved by fiat. The growing popularity of avant-garde management structures such as matrix management, in which many corporate employees wind up reporting to two bosses, has reduced many executives' authority to issue orders, making their interpersonal skills far more important. And in general, corporate management over the last decade has become far more amenable to judging managers by their behavior patterns as well as by bottom-line performance and has shown an increasing willingness to spend time and money on behaviorally oriented programs.

John W. Humphrey, president of Forum Corp., a Boston behavioral consulting firm, calls the trend an evolution from resolving conflict to managing conflict to working with conflict. "We've gone," he says, "from something that says, 'Get it out!' to something that says, 'Learn how to use it.'"

Acting It Out

The techniques of teaching managers how to use conflict vary as much as the consultants who develop them. Vector, for example, includes a commercial movie, *Twelve Angry Men*, in its course because the jury members in the film use a variety of styles to resolve their conflicts. After each showing, the course participants analyze the conflicts and how to resolve them.

Other consultants rely more heavily on role-playing. In one exercise, Forum Corp. sets up groups of three people and gives them a hypothetical problem. One participant might play the part of a research manager, another a product manager, and a third an engineering department head. They have to figure out how to allocate scarce resources for each department. Situation Management Systems Inc., of Boston, offers courses on "Positive Power and Influence" and "Negotiating Skills" that deal heavily with resolving conflicts. They wind up with each trainee playing himself or herself, and a fellow participant acting as the trainee's boss or subordinate.

Not surprisingly, such methods have their detractors. One of them, Kenneth R. Hammond, director of the University of Colorado's Center for Research on Judgment & Policy, has been a conflict troubleshooter for such disparate organizations as the Denver Police Dept. and an international pharmaceutical company. He pays little attention to behavioral styles, concentrating instead on separating facts from values. "People assume that if they solve the emotional problems, the cognitive aspect will solve itself, but then nobody focuses on issues," he maintains.

By focusing on issues, Hammond says, he resolved a two-year conflict between the Denver Police Dept., which wanted a new bullet with greater stopping power, and community leaders, who saw the request as bloodthirsty and possibly racist. He got the warring parties to rank in importance such values as stopping power, injury, and threat to bystanders. He discovered that the community as a whole would accept a bullet that had increased stopping effectiveness without increasing injury. Within six weeks, the police settled on ammunition that would flatten out and knock a person over on impact. As Hammond saw it, the solution had been elusive because of emotions. "When they couldn't agree," he says, "they attributed it to unpleasant motives, such as 'You hate blacks' or 'You want a lawless society.'"

To NTL's Sole, such real-life issues are the stuff of which conflict courses must be made. He also eschews role-playing and artificially created situations and arranges to have an equal distribution of warring factions in his workshops, allowing conflicts to arise naturally. He tries to have the same number of men and women, for instance, and to include a large smattering of minorities. With the participant distribution forming a built-in powder keg, he lets simple issues—such as whether or not to allow smoking—form the conflicts that will be analyzed. "We get a participant pool that guarantees differences but also guarantees pools of support," he explains. "My workshops are kind of a social microcosm, and the issues that emerge mirror issues in society."

Racism and Sexism

In contrast to comprehensive efforts such as Sole's nine-day workshop, a number of corporations are putting in less sweeping programs of their own. More often than not, they are designed to resolve specific conflict problems within an organization. Northwestern Bell Telephone Co., for instance, has a program to combat racism and sexism. "We teach women and minorities to develop support systems and to confront people who use sexist or racist language," Larry L. Waller, staff manager for awareness training, explains.

At Sperry Vickers, a Troy (Mich.) division of Sperry Corp., a switch to matrix management, with its dual ladder of authority, dramatically increased conflict two years ago. B. Richard Templeton, manager of human resources and organization development, has since distributed conflict analysis questionnaires to managers and their subordinates and has been holding informal self-assessment meetings to help them understand how their behavior is perceived by their colleagues.

Templeton grants that the matrix system still causes clashes, but he says that his program is helping resolve the conflicts at an early stage. "It's like setting a course for the moon," he says. "The best place to make a course correction is as early as possible, before you're hopelessly off track."

Tailor-Made Seminars

Conflict consultants sometimes develop seminars to a company's specifications. Union Carbide Corp., for one, has sent nearly 200 managers through a tailor-made Vector course over the last two years. Stephen J. Wall, Carbide's manager of corporate management development, reports that informal feedback has been very positive. "The thread that runs through the comments is that people are startled to discover their own patterns of response to conflicts," he says. "Now they say they can see what's coming and actually plan strategies to deal with it." Wall, who took the course before he bought it for Carbide, says he discovered that he had a tendency to be an accommodator and used to give in to unreasonable requests. "Now whenever I feel I'm about to give in, I roll it around in my head first," he says.

It is almost impossible to put a dollars-and-cents value on such behavioral awareness, but every conflict course graduate with whom BUSINESS WEEK spoke insisted that the course was worth the few hundred dollars it typically cost. Marilyn Loden, an organization development specialist at New York Telephone Co. and a graduate of Sole's program, noted that she had just had a conversation with a recalcitrant employee; it was difficult for her, but it cleared the air in the office. "A year ago I would have been stewing about the fact that he wasn't working out, but I would have said nothing," she says.

Raymond A. Murphy, a Carbide manager of systems software, and Leicia Marlow, a Carbide data processing applications manager, liked the Vector course so much that they have assigned several of their own employees to attend it. "Watching my people at staff meetings now, I see more conscious attempts to understand where the other guy is coming from," Murphy notes. "We've had people who were overassertive before who are now curbing their responses, while others who had sat back and watched have learned to be assertive."

The ability to choose among several styles as the situation requires is probably the most important result of all the courses. Marlow, who concedes that she needed help in becoming more assertive, insists that the course was far more complete than standard assertiveness training. As she sums it up: "It wasn't necessarily altering behavior; it was broadening it."

Issues

1. How does an individual's perception affect conflict in an organization?
2. How does an individual's personality affect conflict in an organization?
3. Why does a matrix organization create conflict?
4. Give an example of a conflict between cognitive and emotional aspects of a situation.
5. Why should competition with another team create conflict within the competing team?

16

Pygmalion in Management

A Manager's Expectations Are the Key to a Subordinate's Performance and Development

In George Bernard Shaw's *Pygmalion*, Eliza Doolittle explains:

You see, really and truly, apart from the things anyone can pick up (the dressing and the proper way of speaking, and so on), the difference between a lady and a flower girl is not how she behaves, but how she's treated. I shall always be a flower girl to Professor Higgins, because he always treats me as a flower girl, and always will; but I know I can be a lady to you, because you always treat me as a lady, and always will."

Some managers always treat their subordinates in a way that leads to superior performance. But most managers, like Professor Higgins, unintentionally treat their subordinates in a way that leads to lower performance than they are capable of achieving. The way managers treat their subordinates is subtly influenced by what they expect of them. If a manager's expectations are high, productivity is likely to be excellent. If his expectations are low, productivity is likely to be poor. It is as though there were a law that caused a subordinate's performance to rise or fall to meet his manager's expectations.

The powerful influence of one person's expectations on another's behavior has long been recognized by physicians, and behavioral scientists and, more recently, by teachers. But heretofore the importance of managerial expectations for individual and group performance has not been widely understood. I have documented this phenomenon in a number of case studies prepared during the past decade for major industrial concerns. These cases and other evidence available from scientific research now reveal:

Reprinted by permission of the Harvard Business Review. "Pygmalion in Management" by J. Sterling Livingston (July-August 1969). Copyright © 1969 by the President and Fellows of Harvard College; all rights reserved.

Author's note: This article is a condensation of my book, *High Expectations in Management,* published by the Sterling Institute Press.

What a manager expects of his subordinates and the way he treats them largely determine their performance and career progress.

A unique characteristic of superior managers is their ability to create high performance expectations that subordinates fulfill.

Less effective managers fail to develop similar expectations, and, as a consequence, the productivity of their subordinates suffers.

Subordinates, more often than not, appear to do what they believe they are expected to do.

Impact on Productivity

One of the most comprehensive illustrations of the effect of managerial expectations on productivity is recorded in studies of the organizational experiment undertaken in 1961 by Alfred Oberlander, manager of the Rockaway District Office of the Metropolitan Life Insurance Company.[1] He had observed that outstanding insurance agencies grew faster than average or poor agencies and that new insurance agents performed better in outstanding agencies than in average or poor agencies, regardless of their sales aptitude. He decided, therefore, to group his superior men in one unit to stimulate their performance and to provide a challenging environment in which to introduce new salesmen.

Accordingly, Oberlander assigned his six best agents to work with his best assistant manager, an equal number of average producers to work with an average assistant manager, and the remaining low producers to work with the least able manager. He then asked the superior group to produce two thirds of the premium volume achieved by the entire agency the previous year. He described the results as follows:

Shortly after this selection had been made, the men in the agency began referring to this select group as a 'super-staff' since, due to the fact that we were operating this group as a unit, their esprit de corps was very high. Their production efforts over the first 12 weeks far surpassed our most optimistic expectations . . . proving that groups of men of sound ability can be motivated beyond their apparently normal productive capacities when the problems created by the poor producer are eliminated from the operation.

Thanks to this fine result, over-all agency performance improved 40 percent and stayed at this figure.

In the beginning of 1962 when, through expansion, we appointed another assistant manager and assigned him a staff, we again utilized this same concept, arranging the men once more according to their productive capacity.

The assistant managers were assigned . . . according to their ability, with the most capable assistant manager receiving the best group, thus playing strength to

---

[1] See "Jamesville Branch Office (A)," MET003A, and "Jamesville Branch Office (B)," MET003B (Boston, Sterling Institute, 1969).

strength. Our agency over-all production again improved by about 25–30 percent, and so this staff arrangement was continued until the end of the year.

Now in this year of 1963, we found upon analysis that there were so many men . . . with a potential of half a million dollars or more that only one staff remained of those men in the agency who were not considered to have any chance of reaching the half-million-dollar mark.[2]

Although the productivity of the "super-staff" improved dramatically, it should be pointed out that the productivity of men in the lowest unit, "who were not considered to have any chance of reaching the half-million-dollar mark," actually declined and that attrition among these men increased. The performance of the superior men rose to meet their managers' expectations, while that of the weaker men declined as predicted.

Self-Fulfilling Prophesies

However, the "average" unit proved to be an anomaly. Although the district manager expected only average performance from this group, its productivity increased significantly. This was because the assistant manager in charge of the group refused to believe that he was less capable than the manager of the "super-staff" or that the agents in the top group had any greater ability than the agents in his group. He insisted in discussions with his agents that every man in the middle group had greater potential than the men in the "super-staff," lacking only their years of experience in selling insurance. He stimulated his agents to accept the challenge of out-performing the "super-staff." As a result, in each year the middle group increased its productivity by a higher percentage than the "super-staff" did (although it never attained the dollar volume of the top group).

It is of special interest that the self-image of the manager of the "average" unit did not permit him to accept others' treatment of him as an "average" manager, just as Eliza Doolittle's image of herself as a lady did not permit her to accept others' treatment of her as a flower girl. The assistant manager transmitted his own strong feelings of efficacy to his agents, created mutual expectancy of high performance, and greatly stimulated productivity.

Comparable results occurred when a similar experiment was made at another office of the company. Further confirmation comes from a study of the early managerial success of 49 college graduates who were management-level employees of an operating company of the American Telephone and Telegraph Company. David E. Berlew and Douglas T. Hall of the Massachusetts Institute of Technology examined the career progress of these managers over a period of five years and discovered that their relative success, as measured by salary increases and the company's estimate of each man's per-

[2]"Jamesville Branch Office (B)," p. 2.

formance and potential, depended largely on the company's expectations of them.[3]

The influence of one person's expectations on another's behavior is by no means a business discovery. More than half a century ago, Albert Moll concluded from his clinical experience that subjects behaved as they believed they were expected to.[4] The phenomenon he observed, in which "the prophecy causes its own fulfillment," has recently become a subject of considerable scientific interest. For example:

In a series of scientific experiments, Robert Rosenthal of Harvard University has demonstrated that a "teacher's expectation for her pupils' intellectual competence can come to serve as an educational self-fulfilling prophecy."[5]

An experiment in a summer Headstart program for 60 preschoolers compared the performance of pupils under (a) teachers who had been led to expect relatively slow learning by their children, and (b) teachers who had been led to believe their children had excellent intellectual ability and learning capacity. Pupils of the second group of teachers learned much faster.[6]

Moreover, the healing professions have long recognized that a physician's or psychiatrist's expectations can have a formidable influence on a patient's physical or mental health. What takes place in the minds of the patients and the healers, particularly when they have congruent expectations, may determine the outcome. For instance, the havoc of a doctor's pessimistic prognosis has often been observed. Again, it is well known that the efficacy of a new drug or a new treatment can be greatly influenced by the physician's expectations—a result referred to by the medical profession as a "placebo effect."

Pattern of Failure

When salesmen are treated by their managers as supersalesmen, as the "super-staff" was at Metropolitan Rockaway District Office, they try to live up to that image and do what they know supersalesmen are expected to do. But when salesmen with poor productivity records are treated by their managers as *not* having "any chance" of success, as the low producers at Rockaway were, this negative expectation also becomes a managerial self-fulfilling prophecy.

Unsuccessful salesmen have great difficulty maintaining their self-image and self-esteem. In response to low managerial expectations, they typically

---

[3]"Some Determinants of Early Managerial Success," Alfred P. Sloan School of Management Organization Research Program #81–64 (Cambridge, Massachusetts Institute of Technology, 1964), pp. 13–14.

[4]Robert Rosenthal and Lenore Jacobson, *Pygmalion in the Classroom* (New York, Holt, Rinehart, and Winston, Inc., 1968), p. 11.

[5]Ibid., Preface, p. vii.

[6]Ibid., p. 38.

attempt to prevent additional damage to their egos by avoiding situations that might lead to greater failure. They either reduce the number of sales calls they make or avoid trying to "close" sales when that might result in further painful rejection, or both. Low expectations and damaged egos lead them to behave in a manner that increases the probability of failure, thereby fulfilling their managers' expectations. Let me illustrate:

Not long ago I studied the effectiveness of branch bank managers at a West Coast bank with over 500 branches. The managers who had had their lending authority reduced because of high rates of loss became progressively less effective. To prevent further loss of authority, they turned to making only "safe" loans. This action resulted in losses of business to competing banks and a relative decline in both deposits and profits at their branches. Then, to reverse that decline in deposits and earnings, they often "reached" for loans and became almost irrational in their acceptance of questionable credit risks. Their actions were not so much a matter of poor judgment as an expression of their willingness to take desperate risks in the hope of being able to avoid further damage to their egos and to their careers.

Thus, in response to the low expectations of their supervisors, who had reduced their lending authority, they behaved in a manner that led to larger credit losses. They appeared to do what they believed they were expected to do, and their supervisors' expectations became self-fulfilling prophecies.

Power of Expectations

Managers cannot avoid the depressing cycle of events that flow from low expectations merely by hiding their feelings from subordinates. If a manager believes a subordinate will perform poorly, it is virtually impossible for him to mask his expectations, because the message usually is communicated unintentionally, without conscious action on his part.

Indeed, a manager often communicates most when he believes he is communicating least. For instance, when he says nothing, when he becomes "cold" and "uncommunicative," it usually is a sign that he is displeased by a subordinate or believes he is "hopeless." The silent treatment communicates negative feelings even more effectively, at times, than a tongue-lashing does. What seems to be critical in the communication of expectations is not what the boss says, so much as the *way he behaves.* Indifferent and noncommittal treatment, more often than not, is the kind of treatment that communicates low expectations and leads to poor performance.

Common Illusions

Managers are more effective in communicating low expectations to their subordinates than in communicating high expectations to them, even though most managers believe exactly the opposite. It usually is astonishingly difficult for them to recognize the clarity with which they transmit negative feelings to subordinates. To illustrate again:

The Rockaway district manager vigorously denied that he had communicated low expectations to the men in the poorest group who, he believed, did not have "any chance" of becoming high producers. Yet the message was clearly received by those men. A typical case was that of an agent who resigned from the low unit. When the district manager told the agent that he was sorry he was leaving, the agent replied, "No, you're not, you're glad." Although the district manager previously had said nothing to the man, he had unintentionally communicated his low expectations to his agents through his indifferent manner. Subsequently, the men who were assigned to the lowest unit interpreted the assignment as equivalent to a request for their resignation.

One of the company's agency managers established superior, average, and low units, even though he was convinced that he had no superior or outstanding subordinates. "All my assistant managers and agents are either average or incompetent," he explained to the Rockaway district manager. Although he tried to duplicate the Rockaway results, his low opinions of his men were communicated—not so subtly—to them. As a result, the experiment failed.

Positive feelings, on the other hand, often do not come through clearly enough. For example:

Another insurance agency manager copied the organizational changes made at the Rockaway District Office, grouping the salesmen he rated highly with the best manager, the average salesmen with an average manager, and so on. However, improvement did not result from the move. The Rockaway district manager therefore investigated the situation. He discovered that the assistant manager in charge of the high-performance unit was unaware that his manager considered him to be the best. In fact, he and the other agents doubted that the agency manager really believed there was any difference in their abilities. This agency manager was a stolid, phlegmatic, unemotional man who treated his men in a rather pedestrian way. Since high expectations had not been communicated to the men, they did not understand the reason for the new organization and could not see any point in it. Clearly, the way a manager *treats* his subordinates, not the way he organizes them, is the key to high expectations and high productivity.

Impossible Dreams

Managerial expectations must pass the test of reality before they can be translated into performance. To become self-fulfilling prophecies, expectations must be made of sterner stuff than the power of positive thinking or generalized confidence in one's fellow men—helpful as these concepts may be for some other purposes. Subordinates will not be motivated to reach high levels of productivity unless they consider the boss's high expectations realistic and achievable. If they are encouraged to strive for unattainable goals, they eventually give up trying and settle for results that are lower than they are capable of achieving. The experience of a large electrical manufacturing company demonstrates this; the company discovered that production actually declined if production quotas were set too high, because the workers simply stopped trying to meet them. In other words, the practice of "dangling the carrot just beyond the donkey's reach," endorsed by many managers, is not a good motivational device.

Scientific research by David C. McClelland of Harvard University and John W. Atkinson of the University of Michigan[7] has demonstrated that the relationship of motivation to expectancy varies in the form of a bell-shaped curve, like this:

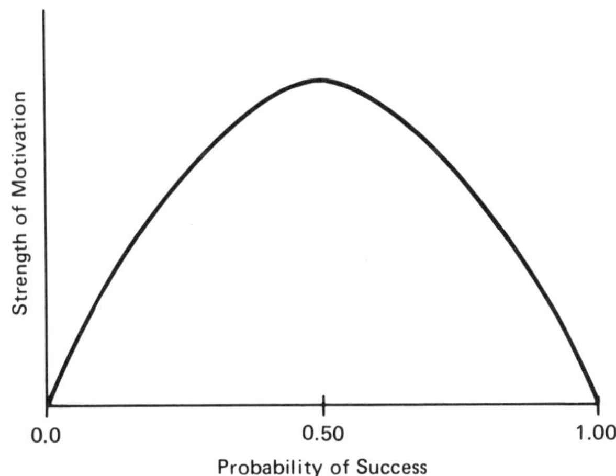

The degree of motivation and effort rises until the expectancy of success reaches 50%, then begins to fall even though the expectancy of success continues to increase. No motivation or response is aroused when the goal is perceived as being either virtually certain or virtually impossible to attain.

Moreover, as Berlew and Hall have pointed out, if a subordinate fails to meet performance expectations that are close to his own level of aspirations, he will "lower his personal performance goals and standards, his . . . performance will tend to drop off, and he will develop negative attitudes toward the task activity or job."[8] It is therefore not surprising that failure of subordi-

---

[7] See John W. Atkinson, "Motivational Determinants of Risk-Taking Behavior," *Psychological Review*, Vol. 64, No. 6, 1957, p. 365.

[8] David E. Berlew and Douglas T. Hall, "The Socialization of Managers: Effects of Expectations on Performance," *Administrative Science Quarterly*, September 1966, p. 208.

---

nates to meet the unrealistically high expectations of their managers leads to high rates of attrition; such attrition may be voluntary or involuntary.

Secret of Superiority

Something takes place in the minds of superior managers that does not occur in the minds of those who are less effective. While superior managers are consistently able to create high performance expectations that their subordinates fulfill, weaker managers are not successful in obtaining a similar response. What accounts for the difference?

The answer, in part, seems to be that superior managers have greater confidence than other managers in their own ability to develop the talents of their subordinates. Contrary to what might be assumed, the high expectations of superior managers are based primarily on what they think about themselves—about their own ability to select, train, and motivate their subordinates. What the manager believes about himself subtly influences what he believes about his subordinates, what he expects of them, and how he treats them. If he has confidence in his ability to develop and stimulate them to high levels of performance, he will expect much of them and will treat them with confidence that his expectations will be met. But if he has doubts about his ability to stimulate them, he will expect less of them and will treat them with less confidence.

Stated in another way, the superior manager's record of success and his confidence in his ability give his high expectations credibility. As a consequence, his subordinates accept his expectations as realistic and try hard to achieve them.

The importance of what a manager believes about his training and motivational ability is illustrated by "Sweeney's Miracle,"[9] a managerial and educational self-fulfilling prophecy:

James Sweeney taught industrial management and psychiatry at Tulane University, and he also was responsible for the operation of the Biomedical Computer Center there. Sweeney believed that he could teach even a poorly educated man to be a capable computer operator. George Johnson, a black man who was a former hospital porter, became janitor at the computer center; he was chosen by Sweeney to prove his conviction. In the morning, George Johnson performed his janitorial duties, and in the afternoon Sweeney taught him about computers.

Johnson was learning a great deal about computers when someone at the university concluded that, to be a computer operator, one had to have a certain I.Q. score. Johnson was tested, and his I.Q. indicated that he would not be able to learn to type, much less operate a computer.

But Sweeney was not convinced. He threatened to quit unless Johnson was permitted to learn to program and operate the computer. Sweeney pre-

[9]See Robert Rosenthal and Lenore Jacobson, op. cit., pp. 3–4.

Experiential Organizational Behavior

vailed, and he is still running the computer center. Johnson is now in charge of the main computer room and is responsible for training new employees to program and operate the computer.

Sweeney's expectations were based on what he believed about his own teaching ability, not on Johnson's learning credentials. What a manager believes about his ability to train and motivate subordinates clearly is the foundation on which realistically high managerial expectations are built.

The Critical Early Years

Managerial expectations have their most magical influence on young men. As subordinates mature and gain experience, their self-image gradually hardens, and they begin to see themselves as their career records imply. Their own aspirations, and the expectations of their superiors, become increasingly controlled by the "reality" of their past performance. It becomes more and more difficult for them, and for their managers, to generate mutually high expectations unless they have outstanding records.

Incidentally, the same pattern occurs in school. Rosenthal's experiments with educational self-fulfilling prophecies consistently demonstrate that teachers' expectations are more effective in influencing intellectual growth in younger children than in older children. In the lower grade levels, particularly in the first and second grades, the effects of teachers' expectations are dramatic.[10] In the upper grade levels, teachers' prophecies seem to have little effect on a child's intellectual growth, although they do affect his motivation and attitude toward school. While the declining influence of teachers' expectations cannot be completely explained, it is reasonable to conclude that younger children are more malleable, have fewer fixed notions about their abilities, and have less well-established reputations in the schools. As they grow, particularly if they are assigned to "tracks" on the basis of their records, as is now often done in public schools, their beliefs about their intellectual ability and their teachers' expectations of them begin to harden and become more resistant to influence by others.

Key to Future Performance

The early years in a business organization, when a young man can be strongly influenced by managerial expectations, are critical in determining his future performance and career progress. This is shown by a study at American Telephone and Telegraph Company:

Berlew and Hall found that what the company initially expected of 49 college graduates who were management-level employees was the most crit-

[10]Ibid., pp. 74–81.

---

ical factor in their subsequent performance and success. The researchers concluded: "The .72 correlation between how much a company expects of a man in his first year and how much he contributes during the next five years is too compelling to be ignored."[11]

Subsequently, the two men studied the career records of 18 college graduates who were hired as management trainees in another of the American Telephone and Telegraph Company's operating companies. Again they found that both expectations and performance in the first year correlated consistently with later performance and success.[12]

Berlew and Hall summarized their research by stating:

Something important is happening in the first year. . . . Meeting high company expectations in the critical first year leads to the internalization of positive job attitudes and high standards; these attitudes and standards, in turn, would first lead to and be reinforced by strong performance and success in later years. It should also follow that a new manager who meets the challenge of one highly demanding job will be given subsequently a more demanding job, and his level of contribution will rise as he responds to the company's growing expectations of him. The key . . . is the concept of the first year as a *critical period for learning*, a time when the trainee is uniquely ready to develop or change in the direction of the company's expectations.[13]

Most Influential Boss

A young man's first manager is likely to be the most influential person in his career. If this manager is unable or unwilling to develop the skills the young man needs to perform effectively, the latter will set lower standards for himself than he is capable of achieving, his self-image will be impaired, and he will develop negative attitudes toward his job, his employer, and—in all probability—his career in business. Since his chances of building a successful career with his employer will decline rapidly, he will leave, if he has high aspirations, in hope of finding a better opportunity. If, on the other hand, his manager helps him achieve his maximum potential, he will build the foundation for a successful career. To illustrate:

With few exceptions, the most effective branch managers at a large West Coast bank were mature men in their forties and fifties. The bank's executives explained that it took considerable time for a man to gain the knowledge, experience, and judgment required to handle properly credit risks, customer relations, and employee relations.

However, one branch manager, ranked in the top 10% of the managers in terms of effectiveness (which included branch profit growth, deposit growth, scores on administrative audits, and subjective rankings by superiors), was only 27 years old. This young man had been made a branch manager at 25, and in two years he not only improved the performance of his branch sub-

[11]"Some Determinants of Early Managerial Success," pp. 13–14.
[12]"The Socialization of Managers: Effects of Expectations on Performance," p. 219.
[13]Ibid., pp. 221–222.

stantially but also developed his younger assistant manager so that he, in turn, was made a branch manager at 25.

The man had had only average grades in college, but, in his first four years at the bank, he had been assigned to work with two branch managers who were remarkably effective teachers. His first boss, who was recognized throughout the bank for his unusual skill in developing young men, did not believe that it took years to gain the knowledge and skill needed to become an effective banker. After two years, the young man was made assistant manager at a branch headed by another executive, who also was an effective developer of his subordinates. Thus it was that when the young man was promoted to head a branch, he confidently followed the model of his two previous superiors in operating his branch, quickly established a record of outstanding performance, and trained his assistant (as he had been trained) to assume responsibility early.

Contrasting Records

For confirming evidence of the crucial role played by a person's first bosses, let us turn to selling, since performance in this area is more easily measured than in most managerial areas. Consider the following investigations:

In a study of the careers of 100 insurance salesmen who began work with either highly competent or less-than-competent agency managers, the Life Insurance Agency Management Association found that men with average sales aptitude test scores were nearly five times as likely to succeed under managers with good performance records as under managers with poor records; and men with superior sales aptitude scores were found to be twice as likely to succeed under high-performing managers as under low-performing managers.[14]

The Metropolitan Life Insurance Company determined in 1960 that differences in the productivity of new insurance agents who had equal sales aptitudes could be accounted for only by differences in the ability of managers in the offices to which they were assigned. Men whose productivity was high in relation to their aptitude test scores invariably were employed in offices that had production records among the top third in the company. Conversely, men whose productivity was low in relation to their test scores typically were in the least successful offices. After analyzing all the factors that might have accounted for these variations, the company concluded that differences in the performance of new men were due primarily to differences in the "proficiency in sales training and direction" of the local managers.[15]

A study I conducted of the performance of automobile salesmen in Ford dealerships in New England revealed that superior salesmen were concentrated in a few outstanding dealerships. For instance, 10 of the top 15 sales-

[14] Robert T. Davis, "Sales Management in the Field," HBR January-February 1958, p. 91.
[15] Alfred A. Oberlander, "The Collective Conscience in Recruiting," address to Life Insurance Agency Management Association Annual Meeting, Chicago, Illinois, 1963, p. 5.

---

men in New England were in 3 (out of approximately 200) of the dealerships in this region; and 5 of the top 15 men were in one highly successful dealership; yet 4 of these men previously had worked for other dealers without achieving outstanding sales records. There seemed to be little doubt that the training and motivational skills of managers in the outstanding dealerships were the critical factor.

Astute Selection

While success in business sometimes appears to depend on the "luck of the draw," more than luck is involved when a young man is selected by a superior manager. Successful managers do not pick their subordinates at random or by the toss of a coin. They are careful to select only those who they "know" will succeed. As Metropolitan's Rockaway district manager, Alfred Oberlander, insisted: "Every man who starts with us is going to be a topnotch life insurance man, or he would not have received an invitation to join the team."[16]

When pressed to explain how they "know" whether a man will be successful, superior managers usually end up by saying something like, "The qualities are intangible, but I know them when I see them." They have difficulty being explicit because their selection process is intuitive and is based on interpersonal intelligence that is difficult to describe. The key seems to be that they are able to identify subordinates with whom they can probably work effectively—men with whom they are compatible and whose body chemistry agrees with their own. They make mistakes, of course. But they "give up" on a subordinate slowly because that means "giving up" on themselves—on their judgment and ability in selecting, training, and motivating men. Less effective managers select subordinates more quickly and give up on them more easily, believing that the inadequacy is that of the subordinate, not of themselves.

Developing Young Men

Observing that his company's research indicates that "initial corporate expectations for performance (with real responsibility) mold subsequent expectations and behavior," R. W. Walters, Jr., director of college employment at the American Telephone and Telegraph Company, contends that: "Initial bosses of new college hires must be the best in the organization."[17] Unfortunately, however, most companies practice exactly the opposite.

Rarely do new graduates work closely with experienced middle managers or upper-level executives. Normally, they are bossed by first-line managers

---

[16] Ibid., p. 9.
[17] "How to Keep the Go-getters," *Nation's Business*, June 1966, p. 74.

    Experiential Organizational Behavior

who tend to be the least experienced and least effective in the organization. While there are exceptions, first-line managers generally are either "old pros" who have been judged as lacking competence for higher levels of responsibility, or they are younger men who are making the transition from "doing" to "managing." Often, these managers lack the knowledge and skill required to develop the productive capabilities of their subordinates. As a consequence, many college graduates begin their careers in business under the worst possible circumstances. Since they know their abilities are not being developed or used, they quite naturally soon become negative toward their jobs, employers, and business careers.

Although most top executives have not yet diagnosed the problem, industry's greatest challenge by far is the underdevelopment, underutilization, and ineffective management and use of its most valuable resource—its young managerial and professional talent.

Disillusion and Turnover

The problem posed to corporate management is underscored by the sharply rising rates of attrition among young managerial and professional personnel. Turnover among managers one to five years out of college is almost twice as high now as it was a decade ago, and five times as high as two decades ago. Three out of five companies surveyed by *Fortune* magazine in the fall of 1968 reported that turnover rates among young managers and professionals were higher than five years ago.[18] While the high level of economic activity and the shortage of skilled personnel have made job-hopping easier, the underlying causes of high attrition, I am convinced, are underdevelopment and underutilization of a work force that has high career aspirations.

The problem can be seen in its extreme form in the excessive attrition rates of college and university graduates who begin their careers in sales positions. Whereas the average company loses about 50% of its new college and university graduates within three to five years, attrition rates as high as 40% in the *first* year are common among college graduates who accept sales positions in the average company. This attrition stems primarily, in my opinion, from the failure of first-line managers to teach new college recruits what they need to know to be effective sales representatives.

As we have seen, young men who begin their careers working for less-than-competent sales managers are likely to have records of low productivity. When rebuffed by their customers and considered by their managers to have little potential for success, the young men naturally have great difficulty in maintaining their self-esteem. Soon they find little personal satisfaction in their jobs and, to avoid further loss of self-respect, leave their employers for jobs that look more promising. Moreover, as reports about the

[18] Robert C. Albrook, "Why It's Harder to Keep Good Executives," *Fortune,* November 1968, p. 137.

---

high turnover and disillusionment of those who embarked on sales careers filter back to college campuses, new graduates become increasingly reluctant to take jobs in sales.

Thus, ineffective first-line sales management sets off a sequence of events that ends with college and university graduates avoiding careers in selling. To a lesser extent, the same pattern is duplicated in other functions of business, as evidenced by the growing trend of college graduates to pursue careers in "more meaningful" occupations, such as teaching and government service.

A serious "generation gap" between bosses and subordinates is another significant cause of breakdown. Many managers resent the abstract, academic language and narrow rationalization typically used by recent graduates. As one manager expressed it to me: "For God's sake, you need a lexicon even to talk with these kids." Noncollege managers often are particularly resentful, perhaps because they feel threatened by the bright young men with book-learned knowledge that they do not understand.

For whatever reason, the "generation gap" in many companies is eroding managerial expectations of new college graduates. For instance, I know of a survey of management attitudes in one of the nation's largest companies which revealed that 54% of its first-line and second-line managers believed that new college recruits were "not as good as they were five years ago." Since what a manager expects of a subordinate influences the way he treats him, it is understandable that new graduates often develop negative attitudes toward their jobs and their employers. Clearly, low managerial expectations and hostile attitudes are not the basis for effective management of new men entering business.

Conclusion

Industry has not developed effective first-line managers fast enough to meet its needs. As a consequence, many companies are underdeveloping their most valuable resource—talented young men and women. They are incurring heavy attrition costs and contributing to the negative attitudes young people often have about careers in business.

For top executives in industry who are concerned with the productivity of their organizations and the careers of young employees, the challenge is clear: it is to speed the development of managers who will treat their subordinates in ways that lead to high performance and career satisfaction. The manager not only shapes the expectations and productivity of his subordinates, but also influences their attitudes toward their jobs and themselves. If he is unskilled, he leaves scars on the careers of the young men, cuts deeply into their self-esteem, and distorts their image of themselves as human beings. But if he is skillful and has high expectations of his subordinates, their

Experiential Organizational Behavior

self-confidence will grow, their capabilities will develop, and their productivity will be high. More often than he realizes, the manager is Pygmalion.

"O the despair of Pygmalion, who might have created a statue and only made a woman!"

Alfred Jarry, 1873–1907
L'Amour Absolu

Issues

1. In the model, Antecedents → Behavior → Consequences, how does the managers' expectations affect subordinate performance?
2. What is more likely to change, the manager's expectations or the subordinate's performance? Why? What would you recommend (if corrective action is needed)?
3. What are the characteristics of the 'ideal' boss for the new, young manager?
4. How does an individual's expectations affect turnover behavior?

17

E. Allen Slusher and
Henry P. Sims, Jr.

Setting Individual Objectives

Introduction

You are beginning an exercise especially designed to give you and others a chance to experience the crucial steps in setting individual objectives within a Management by Objectives (MBO) system. The setting for the exercise is Alsim, Inc., a large manufacturing and wholesaling firm.

In this exercise a number of decisions are necessary. *First,* you will be asked to make an individual decision. *Second,* you will have the opportunity to exchange ideas with your associates in a group discussion. *Third,* the group will then agree upon a solution. The group discussions will be most helpful for learning about MBO if all issues and viewpoints are thoroughly examined and full agreement on a solution is reached. Avoid, if possible, using majority rule to make group decisions.

The basic purpose of this exercise is to stimulate discussion between you and your associates. The more involved you become in the situation depicted by the exercise, the more meaningful will be your contribution to group discussion. The answers given are offered as guides to your thinking. These answers cannot always be "right" because groups typically define the situations depicted differently. Whether the exercise is successful really depends on how much you learn about MBO.

Background

Alsim, Inc. is a large and diversified manufacturing and wholesaling firm. Current sales are in excess of $600 million as a result of a 40-year history of successful and growing operation. However, current economic conditions have made funds for expansion and modernization very limited.

Alsim is organized into four major divisions, each headed by a vice-president. These divisions are Consumer Products, Industrial Products, Sales, and International. For the purposes of this exercise, you will imagine

Used by permission.

that you are a newly appointed plant manager in the Industrial Products Division. This division consists of ten plants located in the mid-west and the southeast.

Your plant (the Middletown Plant) is one of the oldest in the Industrial Products Division. With the exception of a few equipment replacements, the plant was constructed in the mid-1950s. Most other divisional plants and those of your competitors were built in the past seven years. For the previous year, before you assumed this new position, performance of the Middletown Plane had been below forecast. Neither production goals or cost goals had been fully met.

The plant employs approximately 500 people of which about 70 were classified as managerial and professional. You directly supervise a three man administrative staff and seven department heads. The labor force has been recruited largely from nearby rural areas and there have been numerous hourly employees that have assumed first line supervisory positions. Although the local union has not been militant, the labor wage rates have consistently risen with the national trend. Thus, it is becoming increasingly difficult to keep production costs at a competitive level. However, the plant's ability to handle special orders and meet increasingly stringent product specifications has kept its profitability at an acceptable, if unimpressive, level.

You have been Plant Manager since the first of the year, and you've been spending considerable time over the past four months with your staff in developing improved operating procedures throughout the plant. To date there has been some progress in reducing the excessive machine downtime and lowering inventory costs. The Industrial Products Division has been directed by corporate management to implement a Management by Objectives System in each of its plants. You welcome the introduction of MBO as a means of insuring continued improvements in your plant operations. MBO has been used very successfully for several years in other Alsim divisions and corporate management is committed to implementing MBO throughout the company by the end of the coming year.

The Implementation program has been underway at your plant for six weeks and, with the help of MBO consultants retained by corporate headquarters, you feel you are making good progress in implementing MBO with those managers who report directly to you.

For purposes of this exercise, you are acting as the Plant Manager of the Middletown Plant.

Defining Key Result Areas

Dave Rogers is the Manager of the Production Department for your plant and reports directly to you, as plant manager. In preparation for setting his objectives, Rogers has provided you with a list of his major job responsibili-

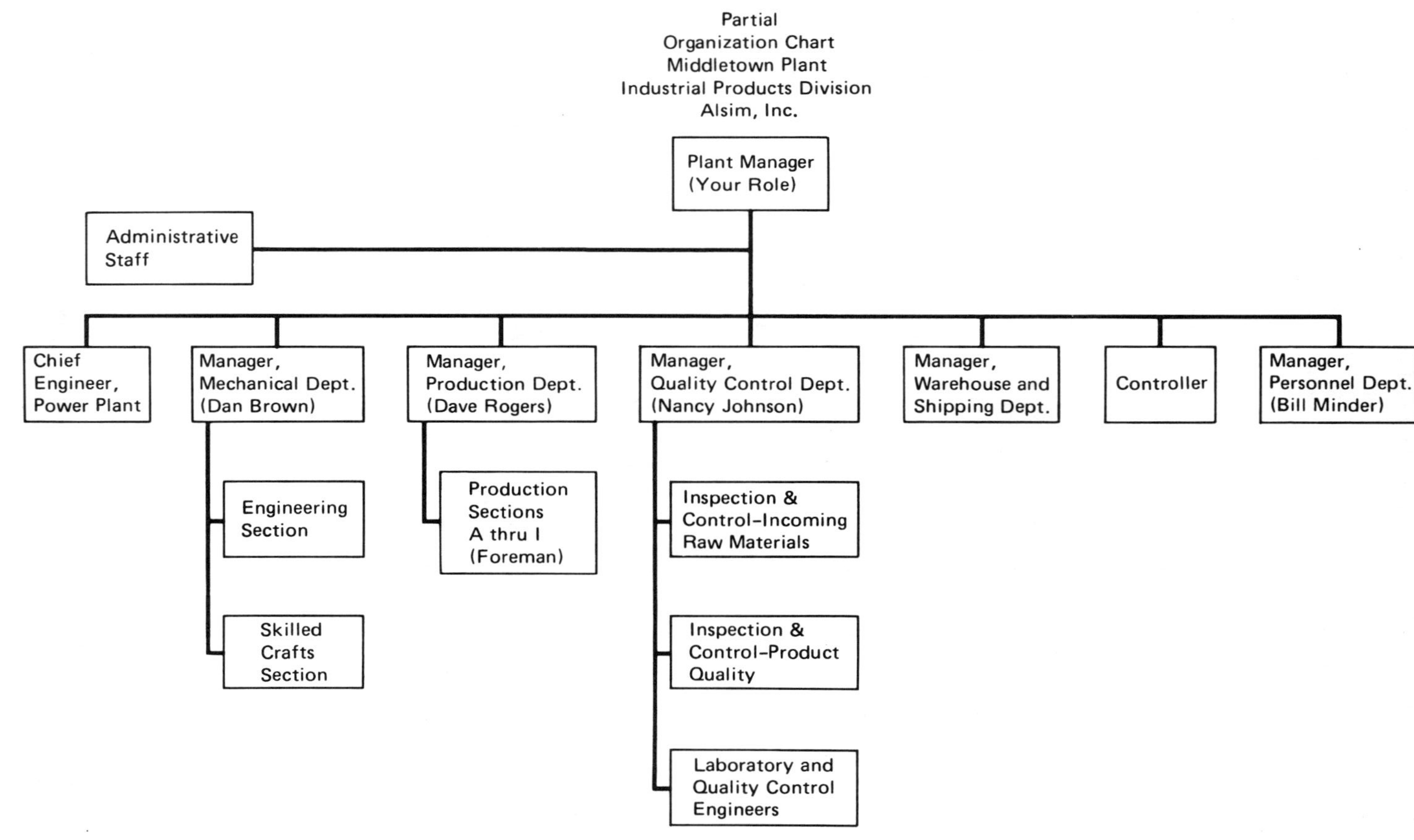

Partial
Organization Chart
Middletown Plant
Industrial Products Division
Alsim, Inc.
Plant Manager
(Your Role)
Administrative
Staff
Chief
Engineer,
Power Plant
Manager,
Mechanical Dept.
(Dan Brown)
Manager,
Production Dept.
(Dave Rogers)
Manager,
Quality Control Dept.
(Nancy Johnson)
Manager,
Warehouse and
Shipping Dept.
Controller
Manager,
Personnel Dept.
(Bill Minder)
Engineering
Section
Skilled
Crafts
Section
Production
Sections
A thru I
(Foreman)
Inspection &
Control–Incoming
Raw Materials
Inspection &
Control–Product
Quality
Laboratory and
Quality Control
Engineers

ties. You have previously reviewed the list and concur with Dave's analysis. This list of major job responsibilities for Dave Rogers is given on the next page.

Soon you will be meeting with Dave Rogers to jointly determine his objectives. It is important that you be very well prepared to discuss with Rogers the Key Result Areas in which you expect him to set objectives.

As an individual, and *without* discussion with your associates, decide which *four* of the major job responsibilities for Dave Rogers should be his Key Result Areas. Indicate your choice by placing a check mark (√) in the Individual Choice column on the next page opposite the four major job responsibilities which are Key Result Areas for Dave Rogers.

After each member of the group has made his individual choice, discuss Rogers' job responsibilities as a group. The group should then select the four major job responsibilities that the group believes are Dave's Key Result Areas. Indicate the group choices by check marks (√) in the Group Choice column opposite the appropriate job responsibility.

Major Job Responsibilities for Dave Rogers, Production Department Manager	Key Result Areas	
	Individual Choice	Group Choice
1. Scheduling the work force	_______________	_______________
2. Quality control	_______________	_______________
3. Prepare cost estimates for special runs	_______________	_______________
4. Deciding first level union grievances	_______________	_______________
5. Supervise nine shift foremen	_______________	_______________
6. Approve shipments	_______________	_______________
7. Order necessary raw materials	_______________	_______________
8. Supervise production clerks	_______________	_______________
9. Direct prevention maintenance program	_______________	_______________
10. Safety	_______________	_______________
11. Training the workforce	_______________	_______________
12. Housekeeping	_______________	_______________

Issues

1. When should a manager pay more attention to *general* goals rather than *specific* goals?
2. How do we translate *activities* into *goals?*
3. One student pointed out the problem associated with having demanding goals as follows: "The deadline rather than the achievement of a necessary task becomes the goal. The deadline can be used as an excuse for turning in incomplete work, simply by saying: 'I didn't have the time to do a complete job.' How do you deal with this problem?" Discuss the student's point of view.

Peter Lorenzi

Performance Appraisal and the Design of Work

The manager of a large local supermarket is seeking your help in assisting her in managing her employees. Historically, the large pool of student employees available has created a general managerial attitude of "if they don't work hard, we can replace them easily. Motivation is no problem here." Her main concerns are low productivity, poor quality of work, high absenteeism, and very high turnover.

In particular, the manager deals with and has to be responsible for stock persons, clerks, and cashiers. Stock persons are responsible for stocking shelves, unloading and storing groceries, sweeping and general maintenance, and assisting in bagging, carrying groceries out to cars, and some cashiering. Cashiers staff the cash registers, recording customer purchases accurately and pleasantly. Unlike the other jobs, which are almost exclusively male, cashiers are exclusively female. Clerks are responsible for store departments, e.g. meat, dairy, produce, sundries. The manager and her assistants directly supervise the stock persons, clerks, and cashiers.

Employees are hired and tend to stay at minimum or low wage levels. The company encourages longevity in the firm by a good pension and benefits plan and big wage increases after five years of employment.

Issues

1. Your assignment is to design a managerial system that effectively promotes motivation and work behavior. How would you proceed? What variables will you focus your efforts on? What structures or processes would you include?
2. What role does technology play? Clearly specify the goals/objectives of your design and explain your recommendations in terms that are relevant and understandable to the manager and your instructor.

19

Value Systems: Managerial Attitudes and Behavior

Overview

Managerial behavior is affected by general value systems and specific attitudes in organizations. This exercise is designed to provide a better understanding of the relationship between attitudes and behavior.*

Behavior refers to "the way one acts," especially to actions that can be observed. For example, we could observe the way a manager behaves in conducting a staff meeting. Similarly, we can observe the way a professor teaches a class or the way a basketball coach acts on the bench during a game.

Values and attitudes are more difficult concepts because we can't see them; they must be inferred from actual behavior, verbal descriptions, and/or written statements. An individual's total past experience provides a value framework (a propensity to think or act) by which the person evaluates the relative merit, usefulness, or importance of things, ideas, or alternative courses of action. Value systems (for groups and individuals) represent a general view of what is desirable or undesirable. Attitudes are more specific; they refer to a person's disposition, opinion, or mental set concerning objects such as things, people, ideas, or policies. Free enterprise might be considered generally desirable or undesirable by someone who has a specific opinion about farm subsidies or import tariffs on electronic equipment.

In this exercise we will look at both attitudes and behavior as well as the relationship between them. For maximum learning, it is best not to read further until the class meets and everyone proceeds simultaneously.

*Adapted from Patrick Suessmuth and Marit Stengels, "Attitudes vs. Behavior," *Training*, March 1973, pp. 38–39.

Step 1

In class, complete the Behavior Check Questionnaire.

Step 2

Complete the Attitude Check Questionnaire by estimating where your attitude is on the continuum. Write A (for Attitude) at the appropriate point on the continuum.

Behavior Checklist

Instructions: For each question, check the choice that most accurately describes your behavior. Be sure to check one box for each question.

	Always	Often	Sometimes	Seldom	Never
1. I would supervise my subordinates closely in order to get their best work.	☐	☐	☐	☐	☐
2. I would simply inform my subordinates of my goals and objectives and not have to sell them on the merit of my plans.	☐	☐	☐	☐	☐
3. I would set up careful controls to assure that my subordinates are getting the job done.	☐	☐	☐	☐	☐
4. I believe that, since I carry the responsibility, my subordinates accept my decisions.	☐	☐	☐	☐	☐
5. I would make sure that my subordinates' major workload is well-planned for them.	☐	☐	☐	☐	☐
6. I would check with my subordinates daily to make sure they were on schedule.	☐	☐	☐	☐	☐
7. I would step in as soon as reports indicate that the performance is slipping.	☐	☐	☐	☐	☐
8. I would have frequent meetings to control what is going on.	☐	☐	☐	☐	☐
9. I would rescind unauthorized decisions made by my employees.	☐	☐	☐	☐	☐
10. I would push my people to meet schedules whenever necessary	☐	☐	☐	☐	☐

Step 3

Place an S on the Theory X–Theory Y continuum (Attitude Check form) at a point representing where you would like your supervisor's attitude to be.

Attitude Check Questionnaire

Instructions: Read the definitions of Theory X and Theory Y and then, on the scale below, estimate where your attitude lies. Write A (for Attitude) at that point.

Theory X		Neutral		Theory Y
10	20	30	40	50

Theory X

- The average human being has an inherent dislike of work and will avoid it if possible.
- Because of this human characteristic of dislike of work, most people must be coerced, controlled, directed, or threatened with punishment to get them to put forth adequate effort toward the achievement of organizational objectives.
- The average human being prefers to be directed, wishes to avoid responsibility, has relatively little ambition, and wants security above all.

Theory Y

- The expenditure of physical and mental effort in work is as natural as play or rest.
- External control and the threat of punishment are not the only means of inducing effort toward organizational objectives. People will exercise self-direction and self-control in the service of objectives to which they are committed.
- Commitment to objectives is a function of the rewards associated with their achievement.
- The average human being learns, under proper conditions, not only to accept but to seek responsibility.
- The capacity to exercise a high degree of imagination, ingenuity, and creativity in the solution of organizational problems is widely, not narrowly, distributed in the population.
- Under the conditions of modern industrial life, the intellectual potentialities of the average human being are only partially utilized.

Step 4

Score the Behavior Check Questionnaire as follows:

1 for Always
2 for Often
3 for Sometimes
4 for Seldom
5 for Never

Write B (for Behavior) at the point on the continuum represented by your total score.

Step 5

Compare A (Attitude), B (Behavior), and S (Supervisor's attitude). Discuss the results in subgroups of five or six and/or the total class.

a. Identify specific personal experiences (your association with organizations) that may have influenced your B, A, and S scores.
b. Is there a general pattern for the group as a whole? For example, is the Behavior score (B) typically to the left of A and S?
c. What factors might account for the results?
d. Discuss specific examples of situations that you have observed where expressed attitudes seemed to differ from actual behavior. To what do you attribute the differences?
e. List the forces in an organization (e.g., this class) that may make it difficult for us to translate our professed attitudes into actual behavior.

Summary and Conceptualization

Did your results on the two questionnaires fit the general pattern as indicated below?

	Own Behavior B		Own Attitude A	Supervisor's Attitude S
Theory X		Neutral		Theory Y
10		30		50

What factors might account for such results? Several problems are apparent in responding to questionnaires of this sort. We are trying to ascertain as accurately as possible both attitudes and behavior. Some people are able to define them better than others. In some cases, people respond in terms of how they "wish" they behaved as managers or of what they think is the "correct" behavior according to the current popular theory. The same problem exists with regard to attitudes: Do we respond in terms of our actual attitude or in terms of the correct attitude for this course or this occasion?

For example, one participant in a management development program for the U.S. Navy suggested, after the session in which we used this exercise, that his responses were biased somewhat because this was the third day in a 5-day program and he felt that there must be some implied best answers. Even though we continually profess that there is no "one best way," much of the current literature does seem to suggest moving toward a Theory Y approach in attitude and behavior.[1] Alternative views have been expressed, but they seem to appear less frequently.[2]

Do you see any discrepancies in professed attitudes and actual behavior in the world around you—among parents, friends, business executives, politicians, etc.? Why do such discrepancies exist? One overriding issue is the difference between theorizing and practicing. It is easy to espouse the Golden Rule; it is more difficult to live by it. Or, as Mark Twain put it, "To be good is noble. To tell people how to be good is even nobler, and much less trouble." We judge ourselves according to our intentions; we judge others according to their actions. Theory Y is essentially an optimistic view of the nature of human beings. It assumes that people are basically good, industrious, intelligent, and responsible—as opposed to bad, lazy, dumb, and irresponsible. Most of us would like to believe the optimistic view, and yet we know individuals who are indeed lazy and irresponsible; thus we have a difficult time implementing a Theory Y approach to management.

A typical explanation of why behavior seems to support Theory X more than attitude goes as follows:

I am good, industrious, intelligent, and responsible. Thus, I know that at least some people can be trusted and therefore I would like to maintain an optimistic view of the nature of human beings. This pushes my attitude toward the Theory Y end of the spectrum. And, it explains why my supervisor should have an optimistic view. Obviously, my boss can trust me.

On the other hand, I am not so sure about the people that work for me. Can they be trusted? Shouldn't I check up on them to make sure they are doing OK?

We have found that this explanation is offered by managers at all levels. In essence, it says that those above me should have an optimistic Theory Y attitude but that I can't afford to because I am not sure about the people below me.

Other explanations for the difference in behavior and attitude revolve

---

[1] Douglas McGregor, *The Human Side of Enterprise,* New York, McGraw-Hill, 1960. His Theory X–Theory Y conceptual model has been used extensively in research and training over the past 15 years.

[2] See, for example, "McClelland: An Advocate of Power," *International Management,* July 1975, pp. 27–29; and Robert N. McMurray, "Power and the Ambitious Executive," *Harvard Business Review,* November–December 1973, pp. 140–145.

Experiential Organizational Behavior

around built-in organizational constraints. Traditional organizational processes (e.g., rules and regulations) may favor Theory X and preclude Theory Y managerial behavior. Long-standing union versus management antagonisms and contract provisions may also get in the way of an approach more supportive of Theory Y.

These factors are all reasonable explanations for significant differences between professed attitudes and actual managerial behavior. Behaving in a particular way e.g., choosing a leadership style is affected by forces in the leader, in the followers, and in the situation. A change cannot be accomplished by merely vowing to change one's attitude. Ingrained personal habits must be unfrozen, changed, and refrozen. This change usually cannot be accomplished unilaterally. It is much easier if the total organizational climate is changed, including the attitudes and behaviors of superiors, peers, and subordinates.

In deciding on a particular managerial style, individuals must include enough flexibility so that they can behave appropriately in a variety of situations. Managers would be well advised to adopt a contingency view that calls for a situational diagnosis as the basis for managerial behavior. A crisis situation, such as mechanical failure on an assembly line, calls for a different approach from day-to-day clerical operations in the finance department. Different tasks (production, sales, research, etc.) call for different approaches; one's own basic personality cannot be modified too greatly, and subordinates vary on a wide range of dimensions (age, education, temperament, etc.). As an example, in one of our workshops a vice president for a large industrial firm seemed to take forever to complete the Behavior Check Questionnaire—in spite of our suggestions to work quickly without pondering each response. Later, he told us that he had to fill out the questionnaire four times, a different response for each of his division managers. He rationalized that his behavior was significantly different toward each person because of their individual differences in personality and experience. This latter factor was particularly important—one person had been with the company 25 years, whereas another had been there only 4 months. We suggested that his approach was realistic and appropriate (even if it did hold up the completion of the exercise).

Are there any guidelines that might be suggested in terms of Theory X and Theory Y? Our answer is yes. Our bias leans toward an optimistic view of people, and we suggest that managers should behave in a way that reflects that optimism as much as possible. The phrase "as much as possible" allows situational analysis and a realistic approach that recognizes variations in goodness, industriousness, intelligence, and responsibleness. One important reason for being as optimistic as possible is that pessimism can be a self-fulfilling prophecy.

It makes a great deal of difference in systems of social control whether those involved tend to view man, in general, as good or evil. If we assume that man is good, we can believe that misbehavior is a reactive response rather than a manifestation of character. This will lead to a search for causes in his experience rather than in his nature. If we are to find a cause for behavioral failure, we are more apt to look outside the offender than inside and thus consider a whole new range of variables as contributory circumstances.

If, on the other hand, we assume that man himself is bad, a priori, then we are prone to assume that misbehavior is caused by something within him which we cannot alter directly. Accordingly, our attention will focus on limiting his freedom to choose and to act through external curbs or controls. In limiting the causes of behavior, we exclude ourselves from powerful internal sources of control.[3]

These summary statements reflect polar positions which, admittedly, are unrealistic. People are neither completely good nor completely evil. There are obvious spectra for behavior in terms of cooperation–competition, love–hate, friendship–enmity, or harmony–discord. Given a particular issue, an individual's behavior will reflect a position on one or more of these continua. However, the basic assumption one makes can have a significant impact on organization and management. Relationships are structured in certain ways; compensation systems are designed; communication patterns are established; authority-responsibility relationships are identified; planning and control processes are established; and many other pertinent organizational considerations are affected by management's basic assumption with regard to the nature of human beings.

McGregor saw Theory X and Theory Y as more than polar extremes of human nature. He considered those who held a Theory X view as relatively closed-minded and less able to cope with dynamic situations and complex problem solving. He saw the advocates of Theory Y as more open-minded, flexible, and dynamic. Theory Y fosters situational diagnosis and problem solving while recognizing variations in task, technology, and human resources. Rather than being a utopian view, it tempers optimism with pragmatism.

---

[3] Henry P. Knowles and Borje O. Saxberg. "Human Relations and the Nature of Man," *Harvard Business Review*, March–April 1967, p. 178.

Elizabeth Brenner

20

How to Make a Point Logically and Clearly

You're daydreaming during a business review meeting. Suddenly the vice president turns to you for the first time. Not only does he know your name, but also he wants your opinion on the last point.

The last point. Your mouth goes dry. What was the last point?

Business meetings can bode success or disaster for fledgling executives, especially women, says Virginia Johnson, marketing supervisor of overhead systems for Minnesota Mining and Manufacturing Co.

Few settings offer women as much opportunity for exposure and visibility— if they're well-prepared and know how to use the meeting to highlight their own strengths.

If they don't, failure in front of the top brass can significantly hinder career growth.

"Management uses meetings as an assessment tool," Ms. Johnson said. "They use them to groom people, to see how people work with each other, who are the potential leaders and who can communicate on paper or in writing. They need to see who's competent and who's articulate."

Unfortunately, few women really are comfortable speaking in front of groups, because they've never received the informal development of speaking skills that men absorb all through their careers.

"Men learn these things through Toastmasters, through Dale Carnegie courses or through their fraternities," Ms. Johnson said. "They made assumptions when they were 12 years old about how to lead business meetings, but when I was 12, no one ever thought to teach me these things."

It was precisely for that reason that she began studying how women can become more effective speakers.

Her first rule is that women should seek ways to make themselves more visible to top management before the meetings ever begin. They should be asking for new duties or expanding their own duties to include new areas of responsibility. She recommends paying attention to what's going on in the

Copyrighted ©, Chicago Tribune. All rights reserved. Reprinted by permission.

job they think they want. That way, no woman can ever be accused of coming unprepared to a meeting.

Ms. Johnson offers these suggestions for women, once they get inside the crucial session:

Don't give out handouts. People tend to rustle papers, read ahead and not listen to what you're saying.

Make clear your first and last points; summarize them before you begin.

Set a time frame and stick to it, giving your audience a road map with which to follow you in the major points you've outlined.

Use visual aids. "Good visuals show you've thought enough about your audience to come prepared," she said.

The most important objective that everyone—not just women—should maintain in planning meeting presentations is to focus on action plans.

"A meeting isn't effective unless people come out of it with a new idea or a plan of action," she said. "It's good to identify the major points and to summarize the status quo, but spend most of your time dealing with recommendations."

Issues

A common complaint by employers concerning recent college graduates is that these new managers have a great difficulty in communicating effectively.

1. Prepare a list of causes of poor communication habits for new managers.

2. Prepare a plan of action for remedying the communication deficiencies listed above.

3. Prepare a plan of action or list of recommendations for making group meetings more effective.

21

Analysis of Job-Related Stress

Objectives

1. To illustrate that individuals view job-related stress factors differently.
2. To display how groups can reach different conclusions than individuals about job-related stress.
3. To emphasize how positive job-related factors can initiate some amount of stress within individuals.
4. To understand the role of stress in organizations and individual performance.

Related Topics

Life event changes influence the behavior and performance of employees. They are important and vary in the amount of influence that they exert physiologically.

Starting the Exercise

Allow individuals to complete Phase I of the exercise without any consultation between each other. Then set up small groups to complete Phase II. In Phase III individuals will be involved in reviewing the work of the groups.

The Facts

Thomas Holmes and other researchers at the University of Washington School of Medicine have developed a stress scaling system that can be used

James Gibson, John Ivancevich, and James Donnelly, Jr., *Organizations: Behavior, Structure, Processes* (Dallas, Tx.: Business Publications, 1979), pp. 94–96. © 1979 by Business Publications, Inc.

TABLE A
Scaling of Life-Change Units for Various Experiences

Life Event	Scale Value
Death of spouse	100
Divorce	73
Marital separation	65
Jail term	63
Death of a close family member	63
Major personal injury or illness	53
Marriage	50
Fired from work	47
Marital reconciliation	45
Retirement	45
Major change in health of family member	44
Pregnancy	40
Sex difficulties	39
Gain of a new family member	39
Business readjustment	39
Change in financial state	38
Death of a close friend	37
Change to a different line of work	36
Change in number of arguments with spouse	35
Mortgage over $10,000	31
Foreclosure of mortgage or loan	30
Change in responsibilities at work	29
Son or daughter leaving home	29
Trouble with in-laws	29
Outstanding personal achievement	28
Wife begins or stops work	26
Begin or end school	26
Change in living conditions	25
Revision of personal habits	24
Trouble with boss	23
Change in work hours or conditions	20
Change in residence	20
Change in schools	20
Change in recreation	19
Change in church activities	19
Change in social activities	18
Mortgage or loan less than $10,000	17
Change in sleeping habits	16
Change in number of family get-togethers	15
Change in eating habits	15
Vacation	13
Christmas	12
Minor violations of the law	11

Source From L. O. Ruch and T. H. Holmes, "Scaling of Life Change: Comparison of Direct and Indirect Methods," Journal of Psychosomatic Research, 1971, 15, 224.

to address the issue of life change stressors. Table A shows the relative impact of different life changes, with the most stressful life event—death of a spouse—given a scale value of 100 points. Some of the events listed are generally considered to be positive life events—outstanding personal achievement (28), gain of a new family member (44), and marital reconciliation (45). Even these positive events generate stress because of new roles, expectations, and activities that go along with the changes. Holmes has found through empirical analysis that the accumulation of more than 200 scale points in a year results in a better than 50 percent chance that the individual will sustain some type of major illness in the following year. The assumption offered is that when a person's endocrine system is overburdened with stressfull events, the body cannot perform its normal function of fighting off diseases.

Perhaps an accumulation of job related stresses could also result in overburdening the body's disease resistant mechanisms. Listed in Table B are some job factors that could cause stress. The three sets of factors are supervisor, individual, and peer initiated. Assume that these factors apply to an individual working in a typical organization. Also assume that the individual is relatively young and has about six years experience in the organization.

Exercise Procedures

Phase I: 20 Minutes

1. Individually place scale values on each of the job factors listed in Table B. Place 100 points on the factors you consider to be the most potentially stressful.
2. Record your individual evaluations on a separate sheet of paper.

TABLE B
A List of Job Factors

Supervisor Initiated	Individually Initiated	Peer Initiated
Demotion	Challenging production goals	Production norms
Criticism	Challenging career goals	Praise
Suspension	High effort	Acceptance
Probation	Poor attitudes	Cohesiveness
Praise	Personal development	Reprimand
Recognition	Self-assessment	Improved status
A bonus	Request for pay raise	
Promotion		
Positive performance evaluation session		
Negative performance evaluation session		

Phase II: 40 Minutes

1. Set up groups of 5 to 6 people and discuss the individual assignments of scale points made by members.
2. Reach some type of group consensus on what is a reasonable value for each of the items.

Phase III: 30 Minutes

1. Each group places the group consensus for the scale values on the board or a chart for each class member to review.
2. Discuss the different values developed by each of the groups.

Issues

1. Define stress. Is stress always dysfunctional?
2. Draw a figure of the relationship between organizational or life stress and
   a. motivation
   b. organizational conflict
   c. individual performance
   d. health of the individual
   What is the nature of each relationship? Positive? Negative? Curvilinear (U-shaped)?
3. Some researchers have suggested that there are different personality types (Type A versus Type B) concerning an individuals ability to deal effectively with stress. What do you think? Is the ability of the individual to deal with stress determined by her personality?

Section **IV**

The Social System

22

Group Ranking Task: Subarctic Survival

Introduction

Research has shown that groups are frequently more effective than individuals in solving complex problems. This is especially true when the problem requires a quality decision. Groups may be more accurate and bring more knowledge to bear on the solution.

In this exercise you will have an opportunity to experiment and see whether this is true. In steps 1 and 2, you will be asked to try to solve a problem by yourself. Do not discuss this problem with anyone, either in your group or outside it. Work on the problem by yourself. When you come to your next session you will have an opportunity to solve the problem with a group. What do you expect to happen? Do you think your solution will be better than your group's? *Step 1* consists of reading "The Situation."

The Situation*

It is approximately 2:30 p.m., October 5th, and you have just crash-landed in a float plane on the east shore of Laura Lake in the subarctic region of the northern Quebec-Newfoundland border. The pilot was killed in the crash, but the rest of you are uninjured. Each of you are wet up to the waist and have perspired heavily. Shortly after the crash, the plane drifted into deep water and sank with the pilot's body pinned inside.

The pilot was unable to contact anyone before the crash. However, ground sightings indicated that you are 30 miles south of your intended course and approximately 22 air miles east of Schefferville, your original destination, and the nearest known habitation. (The mining camp on Hol-

Printed with permission of Experiential Learning Methods, Plymouth, Michigan.
*Copyright © 1974 by Experiential Learning Methods.

112

linger Lake was abandoned years ago when a fire destroyed the buildings.) Schefferville (pop. 5,000) is an iron ore mining town approximately 300 air miles north of the St. Lawrence, 450 miles east of the James Bay/Hudson Bay area, 800 miles south of the Arctic Circle, and 300 miles west of the Atlantic Coast. It is reachable only by air or rail, all roads ending a few miles from town. Your party was expected to return from northwestern Labrador to Schefferville no later than October 19th and filed a Flight Notification Form with the Department of Transportation via Schefferville radio to that effect.

The immediate area is covered with small evergreen trees (1½ to 4 inches in diameter). Scattered in the area are a number of hills having rocky and barren tops. Tundra (arctic swamps) make up the valleys between the hills and consist only of small scrubs. Approximately 25 percent of the area in the region is covered by long, narrow lakes which run northwest to southeast. Innumerable streams and rivers flow into and connect the lakes.

Temperatures during October vary between 25°F. and 36°F., although it will occasionally go as high as 50°F. and as low as 0°F. Heavy clouds cover the sky three-quarters of the time, with only one day in ten being fairly clear. Five to seven inches of snow are on the ground; however, the actual depth varies enormously because the wind sweeps the exposed areas clear and builds drifts 3 to 5′ deep in other areas. The wind speed averages 13–15 miles per hour and is mostly out of the west-northwest.

You are all dressed in insulated underwear, sox, heavy wool shirts, pants, knit gloves, sheepskin jackets, knitted wool caps and heavy leather hunting boots. Collectively, your personal possessions include: $153 in bills and two half dollars, four quarters, two dimes, one nickel and three new pennies; one pocket knife (two blades and an awl which resembles an ice pick); one stub lead pencil; and an air map.

While the map you retrieved is soggy and difficult to read, you have been able to determine that: (1) walking distance to Schefferville would be more than 50 miles; (2) you would have several water crossings to make; (3) a 1900-foot hill a mile northeast of Laura Lake is in line of sight with the Schefferville airport.

The Problem

Before the plane drifted away and sank, you were able to salvage 15 items. Your task is to rank these items according to their importance to your survival, starting with "1" the most important, to "15" the least important.

Step 2

Complete the following task individually.

1. Rank the 15 items listed on the "Scoring Sheet" below according to their importance to your survival. Start with "1," the most important, to

"15," the least important. Enter your ranks in the column on the "Scoring Sheet" labeled "Individual Ranking."

  2. You may assume the following:
  a. The number of survivors is seven.
  b. You are the actual people in the situation.
  c. Everyone has agreed to stick together.
  d. All items are in good condition.

Step 3: 30 Minutes

As a team, rank the 15 items according to the *group's consensus* on order of importance to your survival. Do not vote; try to reach agreement on each item. Base your decision on knowledge, logic, or the experiences of group members. Try to avoid basing the decision on personal preference. Enter the group's rankings in the column on the "Scoring Sheet" labeled "Group Ranking."

Temperature Chart for Crash Area

	Mean Daily Temp.	Mean Daily Max. Temp.	Mean Daily Low Temp.	Minimum Temp. Expected
Oct.	30.3	35.8	24.8	0
Nov.	15.6	22.4	9.3	− 33.0
Dec.	− 0.3	7.5	− 8.1	− 42.0
Jan.	− 9.8	− 1.5	− 18.0	− 53.0

Mean Snowfall

Oct. (Avg. 11 days of snowfall) 7.5 inches
Nov. (Avg. 16 days of snowfall) 14.5 inches

Windchill Factor

Exposed flesh will freeze at:

Wind Velocity MPH	Temperature °F
43	20
26	15
18	10
14	5
13	0
9	− 5
7	− 10
6	− 15
5	− 20
4	− 25
3	− 30
2	− 40

Sunrise 6:15 a.m.; **Sunset** 5:45 p.m.

Items	Individual Ranking	Group Ranking	Survival Expert's Ranking	Influence	Individual Accuracy	Group Accuracy
A magnetic compass						
A gallon can of maple syrup						
A sleeping bag per person (arctic type, down-filled, with liner)						
A bottle of water purification tablets						
A 20 × 20' piece of heavy-duty canvas						
13 wood matches in a metal screwtop, waterproof container						
250 ft. of ¼-inch braided nylon rope. 50-lb. test						
An operating 4-battery flashlight						
Three pairs of snowshoes						
A fifth of Bacardi rum (151 proof)						
Safety razor shaving kit with mirror						
A wind-up alarm clock						
A hand axe						
One aircraft inner tube for a 14-inch wheel (punctured)						
A book entitled. <u>Northern Star Navigation</u>						

Your Score   Team Score:

	1	2	3	4	5	6
Average Individual Score: Add up all the individual scores in your group and divide by the number in the group						
Team Score						
Gain Score: The difference between the team score and the Average Individual Score. If the team score is lower than Average Individual Score, then gain is "+". If team score is higher than Average Individual Score, then gain is "−".						
Lowest Individual Score: ("Best" Individual Score)						

Step 4: 5 Minutes

After all teams have finished, your group leader will read the ranking that the items were assigned by an expert. As these are read, please enter the "correct" rank in the "Survival Expert's" ranking column on the "Scoring Sheet."

Step 5: 10 Minutes

Compute the difference between your individual ranking and the group's ranking. Use the *absolute* difference—ignore plus and minus scores. Enter the difference for each item's ranking in the column on the "Scoring Sheet" labeled "Influence."

This score might be called an "influence score." It may represent the extent that you influenced the group to "your way of thinking" about the correct way to rank the alternatives. Discuss for a few minutes in the group the people who you feel were most influential in group discussion. Then share your "influence scores," and see how they compare—the smaller the score, the more the group's score parallels the private ranking of certain individuals.

Step 6: 10 Minutes

Compute the absolute difference between your individual ranking and the expert's ranking. Again, ignore the plus or minus scores. Enter the difference for each item's ranking in the column labeled "Individual Accuracy." This score might best be called your "accuracy" score.

Share with your group your "accuracy" score, and compare these to the "influence" scores from step 5. The difference between these two scores might be called the "appropriateness of influence." If you had a very *low* accuracy score and a *low* influence score, you were really "right" and the group listened to you. If your accuracy score is high but your influence is low, you might try to explore why you had so much influence in spite of not being accurate; similarly, if you were accurate but had very little influence, you might try to find out why you didn't have a bigger impact on the group.

Step 7: 5 Minutes

Compute the absolute difference between your group's rankings and the expert's rankings. Enter these in the column labeled "Group Accuracy" and compute the total. The total is your "Team Score."

Step 8: 5 Minutes

1. Compute the average of the individual accuracy scores of group members, by adding up all of the individual accuracy scores and dividing by the number of members in the group. Enter this in the space for your group's "Average Individual Score" on the "Scoring Sheet."
2. Enter your "Team Score."

Step 9: 2 Minutes

Compute your "gain score." This is the difference between the average individual accuracy score and the group accuracy score. If the score is positive (+), this means that the group's solution to the problem was better than what individuals could do by themselves without discussion. If the score is negative (−), this means that the group discussion did not make good use of the best resources among members, and that the group product was worse than what individuals, on the average, could do by themselves without discussion.

Step 10: 3 Minutes

Enter the lowest individual score in your group. This is the "best" score obtained by any individual alone. Compare this against the average individual score (step 8) and the team accuracy score. If your group worked extremely well in sharing information and making decisions, it is likely that your team score was not only better than the average of individuals, but better than the best individual in the group. This shows that it is often possible for the group to excel even its best individual resource.

Step 11: 5 Minutes

When steps 3 through 10 have been completed, the group leader will record the data from each group for the discussion. One member of your group should be prepared to provide this data.

Step 12: 15 Minutes

Discuss this experience as a total group with the group leader. Try to arrive at some conclusions about group problem solving and the relevance of the exercise to real-world problems in management.

Issues

1. Is there a right or wrong solution to this task? Are most decisions of this type?
2. List the characteristics of a task that would indicate that a group decision is likely to be more effective than a decision made by a single individual for the group.
3. Is participation by individuals in decisions that affect them an individual right, a management responsibility, or simply a "good" idea? Why should management prefer to preclude workers from job decisions?

Robert Schrank

Union Official

After each one of the twenty or thirty departments had elected a steward, we set up classes to explain the meaning of a union contract in terms of pay and working conditions. At a general shop committee meeting it was agreed to hold meetings in each department and ask each member to go over the nature of a union contract, writing out clauses that they wanted in the agreement. It was a slow process, but without any of us realizing it, some interesting changes began to happen.

I remember it climaxing at a general plant meeting with a couple of hundred people present, when old John McDermott, a Scotsman in his sixties with a huge head of white hair, quietly stood up unannounced in the wrong order of business (we were also teaching *Robert's Rules of Order*) and began to speak softly but forcefully in his burr, "I've been workin' here for well on to thirty-two years now. I don't have much time left before I am forced by age to retire with a pittance that I could not even comfortably starve on. So, I am glad that all of you will now have a chance to repay those bastards who made us crawl like beggars in Calcutta, seeking a farthing. In your presence I want to thank God that I have had a chance to become a man again before I die."

He sat down. There was a long silence as the organizing staff just looked at each other in stunned disbelief. I was chairing the meeting and I remembered the difficulties we had had in getting McDermott to sign a union card. He was the most pious and respected old man in the place. Now he had let loose all his pent-up anger. Suddenly, like a wave breaking, the hall of people stood up in a spontaneous demonstration of approval with people shouting, "That's how it was," "He's right," "Now let's get even." I began to rap the gavel for order, but no one heard. People turned to each other, telling how awful it was to be treated as children, to be constantly humiliated. I stopped my gavel rapping, totally disbelieving what was happening. The organizing staff from the union finally gathered together in front of the po-

Reprinted from *Ten Thousand Working Days* by Robert Schrank by permission of The MIT Press, Cambridge, Massachusetts. Copyright © 1978 by The Massachusetts Institute of Technology.

dium. We just laughed at each other as a great glow of joy ran through us. We had witnessed the birth of a people's collective concern. There was nothing to do after McDermott but let people take the floor to tell their own stories of indignities committed against them by foremen, supervisors, the personnel department—the company.

What gradually emerged as a central issue of concern for these workers was a terrible resentment of years of servility to the supervisors on the plant floor. The more those workers expanded their appreciative system, the more militant the most recent company supporters became. In a short period of time this plant that we never thought we could unionize was the base of militancy in our local union. Many of these workers became friends of long years' standing, and I was only to lose the support of some of them in the worst years of the McCarthy witch hunts. The labor movement prepared workers for struggle against the company. Being only narrowly political, as in its favorite slogan, "Support your friends and punish your enemies," it in no way prepared the workers for any political attacks.

André Gorz, the French radical economist, commenting on the workers' dissatisfaction issue, points out that the outcomes will be qualitatively different, depending on whether workers are dealt with as individuals or collectively. Most attitudinal surveys about work satisfaction lose much of their usefulness because they tell nothing about the people in a plant as a collective group. Yet for the most part that is how they work, as an integrated system. Since in workplaces the formal and informal work group is a critical element in how workers feel about their jobs, dissatisfaction beyond griping can be interpreted as disloyalty to the group, and expressing it is therefore not encouraged, particularly to outsiders. The union gives legitimization to the group feeling, extending it beyond the immediate work area, where it tends to form, to the whole plant. The change that occurs when an informal group of people becomes legitimized is one in which they experience a sense of elation, the excitement of new-found allies. This legitimization of feeling unleashes an entirely new source of energy.

Many behavioral scientists studying workplace problems tend to overlook this collective energy when they deal with the issue of participation in decision making. It may be that behavioral scientists and industrial engineers generally have had little experience with the phenomenon of a bunch of individuals coming to sense themselves as a collective. Yet this was the pivotal force that allowed us to organize Bliss.

Thinking back on it, before Bliss was organized, the working conditions, wages, and other benefits were not all that bad. Pay was only slightly under union scale, benefits were not too different from most union shops. What was very different was a subtle system of paternalism and subservience that had gradually emerged. It demanded that employees ingratiate themselves for small favors, almost the way children seduce their parents to gain little rewards. Subservience in adults creates a resentment that may grow quite imperceptibly over time and can burst forth in what appears as an unwarranted, extreme militancy. The source of the action is a resentment against a system of conduct that deprives people of their adulthood. This paternalism is not a case of evil supervision, though on occasion that is possible. It grows out of the institutional arrangements of power and authority. First-line supervision is pressed by managers above them to increase productivity. Supervisors do this by pressuring their subordinates, the workers. In unorganized plants many workers find that one way of dealing with these pressures is through the seduction game of wooing superiors in order to secure favors and obtain recognition. As we all have experienced, being seductive, aside from being degrading, is one helluva lot of work. When workers in Bliss became a collective, they discovered an alternative to the bowing and scraping. The effect was electric when the energy formerly used to control their resentment was suddenly released in the interests of the group. It was an inspirational peak experience as the group gained an awareness of its collective position of strength, which dramatically changed the participants' appreciative system. There was a new insight into the impact of subservience on their behavior. It was a most dramatic example of experiential learning.

When I was in the labor movement, the issue of how much control the workers would gain through their union was probably more significant than it is now. I think it is an issue, though there is a reluctance to recognize it. The issue of who participates in decision making or in general management skirts the problem of who controls what. Within the confines of a rather conservative ideological stance, the AFL-CIO has carried worker participation in management as far as it could. This conservative position grew as a reaction to the early socialist influence in the labor movement. Many of the ideological issues in the early years of the unions revolved around questions of control of the means of production. In the early 1900s the IWW was propagating worker control or the brotherhood of the working man via the One Big Union. Daniel de Leon, Debs, Haywood, and Hillquit, all either in unions or close to them, were advocating the workers' ownership of the means of production as the only real solution to workers' problems.

The employer groups were scared to death of the ideologists and fought them bitterly. (See, for instance, Pinkerton's *Strikers, Communists, and Tramps.*) The employers' efforts against the socialist ideology resulted in the pure and simple trade unionism of Gompers who, unlike the socialists, assured the owners that the AF of L had no interest whatsoever in depriving them of their property rights or their right to manage. I believe much of the present hostility in the American labor movement toward worker participation in management stems from this earlier controversy, even though it may no longer be valid because of the much more public nature of ownership of major corporations. (In *The New Industrial State* Galbraith sees the corporation as a public institution.)

The issue of participation in management as a measure of control becomes even more critical when applied to the public sector, where there are thirty-five million employees ostensibly working for the taxpayer. Who has the right to control this work force? The elected officials? But they are, after all, politically beholden to the civil servants for their election. The way the public employee unions are moving, I am not sure they do not already have control of some institutions, even though they have not assumed its management functions. That may be the next step.

The old AF of L leaders, in their belief that decision making was purely a management function, may prove to have been influential to the extent that we have learned so little about *how* workers can participate in decision making. Since the experience with work reorganization in the socialist countries has been so disappointing, as S. M. Miller notes in his writings on neosocialist thought, the idea of socialism, if it is ever to get off the ground again, will require a lot of work to be done on some new models. The model of worker participation in Europe outside the so-called socialist countries, which gives workers representation on the boards of the corporation and in work councils, is implemented within traditional hierarchical organizational arrangements. Without some real changes in these traditional structures, the arrangement becomes a cooptation, placing the worker representatives in the position of approving the existing drama by making them actors in the play. The issue of worker participation in management might better be framed in terms of some new organizational structures for achieving the work of society. Unfortunately, since the Wobblies and the Socialists, very few people in the labor movement give this issue any serious consideration.

Another observation based on my union experience of the thirties is about work motivation. My work experience has always given me real doubts about man's intrinsic desire to work. In movements like the organizing drives of the thirties, we just worked like hell. How many times in the wee hours of the morning in some godforsaken flea-bag hotel did I gaze at the yellowed, peeling wallpaper and wonder what the hell I was doing here. I was a true believer addressing my coworkers as Sister and Brother in a crusade for the brotherhood of man. Such belief needs to be mythological, so that it cannot be easily reified.

I saw that kind of belief and commitment again in the civil rights movement of the sixties, which motivated people to work with no regard to pay, hours, or working conditions. It seems reasonable to conclude that when people believe, they become highly motivated. Luther and Calvin must have known that when they assured all us poor humans that we would find salvation in work. Now, as long as the workers believed that, there was plenty of motivation to work. What are we in for as religion fades and there are fewer true believers? Will the motivation to work decrease correspondingly? If it turns out that the drive to work is strongly correlated with believing, then I would have some doubts about Herzberg's notion of increasing work motivation by making the work itself more challenging. If believing in work is an important factor in motivation, then it probably cannot be created by some task arrangement. Witness the need to keep people believing in a continuing revolution in China and now in Cuba, in order that the rice continues to be planted and the cane crop maintained. With the advent of the welfare state and the explosion of nonwork-type jobs, the growing prob lem will be who will do the dirty work. We need to understand this as we try to figure out who does what job, and how compensations, benefits, and amenities are distributed.

Issues

1. Compare and contrast the perspectives on participative decision making in (1) the subarctic survival exercise and (2) Schrank's union official story.
2. How does the group influence an individual's attitude? Is there such a thing as a "collective attitude?"
3. Is participation by workers in decisions that affect them a worker's right? Why should management prefer to preclude workers from job decisions?

Furniture Factory

My third or fourth week at the factory found me earnestly launched in my quest for holding the job but doing less work—or working less hard. This was immediately recognized and hailed by the men with "Now you're gettin' smart, kid. Stop bustin' your ass and only do what you have to do. You don't get any more money for bustin' your hump and you might put some other poor bastard outa a job." Remember this was the depression. Most workers, while aware of the preciousness of their jobs, felt that doing more work than necessary could be putting someone else, even yourself, out of a job. "Only do what you have to" became a rule not only to save your own neck but to make sure you were not depriving some other soul like yourself from getting a job.

In the next few weeks, I was to be taught a second important lesson about working. One day while picking up sawdust, I began to "find" pieces in the sawdust or behind a woodpile or under a machine. The first few times, with great delight, I would announce to the operator, "Hey, look what I found!" I should have figured something was wrong by the lack of any similar enthusiasm from the operator. Sam was a generally quiet Midwesterner who never seemed to raise his voice much, but now when I showed him my finished-work discovery behind his milling machine he shouted, "Who the f__k asked you to be a detective? Keep your silly ass out from behind my machine; I'll tell you what to pick up. So don't go being a big brown-nosing hero around here."

Wow, I sure never expected that. Confused, troubled, almost in tears, not knowing what to do or where to go, I went to the toilet to hide my hurt and just sat down on an open bowl and thought what the hell am I doing in this goddamned place anyway? I lit a cigarette and began pacing up and down in front of the three stalls, puffing away at my Camel. I thought, What the hell should I do? This job is terrible, the men are pissed off at me. I hate the place, why don't I just quit? Well, it's a job and you get paid, I said to myself, so take it easy.

Reprinted from *Ten Thousand Working Days* by Robert Schrank by permission of the MIT Press, Cambridge, Massachusetts. Copyright © 1978 by Massachusetts Institute of Technology.

While I'm pacing and puffing, Sam comes in, saying, "Lissen, kid, don't get sore. I was just trying to set you straight. Let me tell you what it's all about. The guys around, that is the machine operators, agree on how much we are gonna turn out, and that's what the boss gets, no more, no less. Now sometimes any one of us might just fall behind a little, so we always keep some finished stuff hidden away just in case." The more he talked, the more I really began to feel like the enemy. I tried to apologize, but he just went on. "Look, kid, the boss always wants more and he doesn't give a shit if we die giving it to him, so we [it was that "we" that seemed to retrieve my soul back into the community; my tears just went away] agree on how much we're going to give him—no more, no less. You see, kid, if you keep running around, moving the stuff too fast, the boss will get wise about what's going on." Sam put his arm on my shoulder. (My God! I was one of them! I love Sam and the place. I am in!) "So look," he says, "your job is to figure out how to move and work no faster than we turn the stuff out. Get it? OK? You'll get it." I said, "Yes, of course, I understand everything." I was being initiated into the secrets of a work tribe, and I loved it.

I was beginning to learn the second work lesson that would be taught me many times over in a variety of different jobs: Don't do more work than is absolutely necessary. Years later I would read about how people in the Hawthorne works of Western Electric would "bank work" and use it when they fell behind or just wanted to take it easy. I have seen a lot of work banking, especially in machine shops. In some way I have felt that banking work was the workers' response to the stopwatches of industrial engineers. It is an interesting sort of game of hide the work now, take it out later. In another plant, would you believe we banked propellor shafts for Liberty ships!

Issues

1. How can the work group affect individual behavior?
2. What limits does the organization put on individual behavior? What limits does the work group put on individual behavior? What is left to the individual?

Robert Schrank

Machinist

There is a production game that is played between workers and their supervisors. The supervisor or foreman almost always wants the people he is responsible for to produce more. Most workers seem to know instinctively that "more production" either leads to the challenging game of "you want more but I don't want to work harder" or to a bottomless pit. The challenge of the game can prove to be the most interesting part of the job. Workers are ingenious at this game.

I was talking with the Greek about how the foreman was catching up with our production innovations. "Look," I said, "we are in a double bind if we do the work as easily and as quickly as possible, maybe just to increase our schmooze[1] time. If the supervisor catches on and says we're real smart and incorporates our shortcuts, we end up doing more work for the same money. This requires that we hide our shortcut timesavers—and that will take our most creative effort." The Greek looked at me for a long time and then said, "Listen, the next time Ramirez is running far ahead of schedule, I am going to show you something you won't believe, Schrank."

A few weeks later on a summer night, the Greek came by and said, "Let's take a walk." We walked to the back end of the plant, out onto the loading platform. There I could not believe my eyes. I saw two guys burying a thirty-foot propeller shaft in the backyard, I burst out with "What the hell are you guys doing?" They said, "Hey fellows, you watch us be heroes at the end of the month when the boss gives us that we-need-to-break-quota bullshit." I admit that this was an extreme case, but if you can get a group of workers to tell work-banking stories, you will hear some fantastic tales.

Banking work in the sawdust, as was done in the furniture factory, or under benches, in machine shop lockers, under loose floor boards, even in car trunks, or by undercounting, are just a few of the ways I observed workers trying to monitor their own work pace to control the amount that they are asked to produce. I remember a typewriter plant where people would get

Reprinted from *Ten Thousand Working Days* by Robert Schrank by permission of the MIT Press, Cambridge, Massachusetts. Copyright © 1978 by Massachusetts Intitute of Technology.

[1]"Schmooze time" is that time spent in social interaction with co-workers or friends rather than in performance of the required or assigned task.

ahead by taking the extra parts home, then on a day they wanted to take it easy, bring them in to be counted.

If you have not experienced a production line, it is very hard to understand the problem of work pacing. I remember doing things in an emergency, like turning out in seven hours a propeller shaft that normally took twelve or fourteen hours. Obviously I could never do that at a steady pace. It would surely end me up like Charlie Chaplin in *Modern Times.* To expect a production worker to work at his peak for a whole day is like asking a long-distance runner to sprint the whole race the way he does in the last 100 yards. It is simply impossible to do, yet some production-hungry industrial engineers expect that. The foreman at Vass would say, "After all, you produced thirty units this morning. How come you only made ten this afternoon?" I answered, "Because I wore myself out this morning." He did not seem to care about my explanation, just sort of shrugged and said, "If you can do it in the morning, you can do it in the afternoon."

I was learning that I might double or triple my productivity for a short, fixed period of time, but I could not possibly keep up that double or triple pace continuously without serious consequences to my health.

Bennet Kremen, writing in the *New York Times* about the Lordstown, Ohio, General Motors assembly plant told how workers doubled up (buddied) to relieve each other on the line. Some people in the Auto Workers Union were peeved at Kremen for suggesting that one employee on an assembly line could do the work of two; this surely could be seen as evidence that GM might be right when they complain that the workers are not giving a day's work. Workers on a production line may help each other by doing two jobs for a given period of time, but that certainly does not mean one person could do both jobs continuously. I can recall times when I did the work of two or even three men for short time periods. Can this possibly suggest that I could do that continuously and hope to survive? I think not. The problem that employees in manufacturing have is that supervisors continue to harass employees for increased production once the idea takes hold that workers can be more productive. They become extremely aggressive in constantly demanding more. That is how workers learn to pace the amount of work done for a day, a week, or a month. As Max said in the furniture factory, "We give just so much and no more."

A few years ago I visited the Volvo truck plant in Goteborg, Sweden. I spent a day observing work teams assembling trucks. In the afternoon, about three o'clock or three-fifteen, the place seemed to come to a halt as workers began to wipe their hands, wash up, and generally to appear as though the day's work was through. I figured my watch was wrong, because time-zone changes throw off my inner clock. Since quitting time was four o'clock, I asked one of the men what was happening. He looked at me quite surprised saying, "We made our thirty trucks today and that's it. Not even another bolt goes on today."

That example of production pacing is common in many parts of Europe. When I asked the Volvo management about it, they acknowledged the problem, yet they had no idea about what to do. As one manager put it, "What good is participation, team building, and all that stuff if I cannot get one more truck a week?"

Workers in manufacturing try to get some control over the work pace because they are fearful that if they do not, the speedup will kill them. Whether it is true or not is of little consequence because the tradition creates a fear that is real.

Issues

1. What limits does management put on performance? On schmoozing? What limits does the worker's group put on performance? On schmoozing? What effect do these limits have on individual worker's discretion?
2. Describe any experiences you have had where your (work) group put a limit on your individual performance.
3. Explore alternatives to the "production game" that can be used to reduce the negative effect of the worker's group on individual performance.

False Promises

The General Motors Assembly Division is a tough, no-nonsense outfit charged with the responsibility "of being able to meet foreign competition." GMAD "adopted 'get tough' tactics to cope with increased worker absenteeism and boost productivity." According to *Business Week*, the new division was set up in 1965 to tighten and revamp assembly operations. "The need for GMAD's belt-tightening role was underscored during the late 1960s when GM's profit margin dropped from 10 percent to 7 percent."[1]

At Lordstown, efficiency became the watchword. At 60 cars an hour, the pace of work had not been exactly leisurely, but after GMAD came in the number of cars produced almost doubled. Making one car a minute had been no picnic, especially on a constantly moving line. Assembly work fits the worker to the pace of the machine. Each work station is no more than 6 to 8 feet long. For example, within a minute on the line, a worker in the trim department had to walk about 20 feet to a conveyor belt transporting parts to the line, pick up a front seat weighing 30 pounds, carry it back to his work station, place the seat on the chassis, and put in four bolts to fasten it down by first hand-starting the bolts and then using an air gun to tighten them according to standard. It was steady work when the line moved at 60 cars an hour. When it increased to more than 100 cars an hour, the number of operations on this job were not reduced and the pace became almost maddening. In 36 seconds the worker had to perform at least eight different operations, including walking, lifting, hauling, lifting the carpet, bending to fasten the bolts by hand, fastening them by air gun, replacing the carpet, and putting a sticker on the hood. Sometimes the bolts fail to fit into the holes; the gun refuses to function at the required torque; the seats are defective or the threads are bare on the bolt. But the line does not stop. Under these circumstances the workers often find themselves "in the hole," which means that they have fallen behind the line.

"You really have to run like hell to catch up, if you're gonna do the whole

From *False Promises* by Stanley Aronowitz. Copyright © 1973 by Stanley Aronowitz. Used with permission of McGraw-Hill Book Company, pp. 22–27.

[1] *Business Week*, "A GM Reorganization Backfires," No. 2221, March 25, 1972, pp. 46–51.

job right," one operator named Jerry told me when I interviewed him in the summer of 1972. "They had the wrong-sized bolt on the job for a whole year. A lot of times we just miss a bolt to keep up with the line."

In all plants workers try to make the work a little easier for themselves. At Lordstown, as in other automobile plants, there are many methods for making the work tolerable. Despite the already accelerated pace, workers still attempt to use the traditional relief mechanism of "doubling up." This method consists of two workers deciding that they will learn each other's operation. One worker performs both jobs while the other worker is spelled. At Lordstown, a half-hour "on" and a half-hour "off" is a fairly normal pattern..The worker who is on is obliged to do both jobs by superhuman effort. But workers would rather race to keep up with the line than work steadily— in anticipation of a half-hour off to read, lie down, go to the toilet, or roam the plant to talk to a buddy. Not all jobs lend themselves to this arrangement, especially those where a specific part like a front seat must be placed on all models; here the work is time consuming, and full of hassles. But there are many operations where doubling up is feasible, particularly light jobs which have few different movements. Fastening seat belts and putting on windshield wipers are examples.

"The only chance to keep from goin' nuts," said one worker, "is to double up on the job. It's the only way to survive in the plant. . . ."

The company claims that doubling up reduces quality. The method engenders a tendency for workers to miss operations, especially when they fall behind, according to one general foreman. Some workers believe that the company blames workers for doubling up as an excuse to explain its own quality control failures. There is a widespread feeling among the line workers that the doubling-up "issue" has more to do with the company's program of harrassment than the problem of quality control.

The tenure of the previous management at the Chevrolet division of GM was characterized by a plethora of shop floor agreements between foremen and line workers on work rules. These agreements were not written down, but were passed from worker to worker as part of the lore of the job. As in many workplaces, a new line supervisor meant that these deals had to be "renegotiated."

When GMAD took over at Lordstown, management imposed new, universally applicable rules which, in fact, were applied selectively. On Mondays, "when there are not many people on the line," the company tolerates lateness. On Tuesdays, when young workers come back from their long weekends, "they throw you out the door" for the rest of the shift for coming in fifteen minutes or a half-hour late. "When the company gets a bug up its ass to improve quality, they come down on you for every little mistake. But then things start goin' good on the cars, so they start to work on other areas. Then you are not allowed to lay down—not allowed to read on the job; no talkin' (you can't talk anyway the noise is so terrific); no doubling up."

Efficiency meant imposing on workers the absolute power of management to control production. GMAD instituted a policy of compulsory overtime at the time of the model changeover. The "normal" shift became ten hours a day and there were no exceptions to the rule. Absenteeism and lateness became the objects of veritable holy crusades for the new management. Nurses refused to grant permission for workers to go home sick. The company began to consider a worker a voluntary quit if he stayed off for three days and failed to bring a doctor's note certifying his illness. Doctors were actually sent to workers' homes to check up on "phony" illnesses in an effort to curb absenteeism.

The average hourly rate for production line workers was $4.56 an hour in mid-1972. In addition, annual cost of living increases geared to the consumer price index had been incorporated into the contract. Gross base weekly earnings for ten hours a day were more than $195. With overtime, some workers had made more than $13,000 a year. Besides, GM workers have among the best pension, health insurance, and unemployment benefits programs in American industry. Certainly, there is no job in the Warren area whose terms compare with the high wages and benefits enjoyed by the GM workers. Equally significant, GM is among the few places in the area still hiring a large number of employees. The steel mills, electrical plants, and retail trades offer lower wages to unskilled workers and less steady employment to low-seniority people. For some, General Motors is "big mother." Many workers echo the sentiment of Joe, a forty-five-year-old assembly line worker who said that GM offered better wages and working conditions than he had ever enjoyed in his life—"I don't know how anybody who works for a living can do better than GM." Compared to the steel mill where he did heavy dirty jobs, GM was "not near as hard."

Of course Joe has had differences with company policies. The job was "too confining." He didn't like to do the same thing every day. He objected to the company harassment of the men and had actually voted for a strike to correct some of the injustices in the plant. But, like many others, Joe had "married the job" because he didn't know where else he could get a retirement plan which would give him substantial benefits after thirty years of service, full hospital benefits, and real job security.

GMAD likes workers like Joe too. They know Joe isn't going anywhere. They believe him when he says he is sick and, if he misses installing parts on a car he can "chalk it up." In such cases, he simply tells the foreman about the missing operation and the "repairmen will take care of it."

Yet high wages and substantial fringe benefits have not been sufficient to allay discontent among the people working on the line. If other area employers paid wages competitive with GM wages, GM would have serious difficulty attracting a labor force. The wages are a tremendous initial attraction for workers and explain why many are reluctant to leave the shop. But even the substantial unemployment in the Warren and Youngstown areas has not succeeded in tempering the spirit of rebellion among young workers or preventing the persistence of turnover among them. The promise of high earnings has not reduced the absentee rate in the plant. One young worker, married with a child, earned a gross income of $10,900 in 1971, a year when overtime was offered regularly to employees. This was a gross pay at least $2,000 below his possible earnings. He had taken at least one day off a week and refused several offers of Saturday work.

GM acknowledges that absenteeism, particularly on Mondays and Fridays, constitutes its most distressing discipline problem. Workers report line shutdowns "for as much as a half hour" on Mondays because there are simply not enough people to perform the operations. But many young people are prepared to sacrifice higher earnings for a respite from the hassles of assembly line work, even for one day.

At Lordstown and other plants where youth constitute either a majority or significant minority of the work force there is concrete evidence that the inducements to hard work have weakened. Older workers in the plant as well as a minority of the youth admit that they have never seen this kind of money in their lives. But the young people are seeking something more from their labor than high wages, pensions, and job security. At Lordstown, they are looking for "a chance to use my brain" and a job "where my high school education counts for something." Even though workers resent the demanding pace of the line, no line job takes more than a half-hour to learn. Most workers achieve sufficient speed in their operation to keep up with the line in about a half a shift. The minute rationalization of assembly line operations to a few simple movements has been perfected by GMAD. One operator whose job was to put two clips on a hose all day long said, "I never think about my job. In fact, I try to do everything I can to forget it. If I concentrated on thinking about it, I'd go crazy. The trouble is I have to look at what I'm doing or else I'd f__k up every time." This worker spent some of his time figuring out ways to get off the line, especially ways to take days off. "I always try to get doctor's slips to take three days if I can." Another worker reported provoking a foreman to give him a disciplinary layoff (DLO) just to avoid the monotony of his tasks.

The drama of Lordstown is the conflict between the old goals of decent income and job security, which have lost their force but are by no means dead, and the new needs voiced by young people for more than mindless labor. The company and the union represent the promise that the old needs can be met on a scale never before imagined for many of the people on the line. The youth are saying that these benefits are not enough.

The picture is complicated by the fact that not all young people share the same attitudes. Even though the overwhelming majority of workers in the shop are between twenty and thirty years old, they are not all cut from the same cloth. The most disaffected group in the plant are the youth who were raised in the Warren-Youngstown area. Their fathers and mothers were industrial workers, or at least had been part of an urban environment for most of their lives. Since the area has had a long industrial tradition (it lies in the heart of the Ohio valley), high wages and traditional union protections and

Experiential Organizational Behavior

benefits are part of the taken-for-granted world of a generation brought up in the shadows of the steel mills and rubber factories. These workers share the same upbringing, went to the same schools, frequented the same neighborhood social centers, and speak the same symbolic languages. When they came to General Motors, they brought with them a set of unspoken expectations about their work and their future. Many were high school graduates; a smaller, but significant number were attending college. Although it cannot be denied that the "good money" paid by GM was an important inducement for these young people to choose to work there, few of them considered steady work and good wages sufficient to satisfy a life's ambition.

Issues

1. Analyze the situation described here in terms of (1) Maslow's hierarchy of needs, (2) Vroom's expectancy theory, and (3) Herzberg's dual-factor theory.
2. Compare the Lordstown practice of "doubling up" with the practice of job enlargement. How are they similar? different?
3. Prepare two lists under the following headings:
   What workers want from their job   *What management wants from the workers*

27

Meg Cox

Staff Reporter of THE WALL STREET JOURNAL

Speedier Chickens Fowl Up Their Jobs, Inspectors Grouse

They Say Agency's Mirrors, Used to Spur Processing, Are a Pain in Their Eyes

CARROLLTON, Ga.—In the old days, a chicken inspector was really something. He'd stand by the side of an overhead conveyor carrying thousands of naked, wobbling upside-down chickens and with the hand movements of a Javanese dancer go through 26 motions to inspect a chicken inside and out.

Oh, how low has the chicken inspector fallen today. Now he must sit or stand beneath the conveyor, moving only his eyes, scanning first one side of the chicken and then the other reflected in a two-foot by three-foot mirror. Here at the super-mechanized Gold Kist processing plant, for example, inspectors are performing these rapid eye movements at the rate of 35,000 birds a day.

The U.S. Department of Agriculture, whose federal Chicken Inspection Service controls the chicken in every pot, is crowing about the recent introduction of these mirrors as the first major innovation in the service's 20-year history. The mirrors, the federal chicken people say, have speeded up production lines, resulting in an average 30% rise in chicken output with 25% fewer inspectors, thus saving the taxpayer millions of dollars. "I'm proud of this," says assistant agriculture secretary Carol Tucker Foreman.

"Line Hypnosis"

But those inspectors who are forced to only stand and stare are viewing the birds with malice through the looking glass. The chicken inspectors' union,

Reprinted by permission of *The Wall Street Journal*, © Dow Jones & Company, Inc. (1979). All Rights Reserved.

the National Joint Council of Food Inspection Locals, has sued the Agriculture Department, contending that the mirrors and the faster lines are causing its members to suffer from "line hypnosis" and "undue inspector fatigue." But a man with the department says he doubts the effects are that fancy. "I think it's just a monotonous job," he says.

A federal judge dismissed the suit. But late last month the union appealed. It also has filed an unfair-labor-practices claim with the National Labor Relations Board. And the chicken inspectors are finding an audience at the National Institute of Occupational Safety and Health, which is investigating to see whether the mirrors do indeed cause undue stress.

Of course, the union doesn't care for the idea of it all being done with mirrors at the expense of 25% of its membership. But, says James Murphy, the union's chairman, the mirrors are causing all manner of complaints, from dizziness to eye strain. "Some people who never wore glasses are getting them," he says.

The chicken inspectors are needed in the first place because the Agriculture Department requires that between slaughtering and supermarket every chicken be inspected for disease, such as a type of arthritis, and for such things as bruises and broken bones. This task gets ever harder the more efficient and automated the $8.5 billion-a-year chicken industry becomes. Last year, 3.5 billion birds passed in front of inspectors, compared with only 2.5 billion in 1970.

A Growing Bill

The solution to dealing with this torrent of chickens has been to speed up the processing equipment and to add more inspectors. There now are about 2,000 inspectors, compared with 1,300 a decade ago, and the bill for their services has grown to $80 million a year from $31 million.

The department has been looking at how to get more birds for the buck since 1968. In 1976 it ordered a $400,000 "efficiency study" from a private firm. This disclosed the startling news that the elaborate chicken inspection with all those hand movements wasn't really necessary; poultry science had made chickens so healthy that the rate of sickly birds discovered on the line was a mere 1%.

Yet another study recommended speeding up the inspection process by having two inspectors instead of one for each bird. One would merely inspect the outside of the bird with the use of a mirror and the other, farther down the line, would check the innards. The department didn't do much with the studies except study them and issue a 73-page report calling for "quite a few studies" more, in the words of one official.

Then, last fall, the agency was stung into action. As the result of a complicated court case, a federal judge ruled that all similar chicken-processing plants had to be run at more or less the same speed. In the confusion that followed, some plants began slowing down and chickens began backing up in the coops.

To get its national chicken system back in order, the department decided to put all those years of studies into action. In April, it issued an emergency order for the use of mirrors to speed up and to simplify the inspection process. Since then, 40% of all chicken processors have installed the mirrors and now have inspectors for the outside of the birds and inspectors to peek at the entrails. Other processors are spending up to $95,000 redesigning their plants so that they also can use the mirror system.

At the modern, highly mechanized poultry-processing plant owned by Gold Kist, a farmers' cooperative that kills, plucks, cleans and chills 230 million chickens a year, the mirror inspectors have to watch the birds whizzing by at the rate of 70 a minute, four birds a minute faster than before. The plant now turns out 128,000 chickens a day, 9,200 more than before, with one-fourth fewer inspectors.

Ester "Rosie" Rosenbaum, one of the 14 inspectors at Gold Kist, sniffs in disgust at the new system. And just to think, she says, she became a chicken inspector back in the 1960s because President Kennedy said "to do something for my country."

Supervisor Jack Kemp, who isn't required to take over the mirror shift very often, says that when he does, it "puts me to sleep." John Simpson, an inspector for three years, declares that "my back hurts a lot." Then he concedes that "it hurt before, too."

But Wilma Hitchcock likes her job. She quit as a production worker for Gold Kist six years ago for the better benefits and pay, averaging $16,000 a year, of an Agriculture Department inspector. I look at it this way," she says, "I'd eat anything going down that line."

The mirror inspectors see the chickens after they have been through the scalder and through the rubber "fingers" of the plucking machine. As the chickens pass by upside-down overhead, a stainless-steel trough to catch the drippings moves below in the opposite direction. The inspectors complain that this two-way movement "hypnotizes" them, producing a sort of dazed condition. But Charles Williams, the supervising Agriculture Department veterinarian at the plant, says he feels that "boredom" is a better explanation.

Farther down the line, the chickens are eviscerated and their innards are inspected for disease by other inspectors. The "inside" inspectors have to view only about half of the 35,000 birds that each mirror inspector has to see every day. Even so, the mirror inspectors apparently refuse to rotate their job. "The mirror job has become the prestige position because you don't have to handle the birds,' says one plant manager.

Bureaucracy being what it is, even something as simple as a mirror can create problems. Mirrors, particularly in chicken plants, tend to get smudged and gooey. To clean them, the department wanted to use Windex. But that wasn't on the list of "chemicals approved for use in chicken-packing plants." As of this date, plants have only temporary approval to use Windex. "They've got to feed it to rats for a year first," says one chicken-plant official sarcastically.

But that's all right. Just think of all the money that taxpayers are going to be saved. Well, perhaps not. The money, says Mrs. Foreman, the assistant agriculture secretary, will go into improved chicken analysis.

One reason fewer inspectors are needed is because chickens are so healthy, and the reason for this is that chickens have a multitude of chemicals pumped into them. Now tests have to be developed to detect the chemicals in the dead birds that made the live birds so healthy in the first place. If you see what we mean.

Issues

1. Describe the pressure(s) for change in the processing plant. Describe the resistance(s) to change. What is the resultant, current state? What options are open to the worker? What behaviors would you predict?

28

Victor H. Vroom

A New Look at Managerial Decision Making

All managers are decision makers. Furthermore, their effectiveness as managers is largely reflected in their "track record" in making the "right decisions." These "right decisions" in turn largely depend on whether or not the manager has utilized the right person or persons in the right ways in helping him solve the problem.

Our concern in this article is with decision making as a social process. We view the manager's task as determining how the problem is to be solved, not the solution to be adopted. Within that overall framework, we have attempted to answer two broad sets of questions: What decision-making processes should managers use to deal effectively with the problems they encounter in their jobs? What decision-making processes do they use in dealing with these problems and what considerations affect their decisions about how much to share their decision-making power with subordinates?

The reader will recognize the former as a normative or prescriptive question. A rational and analytic answer to it would constitute a normative model of decision making as a social process. The second question is descriptive, since it concerns how managers do, rather than should, behave.

Toward a Normal Model

About four years ago, Philip Yetton, then a graduate student at Carnegie-Mellon University, and I began a major research program in an attempt to answer these normative and descriptive questions.

We began with the normative question. What would be a rational way of deciding on the form and amount of participation in decision making that should be used in different situations? We were tired of debates over the

Reprinted, by permission of the publisher, from ORGANIZATIONAL DYNAMICS, Spring 1973, © 1973 by AMACOM, a division of American Management Associations. All rights reserved.

relative merits of Theory X and Theory Y and of the truism that leadership depends upon the situation. We felt that it was time for the behavioral sciences to move beyond such generalities and to attempt to come to grips with the complexities of the phenomena with which they intended to deal.

Our aim was ambitious—to develop a set of ground rules for matching a manager's leadership behavior to the demands of the situation. It was critical that these ground rules be consistent with research evidence concerning the consequences of participation and that the model based on the rules be operational, so that any manager could see it to determine how he should act in any decision-making situation.

Table I shows a set of alternative decision processes that we have employed in our research. Each process is represented by a symbol (e.g., AI, CI, GII) that will be used as a convenient method of referring to each process. The first letter in this symbol signifies the basic properties of the process (A stands for autocratic; C for consultative; and G for group). The Roman numerals that follow the first letter constitute variants on that process. Thus, AI represents the first variant on an autocratic process, and AII the second variant.

TABLE I
Types of Management Decision Styles

AI	You solve the problem or make the decision yourself, using information available to you at that time.
AII	You obtain the necessary information from your subordinate(s), then decide on the solution to the problem yourself. You may or may not tell your subordinates what the problem is in getting the information from them. The role played by your subordinates in making the decision is clearly one of providing the necessary information to you, rather than generating or evaluating alternative solutions.
CI	You share the problem with relevant subordinates individually, getting their ideas and suggestions without bringing them together as a group. Then _you_ make the decision that may or may not reflect your subordinates' influence.
CII	You share the problem with your subordinates as a group, collectively obtaining their ideas and suggestions. Then _you_ make the decision that may or may not reflect your subordinates' influence.
GII	You share a problem with your subordinates as a group. Together you generate and evaluate alternatives and attempt to reach agreement (consensus) on a solution. Your role is much like that of chairman. You do not try to influence the group to adopt "your" solution and you are willing to accept and implement any solution that has the support of the entire group.

(GI is omitted because it applies only to more comprehensive models outside the scope of the article.)

Conceptual and Empirical
Basis of the Model

A model designed to regulate, in some rational way, choices among the decisions processes shown in Table I should be based on sound empirical evidence concerning the likely consequences of the styles. The more complete the empirical base of knowledge, the greater the certainty with which we can develop the model and the greater will be its usefulness. To aid in understanding the conceptual basis of the model, it is important to distinguish among three classes of outcomes that bear on the ultimate effectiveness of decisions. These are:

1. The quality or rationality of the decision.
2. The acceptance or commitment on the part of subordinates to execute the decision effectively.
3. The amount of time required to make the decision.

The effects of participation on each of these outcomes or consequences were summed up by the author in *The Handbook of Social Psychology* as follows:

The results suggest that allocating problem solving and decision-making tasks to entire groups requires a greater investment of man hours but produces higher acceptance of decisions and a higher probability that the decision will be executed efficiently. Differences between these two methods in quality of decisions and in elapsed time are inconclusive and probably highly variable . . . It would be naive to think that group decision making is always more "effective" than autocratic decision making, or vice versa; the relative effectiveness of these two extreme methods depends both on the weights attached to quality, acceptance and time variables and on differences in amounts of these outcomes resulting from these methods, neither of which is invariant from one situation to another. The critics and proponents of participative management would do well to direct their efforts toward identifying the properties of situations in which different decision-making approaches are effective rather than wholesale condemnation or deification of one approach.

We have gone on from there to identify the properties of the situation or problem that will be the basic elements in the model. These problem attributes are of two types: 1) Those that specify the importance for a particular problem of quality and acceptance, and 2) those that, on the basis of available evidence, have a high probability of moderating the effects of participation on each of these outcomes. Table II shows the problem attributes used in the present form of the model. For each attribute a question is provided that might be used by a leader in diagnosing a particular problem prior to choosing his leadership style.

In phrasing the questions, we have held technical language to a minimum. Furthermore, we have phrased the questions in Yes-No form, translating the continuous variables defined above into dichotomous variables. For example, instead of attempting to determine how important the decision quality is to the effectiveness of the decision (attribute A), the leader is asked in the first question to judge whether there is any quality component to the problem. Similarly, the difficult task of specifying exactly how much information the leader possesses that is relevant to the decision (attribute B) is reduced to a simple judgment by the leader concerning whether or not he has sufficient information to make a high quality decision.

We have found that managers can diagnose a situation quickly and accurately by answering this set of seven questions concerning it. But how can such responses generate a prescription concerning the most effective leadership style or decision process? What kind of normative model of participation in decision making can be built from this set of problem attributes?

Figure 1 shows one such model expressed in the form of a decision tree. It is the seventh version of such a model that we have developed over the last three years. The problem attributes, expressed in question form, are arranged along the top of the figure. To use the model for a particular decision-making situation, one starts at the left-hand side and works toward the right asking oneself the question immediately above any box that is encountered. When a terminal node is reached, a number will be found designating the problem type and one of the decision-making processes appearing in Table I. AI is prescribed for four problem types (1, 2, 4, and 5); AII is prescribed for two problem types (9 and 10); CI is prescribed for only one problem type (8); CII is prescribed for four problem types (7, 11, 13, and 14); and GII is prescribed for three problem types (3, 6, and 12). The relative frequency with which each of the five decision processes would be prescribed for any manager would, of course, depend on the distribution of problem types encountered in his decision making.

Rationale Underlying the Model:

The decision processes specified for each problem type are not arbitrary. The model's behavior is governed by a set of principles intended to be consistent with existing evidence concerning the consequences of participation in decision making on organizational effectiveness.

There are two mechanisms underlying the behavior of the model. The first is a set of seven rules that serve to protect the quality and the acceptance of the decision by eliminating alternatives that risk one or the other of these decision outcomes. Once the rules have been applied, a feasible set of decision processes is generated. The second mechanism is a principle for choosing among alternatives in the feasible set where more than one exists.

Let us examine the rules first, because they do much of the work of the model. As previously indicated, the rules are intended to protect both the quality and acceptance of the decision. In the form of the model shown, there are three rules that protect decision quality and four that protect acceptance.

TABLE II
Problem Attributes Used in the Model

Problem Attributes	Diagnostic Questions
A. The importance of the quality of the decision.	Is there a quality requirement such that one solution is likely to be more rational than another?
B. The extent to which the leader possesses sufficient information/expertise to make a high-quality decision by himself.	Do I have sufficient information to make a high-quality decision?
C. The extent to which the problem is structured.	Is the problem structured?
D. The extent to which acceptance or commitment on the part of subordinates is critical to the effective implementation of the decision.	Is acceptance of decision by subordinates critical to effective implementation?
E. The prior probability that the leader's autocratic decision will receive acceptance by subordinates.	If you were to make the decision by yourself, is it reasonably certain that it would be accepted by your subordinates?
F. The extent to which subordinates are motivated to attain the organizational goals as represented in the objectives explicit in the statement of the problem.	Do subordinates share the organizational goals to be obtained in solving this problem?
G. The extent to which subordinates are likely to be in conflict over preferred solutions.	Is conflict among subordinates likely in preferred solutions?

1. The Information Rule

If the quality of the decision is important and if the leader does not possess enough information or expertise to solve the problem by himself, AI is eliminated from the feasible set. (Its use risks a low-quality decision.)

2. The Goal Congruence Rule

If the quality of the decision is important and if the subordinates do not share the organizational goals to be obtained in solving the problem, GII is eliminated from the feasible set. (Alternatives that eliminate the leader's final control over the decision reached may jeopardize the quality of the decision.)

3. The Unstructured Problem Rule

In decisions in which the quality of the decision is important, if the leader lacks the necessary information or expertise to solve the problem by himself, and if the problem is unstructured, i.e., he does not know exactly what information is needed and where it is located, the method used must provide

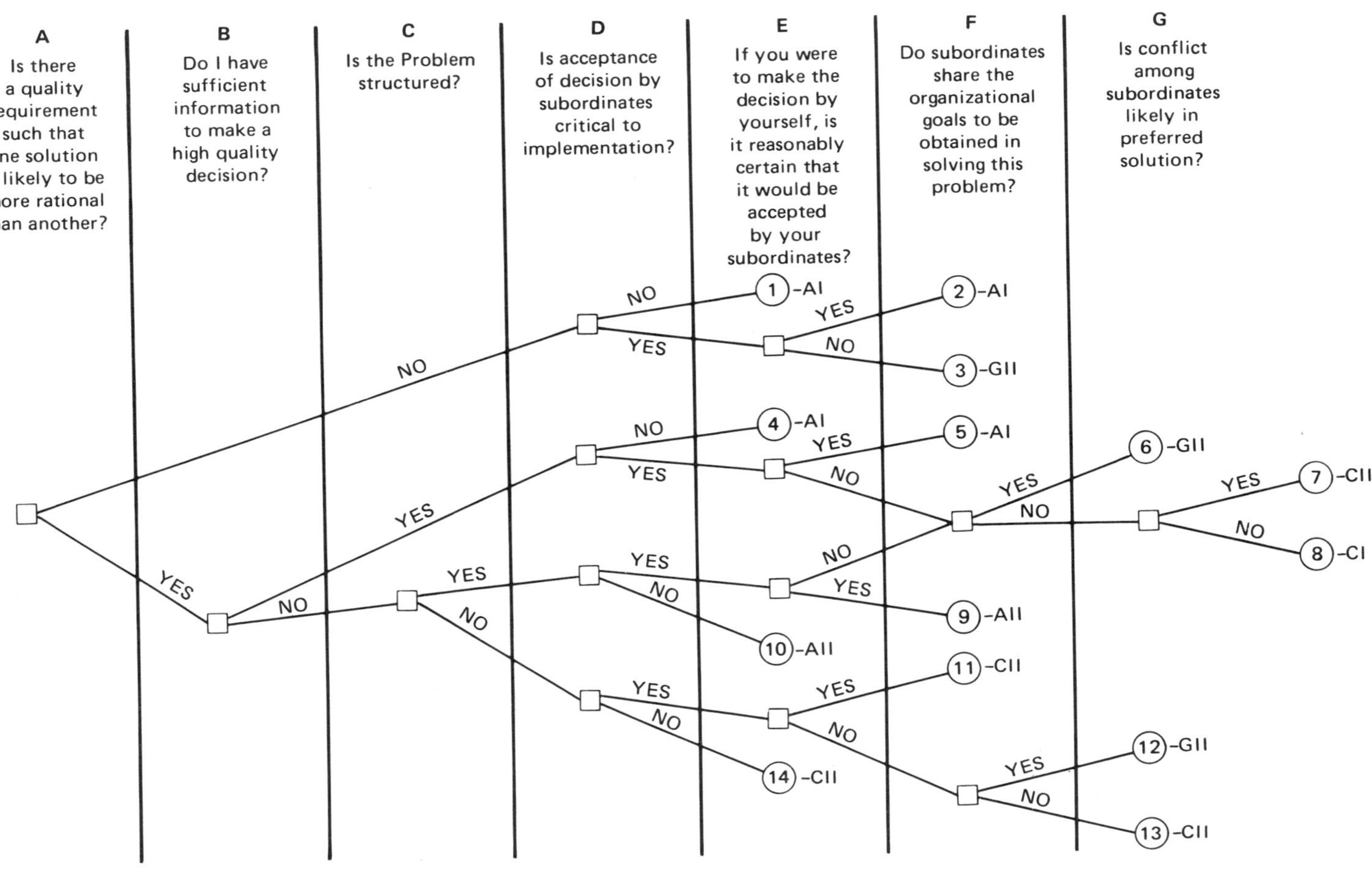

FIGURE 1. Decision Model

not only for him to collect the information but to do so in an efficient and effective manner. Methods that involve interaction among all subordinates with full knowledge of the problem are likely to be both more efficient and more likely to generate a high-quality solution to the problem. Under these conditions, AI, AII, and CI are eliminated from the feasible set. (AI does not provide for him to collect the necessary information, and AII and CI represent more cumbersome, less effective, and less efficient means of bringing the necessary information to bear on the solution of the problem than methods that do permit those with the necessary information to interact.)

4. The Acceptance Rule

If the acceptance of the decision by subordinates is critical to effective implementation, and if it is not certain that an autocratic decision made by the leader would receive that acceptance, AI and AII are eliminated from the feasible set. (Neither provides an opportunity for subordinates to participate in the decision and both risk the necessary acceptance.)

5. The Conflict Rule

If the acceptance of the decision is critical, and an autocratic decision is not certain to be accepted, and subordinates are likely to be in conflict or disagreement over the appropriate solution, AI, AII, and CI are eliminated from the feasible set. (The method used in solving the problem should enable those in disagreement to resolve their differences with full knowledge of the problem. Accordingly, under these conditions, AI, AII, and CI, which involve no interaction or only "one-on-one" relationships and therefore provide no opportunity for those in conflict to resolve their differences, are eliminated from the feasible set. Their use runs the risk of leaving some of the subordinates with less than the necessary commitment to the final decision.)

6. The Fairness Rule

If the quality of decision is unimportant and if acceptance is critical and not certain to result from an autocratic decision, AI, AII, CI, and CII are eliminated from the feasible set. (The method used should maximize the probability of acceptance as this is the only relevant consideration in determining the effectiveness of the decision. Under these circumstances, AI, AII, CI, and CII, which create less acceptance or commitment than GII, are eliminated from the feasible set. To use them is to run the risk of getting less than the needed acceptance of the decision.)

7. The Acceptance Priority Rule

If acceptance is critical, not assured by an autocratic decision, and if subordinates can be trusted, AI, AII, CI, and CII are eliminated from the feasible set. (Methods that provide equal partnership in the decision-making process can provide greater acceptance without risking decision quality. Use of any method other than GII results in an unnecessary risk that the decision will not be fully accepted or receive the necessary commitment on the part of subordinates.)

Once all seven rules have been applied to a given problem, we emerge with a feasible set of decision processes. The feasible set for each of the fourteen problem types is shown in Table III. It can be seen that there are some problem types for which only one method remains in the feasible set, others for which two methods remain feasible, and still others for which five methods remain feasible.

When more than one method remains in the feasible set, there are a number of ways in which one might choose among them. The mechanism we have selected and the principle underlying the choices of the model in Figure 1 utilizes the number of man-hours used in solving the problem as the basis for choice. Given a set of methods with equal likelihood of meeting both quality and acceptance requirements for the decision, it chooses that method that requires the least investment in man-hours. On the basis of the empirical evidence summarized earlier, this is deemed to be the method furthest to the left within the feasible set. For example, since AI, AII, CI, CII, and GII are all feasible as in Problem Types 1 and 2, AI would be the method chosen.

To illustrate application of the model in actual administrative situations, we will analyze two cases with the help of the model. While we attempt to describe these cases as completely as is necessary to permit the reader to make the judgments required by the model, there may remain some room

---

TABLE III

Problem Types and the Feasible Set of Decision Processes

Problem Type	Acceptable Methods
1.	AI, AII, CI, CII, GII
2.	AI, AII, CI, CII, GII
3.	GII
4.	AI, AII, CI, CII, GII*
5.	AI, AII, CI, CII, GII*
6.	GII
7.	CII
8.	CI, CII
9.	AII, CI, CII, GII*
10.	AII, CI, CII, GII*
11.	CII, GII*
12.	GII
13.	CII
14.	CII, GII*

*Within the feasible set only when the answer to question F is Yes.

for subjectivity. The reader may wish after reading the case to analyze it himself using the model and then to compare his analysis with that of the author.

Case I

You are a manufacturing manager in a large electronics plant. The company's management has recently installed new machines and put in a new simplified work system, but to the surprise of everyone, yourself included, the expected increase in productivity was not realized. In fact, production has begun to drop, quality has fallen off, and the number of employee separations has risen.

You do not believe that there is anything wrong with the machines. You have had reports from other companies that are using them and they confirm this opinion. You have also had representatives from the firm that built the machines go over them and they report that they are operating at peak efficiency.

You suspect that some parts of the new work system may be responsible for the change, but this view is not widely shared among your immediate subordinates who are four first-line supervisors, each in charge of a section, and your supply manager. The drop in production has been variously attributed to poor training of the operators, lack of an adequate system of financial incentives, and poor morale. Clearly, this is an issue about which there is considerable depth of feeling within individuals and potential disagreement among your subordinates.

This morning you received a phone call from your division manager. He had just received your production figures for the last six months and was calling to express his concern. He indicated that the problem was yours to solve in any way that you think best, but that he would like to know within a week what steps you plan to take.

You share your division manager's concern with the falling productivity and know that your men are also concerned. The problem is to decide what steps to take to rectify the situation.

Analysis
Questions—
      A (Quality?) = Yes
      B (Managers Information?) = No
      C (Structured?) = No
      D (Acceptance?) = Yes
      E (Prior Probability of Acceptance?) = No
      F (Goal Congruence?) = Yes
      G (Conflict?) = Yes
Problem Type—12
Feasible Set—GII

Analysis
Minimum Man-Hours Solution (from Figure 1)—GII
Rule Violations—
    AI violates rules 1, 3, 4, 5, 7
    AII violates rules 3, 4, 5, 7
    CI violates rules 3, 5, 7
    CII violates rule 7

Case II

You are general foreman in charge of a large gang laying an oil pipeline and have to estimate your expected rate of progress in order to schedule material deliveries to the next field site.

You know the nature of the terrain you will be traveling and have the historical data needed to compute the mean and variance in the rate of speed over that type of terrain. Given these two variables, it is a simple matter to calculate the earliest and latest times at which materials and support facilities will be needed at the next site. It is important that your estimate be reasonably accurate. Underestimates result in idle foremen and workers, and an overestimate results in tying up materials for a period of time before they are to be used.

Progress has been good and your five foremen and other members of the gang stand to receive substantial bonuses if the project is completed ahead of schedule.

Analysis
Questions—
    A (Quality?) = Yes
    B (Manager's Information?) = Yes
    C (Acceptance?) = No
Problem Type—4
Feasible Set—AI, AII, CI, CII, GII
Minimum Man-Hours Solution (from Figure 1)—AI
Rule Violations—None

Class Exercise*

Review the "Decision Process Flowchart" in Figure 1. The instructor will then form groups of four to five people to analyze each of the following three

*James Gibson, John Ivancevich, and James Donnelly, Jr., *Organizations: Behavior, Structure, Processes* (Dallas, Tx., Business Publications, 1979). © 1979 by Business Publications, Inc.

cases. Try to reach a group consensus on which decision style is best for the particular case. You are to select the best style based on use of the Vroom-Yetton model, available styles, and decision rules. Each case should take between 30 and 45 minutes to analyze as a group.

Case I

Setting: Corporate Headquarters
Your Position: Vice President

As marketing vice president, nonroutine requests from customers are frequently sent to your office. One such request, from a relatively new customer, was for extended terms on a large purchase ($2,500,000) involving several of your product lines. The request is for extremely favorable terms which you would not normally consider except for the high inventory level of most product lines at the present time due to the unanticipated slack period which the company has experienced over the last six months.

You realize that the request is probably a starting point for negotiations and you have proven your abilities to negotiate the most favorable arrangements in the past. As preparation for this negotiation, you have familiarized yourself with the financial situation of the customer using various investment reports you regularly receive.

Reporting to you are four sales managers, each of whom has responsibility for a single product line. They know of the order and, like you, believe that it is important to negotiate terms with minimum risks and maximum return to the company. They are likely to differ on what constitutes an acceptable level of risk. The two younger managers have developed a reputation of being "risk takers" whereas the two more senior managers are substantially more conservative.

Case II

Setting: Toy Manufacturer
Your Position: Vice President, Engineering & Design

You are a vice president in a large toy manufacturing company with responsibilities that include the design of new products that will meet the changing demand in this uncertain and very competitive industry. Your design teams, each under the supervision of a department head, are therefore under constant pressure to produce novel, marketable ideas.

At the opposite end of the manufacturing process is the Quality Control Department which is under the authority of the Vice President, Production. When Quality Control has encountered a serious problem that may be due to design features, their staff has consulted with one or more of your department heads to obtain their recommendations for any changes in the production process. In the wake of consumer concern over the safety of children's toys, however, Quality Control responsibilities have recently been expanded to insure not only the quality but the safety of your products. The first major problem in this area has arisen. A preliminary consumer report has "black listed" one of your new products without giving any specific reason or justification. This has upset you and others in the organization since it was believed that this product would be one of the most profitable items in the coming Christmas season.

The consumer group has provided your company the opportunity to respond to the report before it is made public. The head of Quality Control has therefore consulted with your design people, but you are told that they became somewhat defensive and dismissed the report as "overreactive fanatic nonsense." Your people told Quality Control that, while freak accidents are always possible, the product is certainly safe as designed. They argued that the report should simply be ignored.

Since the issue is far from routine, you have decided to give it your personal attention. Because your design teams have been intimately involved in all aspects of the development of the item, you suspect that their response is itself extreme and perhaps governed more by their emotional reaction to the report than by the facts. You are not convinced that the consumer group is totally irresponsible, and you are anxious to explore the problem in detail and recommend to Quality Control any changes that may be required from a design standpoint. The firm's image as a producer of high quality toys could suffer a serious blow if the report is made public and public confidence is lost as a result.

You will have to depend heavily on the background and experience of your design departments to help you in analyzing the problem. Even though Quality Control will be responsible for the decision to implement any changes you may ultimately recommend, your own subordinates have the background of design experience that could help set standards for what is "safe" and to suggest any design modifications that would meet these criteria.

Case III

Setting: Corporate Headquarters
Your Position: Vice President

The sales executives in your home office spend a great deal of the time visiting regional sales offices. As marketing vice president, you are concerned that the expenses incurred on these trips are excessive—especially now when the economic outlook seems bleak and general belt tightening measures are being carried out in every department.

Having recently been promoted from the ranks of your subordinates, you are keenly aware of some cost saving measures that could be introduced. You have, in fact, asked the accounting department to review a sample of past expense reports, and they have agreed with your conclusion that several highly favored travel "luxuries" could be curtailed. Your executives, for example, could restrict first-class air travel to only those occasions when economy class is unavailable, airport limousine service to hotels could be used instead of taxis where possible, etc. Even more savings could be made if your personnel carefully planned trips such that multiple purposes could be achieved where possible.

The success of any cost saving measures, however, depends on the commitment of your subordinates. You do not have the time (nor the desire) to closely review the expense reports of these executives. You suspect, though, that they do not share your concerns over the matter. Having once been in their position, you know they feel themselves deserving of travel amenities.

The problem is to determine which changes, if any, are to be made in current travel and expense account practices in the light of the new economic conditions.

Exercise Procedures

Phase I: 10–15 minutes
  Individually read case and select proper decision style using Vroom-Yetton model.
Phase II: 30–45 minutes
  Join group appointed by instructor and reach group consensus.
Phase III: 20 minutes
  Each group spokesperson presents group's response and rationale to other groups.

These phases should be used for each of the cases.

Issues

1. Discuss the applicability of this model/process to day-to-day decisions by a manager. How does this model help? Where does it fail?
2. Identify crucial and/or difficult decision points in the decision tree. What role does managerial judgment play in this process/model?
3. Describe a recent decision which you faced in terms of the decision tree model.

29

Henry P. Sims, Jr.

Leadership: An Operant Approach

The purpose of this exercise is to introduce the participant to the study of important leader behaviors. The following Supervisory Behavior Questionnaire, scoring key, and discussion will combine the description of leader behaviors with the impact and analysis of these behaviors.

Supervisory Behavior Questionnaire

	Definitely Not True	Not True	Slightly Not True	Uncertain	Slightly True	True	Definitely True
1. My supervisor would pay me a compliment if I did outstanding work.	1	2	3	4	5	6	7
2. My supervisor maintains definite standards of performance.	1	2	3	4	5	6	7
3. My supervisor would give me a reprimand if my work was consistently below standards.	1	2	3	4	5	6	7
4. My supervisor defines clear goals and objectives for my job.	1	2	3	4	5	6	7
5. My supervisor would give me special recognition if my work performance was especially good.	1	2	3	4	5	6	7
6. My supervisor would "get on me" if my work were not as good as the work of others.	1	2	3	4	5	6	7
7. My supervisor would tell others if my work were outstanding.	1	2	3	4	5	6	7
8. My supervisor establishes clear deadlines.	1	2	3	4	5	6	7
9. My supervisor would express his displeasure if I were absent for several days without an excuse.	1	2	3	4	5	6	7

Used by permission of Henry P. Sims, Jr.

This questionnaire is part of an exercise designed to teach about supervisory behavior. It is not a "test": there are no "right" or "wrong" answers. The questionnaire will NOT be collected, so, your answers will remain your own private information.

Please answer the questions on page 151 which are about your supervisor. (If you prefer, you can think about a supervisor you have had at some job or with some organization in the past.) Read each statement carefully, and circle the number indicating *how true* or *how untrue* you believe the statement to be.

Scoring Instructions

For each of the three "scales" (A, B, and C), compute a TOTAL SCORE by summing the answers to the appropriate questions, and then subtracting the number 12.

Question Number	Question Number	Question Number
2. + ( )	1. + ( )	3. + ( )
4. + ( )	5. + ( )	6. + ( )
8. + ( )	7. + ( )	9. + ( )
Sub Total ( )	Sub Total ( )	Sub Total ( )
— 12	— 12	— 12
Total Score ___	Total Score ___	Total Score ___
A	B	C

Next, on the following graph, write in a large "X" to indicate the total score for scales A, B, and C.

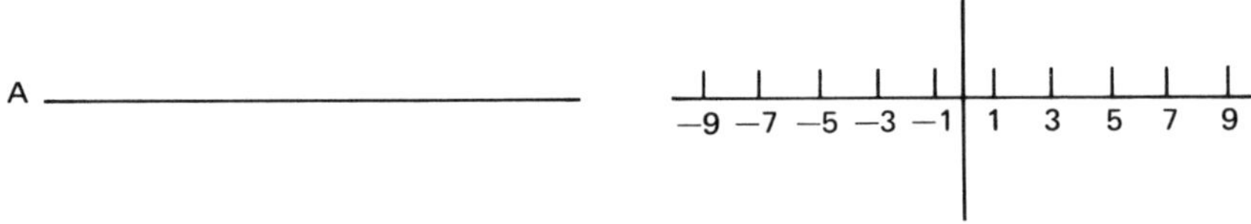

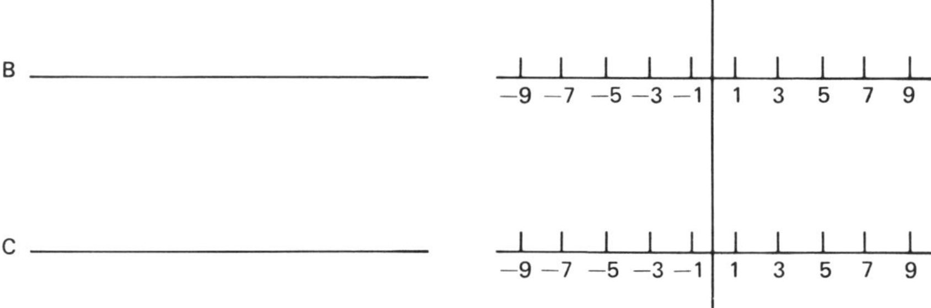

The purpose of this exercise is to introduce participants to instrumented leader behavior, based on an operant theory of leadership (e.g., Mawhinney and Ford, 1977; Scott, 1977; Sims, 1977). This exercise provides a conceptual approach to leadership theory that is different from the traditional approaches of consideration/initiating structure, managerial grid, and/or contingency theory.

Underlying Theory

The exercise assumes a theory of leadership based on operant, or reinforcement principles (Skinner, 1969). According to this viewpoint, behavior within organizations is controlled by "contingencies of reinforcement."

Figure 1 is a diagram representing a positive reinforcement contingency, which consists of three parts. The first part is a "discriminitive stimulus" (S^D), which is an environmental cue providing an individual with information of how behavior will be reinforced. A discriminitive stimulus is environmental information (an antecedent) that *comes before* individual behavior. The second part is the response, or, the behavior of the individual. Last, the behavior is followed by the administration of a reinforcer. A positive reinforcer (a consequence) is a reward that is administered contingent upon a desired behavior, and has the effect of increasing the frequency of the behavior in the future.

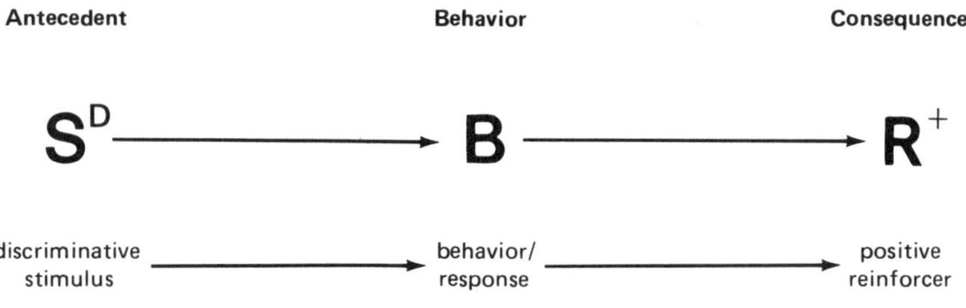

FIGURE 1. Positive Reinforcement Contingency

Reinforcers are frequently thought of as "material"; that is, pay, or some type of extrinsic incentive. In the superior/subordinate dyad, however, interpersonal reinforcers are frequently more potent (at least in the short term). That is, compliments (or statements of recognition) that are given contingent upon good performance (i.e., desirable subordinate behavior) can have reinforcing effects that serve to increase future performance.

Another type of reinforcement contingency is "punishment,"[1] which involves the administration of an aversive stimuli contingent upon a specific response. In leadership terms, punishment is typically used to *decrease* the frequency of an *undesirable* behavior. In using punishment, leaders typically use oral reprimands ("he chewed me out") or undesirable job assignments in an attempt to eliminate undesirable behavior (i.e., behavior that is detrimental to job performance.)

Both punishment and positive reinforcement are actions of the leader that "come after" subordinate behavior. That is, they are administered subsequent to (and contingent upon) a performance-related response by the subordinate. However, the behavior of the leader that occurs prior to subordinate behavior can also have a substantial impact upon performance. Frequently, this type of behavior that "comes before" subordinate behavior can be considered a discriminative stimulus (S^D); an environmental cue that informs the subordinate of what behavior is expected in order to be reinforced.

One important type of leader behavior that can be classified as S^D is connected with goal-setting or objective setting. That is, leaders that set goals, (or, induce the subordinate to set goals) can be said to be providing discriminative stimuli to subordinates. If appropriately followed by contingent reinforcement, goal setting can be an important leader behavior that enhances subordinate performance.

References

BROWN, PAUL L. and PRESBIE, R. J. *Behavior Modification in Business, Industry, and Government.* P.O. Box 296, New Paltz, N.Y.: Behavior Improvement Associates, 1976.

GREENE, C. Contingent relationships between instrumental leader behavior and subordinate satisfaction and performance. *Proceedings: American Institute for Decision Sciences,* 1975.

HAMNER, W. C. Reinforcement theory and contingency management in organization settings. In H. L. Tosi and W. C. Hamner, *Organizational Behavior and Management: A Contingency Approach.* Chicago: St. Clair Press, 1974.

[1]"Punishment" is technically distinct from "negative reinforcement," which involves the *removal* of an aversive stimulus in order to *increase* a target behavior. However, punishment and negative reinforcement are both *aversive* control techniques.

JABLONSKY, S. F. and DEVRIES, D. L. Operant conditioning principles extrapolated to the theory of management. *Organizational Behavior and Human Performance*, 1972, **7**, 340–358.

JOHNSON, R. D. *An Investigation of the Interaction Effects of Ability and Motivational Variables on Task Performance*. Unpublished doctoral dissertation. Indiana University, 1973.

LUTHANS, F. and KREITNER, R. *Organizational Behavior Modification*. Glenview, Ill.: Scott, Foresman and Company, 1975.

MAWHINNEY, T. C. Operant terms and concepts in the description of individual work behavior: some problems of interpretation, application, and evaluation. *Journal of Applied Psychology*, 1975, **60**, 704–714.

MAWHINNEY, T. C. and FORD, J. C. The path goal theory of leader effectiveness: an operant interpretation. *Academy of Management Review*, 1977, **2**, 398–411.

NORD, W. R. Beyond the teaching machine: the neglected area of operant conditioning in the theory and practice of management. *Organizational Behavior and Human Performance*, 1969, **4**, 375–401.

REITZ, H. J. Managerial attitudes and perceived contingencies between performance and organizational response. *Academy of Management Proceedings*, 31st Annual Meeting, 1971, 227–238.

SCOTT, W. G. Leadership: a functional analysis. In Hunt and Larson (eds.), *Leadership: The Cutting Edge*. Carbondale, Illinois: Southern Illinois University Press, 1977.

SIMS, H. P. The leader as a manager of reinforcement contingencies: an empirical example and a model. In Hunt and Larson (eds.), *Leadership: The Cutting Edge*. Carbondale, Illinois: Southern Illinois University Press, 1977.

SIMS, H. P. and SZILAGYI, A. D. Leader reward behavior and subordinate satisfaction and performance. *Organizational Behavior and Human Performance*, 1975, **14**, 426–438.

SKINNER, B. F. *The Contingencies of Reinforcement: A Theoretical Analysis*. New York: Appleton-Century-Crofts, Meredith Corporation, 1969.

Issues

1. How do leader behaviors (e.g., giving rewards, setting goals) affect the performance of subordinates?
2. Why might the study of leader behaviors tell us more about the nature of leadership then the study of leader styles (e.g., task-oriented) or dimensions (e.g., initiating structure)?
3. Discuss the application of operant approaches to leadership to the training of leaders.
4. Give three specific examples of each of the ways a leader can (1) set performance goals, (2) reward the desired behavior (performance), and (3) punish undesired behavior.

Thomas J. Peters

Leadership: Sad Facts and Silver Linings

*The typical CEO has endless interruptions
and limited options for action. In
addition, he may not even hear about
his choices, or any bad news that might
require action, until it is almost too
late. Finally, any decision he does
make will probably require months or
years to implement fully. This author
suggests that this gloomy picture
has another side. In fact, each of
these "sad facts" of managerial life
can be turned into an opportunity to
communicate values and to persuade,
and they add up to a new notion
of the chief executive's function.*

You are executive vice president of a large corporation, challenged by competitors at home and abroad. During the past year, you have tried to get the organization moving on a much-needed overhaul of the product line. Today one of the task forces is to spend all day reviewing its key findings with you.

Twenty minutes into the presentation it is already clear that what it has come up with is a future product array with no apparent flexibility. You are being asked to bet several million dollars on a risky slate that is sure to be challenged in whole or in part long before even the first products hit the marketplace.

Reprinted by permission of the Harvard Business Review. "Leadership: Sad facts and silver linings" by Thomas J. Peters (November–December 1979). Copyright © 1979 by the President and Fellows of Harvard College; all rights reserved.

Then at 9:35 you are pulled out of the review to talk with the vice chairman about a product safety challenge that has just hit the local press. You get back to the meeting at 11:05 only to be pulled out again at 11:40: the president wants to verify the amount of capital spending in next year's budget before a luncheon with an outside board member. Finally, after returning at 12:35, you are pulled out for good at 2:15 to meet a major customer who has flown in unexpectedly to talk about a $20 million bid one of your major divisions just made. So, in the end, the six straight hours you had planned to give to that all-important product line issue were cut down to less than three.

The preceding situation would expose you to attack from two kinds of management thinkers. Decision-making theorists would chide you for failing to develop a wide range of options. Time effectiveness experts would criticize you for not going off-campus and devoting the full six-hour block to such a major issue.

There is, however, another side to the coin: the scenario just sketched is typical of the real world of senior management; it is, in fact, the norm.

Executives have sensed for years that this series of interruptions with the task at hand sandwiched in represents a true picture of the way they do business, but only recently has such a routine been thoroughly documented. In the early 1970s, when studying chief executives' use of time, Canadian researcher Henry Mintzberg noted that they moved in a fragmented fashion through a bewildering array of issues on any given day; in fact, fully half of their activities were completed in less than nine minutes.[1]

Moreover, he argued that such behavior was probably both appropriate and efficient. A chief executive officer provides a unique perspective and is a unique information source, Mintzberg pointed out. His ability to influence a large number of activities through brief contacts may, in fact, be a highly leveraged use of his time. More recently, examining 25 major business decisions, Mintzberg found that, in every case, top management deliberation focused on only one option. They were all go-no-go issues; not a multiple choice question in the lot.

More than a decade ago, H. Edward Wrapp postulated in a much-quoted article that the successful manager "recognizes the futility of trying to push total packages or programs through the organization. . . . Avoiding debates on principles, he tries to piece together particles that may appear to be incidentals into a program that moves at least part way toward [his goals]."[2]

Without offering many prescriptions, other researchers, too, are challenging the conventional organizational wisdom concerning the supposed advantages of orderly decision-making processes and the supposed waste of time

[1] Henry Mintzberg, "The Manager's Job: Folklore and Fact," HBR July–August 1975, p. 49.
[2] H. Edward Wrapp, "Good Managers Don't Make Policy Decisions," HBR September–October 1967, p. 95.

entailed by meetings, telephone conversations, unscheduled interruptions, and so on. The researchers do not deny the *rationality* of accepted notions about how a top executive ought to spend his time, nor do they dismiss out of hand the values of orderly management.

Rather, by challenging the realism of advice based on a model so much less messy than the real world, they suggest that executive behavior that results from an ad hoc adaptation to shifting circumstances is not in itself irrational. Such behavior might, after all, prove to be the expression of a very different organizing principle.

Reckoning with Realities

Over the past two years, several of my colleagues and I have been attempting to anaylze the workings of advanced decision-making systems in some two dozen corporations in the United States and Western Europe. In general, our observations support the views of the realists against the less practical rationalizations of conventional organization theory. Our findings can be summarized under the following four headings:

1. *Senior managers will usually receive for review what amounts to a single option (one new product slate, one acquisition candidate, one major investment proposal), rather than a set of fully developed choices.* They usually face yes or no decisions rather than trade-offs. Rarely, moreover, does the proposal that they see include assessments of possible competitive responses or government constraints that will emerge over the long term.

2. *Senior management will spend most of its time fighting fires and may not come upon critical issues until late in the game.* It is unusual for senior management to get a look at proposals when the options are still wide open. Published scientific papers (the equivalent of polished proposals) typically suggest an "immaculate, rational, step-by-step approach to discovery," notes science historian Robert Merton;[3] the dead ends and assumptions left untested because of time constraints never show up in the finished product.

3. *Senior managers will be shielded from most bad news.* Obviously, the monthly or quarterly revenues and net income figures that top managers see are reasonably straightforward and timely; even by playing with receivables or speeding up deliveries, a division manager cannot hide bad news at this level for long. But *really* bad news—for example, on a share decline in a critical segment of a product line—can be concealed for months, sometimes for years.

4. *Most really important decisions emerge only after top managers have vacillated for months or years, apparently or actually; and the solution they choose at the end may well be indistinguishable from that proposed at the*

[3]Robert K. Merton, *Social Theory and Social Structure* (New York: The Free Press, 1968), p. 4.

 Experiential Organizational Behavior

beginning of the search. In practice, top managers typically respond to major issues with trial balloons. They seldom give public commitment to a choice before they are quite sure that: (a) its wisdom is no longer open to serious question, and (b) the organization is agreeable.

Each of these observations seemingly casts a gloomy cloud over the potential for a rational organization theory. Yet I would argue that each can have a silver lining. The purpose of this article is to point out these silver linings and to suggest how senior executives can take advantage of them.

First, however, an important preliminary point. The four observations appear to be as characteristic of companies that perform well as of those that perform poorly. They are not, in other words, symptoms of some sort of organizational malaise that should be (or could be) "put right."

At first glance, the four observations offer no obvious encouragement to the senior executive who aspires to shape events and to leave a mark of excellence behind. Considered more thoughtfully, however, they do suggest a hopeful hypothesis: *perhaps* the seemingly disorderly bits of the choice process make available to the senior executive a set of opportunities to impart a thrust to, or to fine tune, his organization's sense of direction. I believe that this is indeed the case. Let us examine each observation in turn and try to discover its potential silver lining.

Not Enough Choices

Sad Fact No. 1:

Senior managers get only one option.

Silver Lining:

(a) The option is in accord with senior managers' preferences; (b) there are enough one-option choices in a given period to permit managers to shape them, over time, as a portfolio.

There is nothing wrong with one option, if it is an option the senior manager wants to see. This is an obvious statement, perhaps, but it has not-so-obvious implications. First, it assumes that the senior manager's main business is unearthing concerns, reminding people about past errors, setting directions, and building management capabilities. Chief executives have little enough time to spend "on the issues"—too little to spend it making complex trade-offs between action alternatives. Their real question, then, is less likely to be "Where are the other options?" than "Does this option contain the thrust we want to see?"

Suppose top managers are worried that their company is making a relatively high-cost product in a major line; it is making Oldsmobiles for a Chevrolet (or Honda) market. The new product slate comes up. Broadly, they want to know: Is it a low-cost slate? More important, is it clearly *different* from the slates of past years—different in the way they want to see? Top managers' yes or no decision on the proposal is in no sense a check on its optimality. It is, however, a check on its direction and a signal back to, say, division management that "We think you have (or have not) gotten the message."

Next consider this one-option agenda over six months or so. There may be a half-dozen decisions of note, which add up to a reasonably sizable portfolio of choices. Viewed in this light, the quarterly or annual slate of choices becomes an array of opportunities to communicate, reinforce, or adjust in a direction top management wishes to pursue.

Not Enough Time

Sad Fact No. 2:

Time is fragmented; issues arrive late, fully staffed.

Silver Lining:

(a) Each fragment can be used to convey preferences, so that the calendar or agenda as a whole provides an opportunity to set direction; (b) lateness is relative; each slight modification of the current option becomes a strong signal about what the next one should look like.

The point here is that fragmentation can, if properly managed, be a positive advantage. As Richard Neustadt wrote of Franklin Roosevelt:

"He had a strong feel for the cardinal fact of government: that presidents don't act on policies, programs or personnel in the abstract; they act in the concrete as they meet deadlines set by due dates, act on documents awaiting signatures, vacant posts awaiting appointees, officials seeking interviews, newsmen seeking answers, audiences waiting for a speech, etc."[4]

The fragments that compose the executive's working day can be used as a succession of opportunities to tackle bits of the issue stream. It is precisely the fragmented nature of their activity that permits top managers to fine tune, test, and retest the general strategic direction they are trying to impart to their companies over the longer term.

Moreover, fragmentation of time, properly exploited, can yield a rich variety of information. Within reason, the more views and visits in the top executive's schedule and the more numerous the interruptions and unscheduled encounters, the better informed he is likely to be. As Mintzberg observes, "The chief executive tolerates interruption because he does not wish to discourage the flow of current information."[5]

The potential danger is equally clear: the fragmentation of his time multiplies opportunities for the executive to send inconsistent signals to the organization. To send effective signals to, say, the 25 to 75 key executives in an

---

[4] Richard E. Neustadt, "Approaches to Staffing the Presidency," *American Political Science Review*, December 1963, p. 855.

[5] Henry Mintzberg, *The Nature of Managerial Work* (New York: Harper & Row, 1973), p. 35.

organization, the top management team must obviously be clear on the general message it wants to get across.

The second aspect of this fact of life is late exposure to issues. Senior managers must accept their fate as reviewers of completed staff work. Rarely does a rough draft, rife with contention over key assumptions or problem attributes, reach the executive suite.

Again, fragmentation, used effectively, can provide a partial answer. By their very position, top managers seldom deal with problems in isolation. They deal with a flow. Each brief exposure to an issue becomes an opportunity to express general concerns and to gradually sharpen the responses of the organization to reflect the same concerns. One CEO, in the midst of a strategic crisis, devoted a lot of time to a seemingly insignificant customer complaint because, as he explained afterward, it gave him a chance to demonstrate an approach to broad competitive issues that he was trying to instill throughout the organization.

Too Many Filters

Sad Fact No. 3:
Bad news is normally hidden.

Silver Lining:
Review and comment on details of good news offer a chance to shape attitudes and preferences, so that those down the line will share senior management's assumptions and priorities.

Inevitably, most news sent up the line to senior managers will be "good"; and, in any case, the chief executive is too far removed from daily operations to unerringly ask the crucial question that might open up a Pandora's box. True, he can take advantage of the fragmentation of his time to tap multiple sources of information and catch, by designed chance, a few reviews and analyses while debate is still focused on objectives and assumptions rather than on how to package a chosen option so the "old man" (or the finance staff) will buy it.

More important, however, is the opportunity that the good news presents. Much can be accomplished through a style of good-news review that zeros in on almost any sort of significant subpoint for special attention and comment. In dealing with the problem of how overextended and partially ignorant congressmen can quickly inform themselves on complex issues, political scientist Aaron Wildavsky makes a relevant point:

"Another way of handling complexity is to use actions on simpler items as indices of more complicated ones. Instead of dealing with the cost of a huge atomic installation, Congressmen may seek to discover how personnel and administrative costs or real estate transactions with which they have some familiarity are handled. The reader has probably heard of this practice under some such title as 'straining at gnats.' This practice may at times have greater validity than appears on the surface if it is used as a testing device, and if there is a reasonable connection between the competence shown in handling simple and complex items."[6]

Top managers regularly use forays into detail as a shield against surprise, and, over time, they can learn a lot this way. More important, though, such attention conveys a sense of "how we deal with problems," and indicates the sort of understanding of issues that is expected of managers down the line. If, additionally, top managers' probings clearly reflect concern with a particular issue, the danger that their subordinates will lose sight of that issue will be slight.

Such irregular involvement with detail contrasts markedly with the exclusive use of staff for probing. Obviously, staff probes can be productive in some situations, but in others they may simply drive the bad news further into hiding. While using his staff as merciless probers, ITT's legendary chief executive Harold Geneen was a firm believer in face-to-face reviews because, as he put it, "You can tell by the tone of voice if a fellow is having a problem he hasn't reported yet."

A simple but often overlooked aspect of good-news review is the use of praise. An executive can use detailed good-news review deliberately to reinforce desired patterns of action or response. One CEO, when attending field reviews, always stopped in at a regional sales office or plant. He would dig into the records ahead of time, pick out an exemplary action by some salesman or foreman, and make a point of asking him how he had done this or that so well.

He might then take up the idea in a memo that would be sent all around the company. Again, if in the course of a presentation a junior staff man came up with a particularly clever analysis that fitted in well with the CEO's current main concern—for example, looking at the competitor's position in a new way—he would interrupt the presentation and raise the possibility of introducing the idea into a large class of proposals or reviews.

Too Much Inertia

Sad Fact No. 4:

Major choices take months or years to emerge.

Silver Lining

The process of choosing provides an opportunity to build a strong consensus for consistent implementing actions that will require only minimal correction over time. If enough choices are in the hopper, the lengthy sorting process will be punctuated by fairly frequent decisions that will support (or serve to test) top managers' chosen directions.

An instructive case in point concerns a large industrial products company,

[6] Aaron Wildavasky, *The Politics of the Budgetary Process* (Boston: Little, Brown, 1964), p. 12.

long dominated by engineers, that found itself threatened in frightening new ways. Overseas competitors' products were nicking sizable chunks from previously uncontested market segments. Cash-rich domestic competitors were investing in small companies making promising substitute products for some key lines. The threat was both diffuse and pervasive.

Gradually, over a three- to five-year period, the top team became convinced that its main task was to instill a marketing orientation. Early steps, all in the nature of trial balloons, included: (1) going outside to hire three senior marketers from companies with outstanding marketing reputations; (2) creating a top-level task force to assess the five-year competitive outlook; and (3) giving one of the new marketers a special new product group with a sizable budget to develop a product slate for one of the threatened market niches.

About 18 months later some more definite signals came of what was afoot: a major speech to security analysts outlining the company's new approach to marketing; irregular visits to important customers by the president and top team; the establishment of a monthly president's review, marked by several special sessions on competitive assessment and the beginning of share reporting in certain businesses; the creation of a large number of new assistant regional sales manager jobs and the hiring of highly paid MBAs to fill them. Finally, at about the three-year mark, the top team took some very conspicuous actions. It promoted two of the three marketers who had been recruited on the outside, together with two insiders, to the position of senior vice president, with realigned market responsibilities.

At the annual shareholders meeting the top team launched a new theme: "Our emerging role is to be preeminent in marketing." It brought out a slate of surprisingly good new products, striking back hard at competitors in one or two besieged market segments. Internally, it publicly introduced a new management information and cost system that had been implemented after three years of gradual, incremental development.

Thus, over a 36-month period, without much fanfare, the top team successfully shifted the institution's attention to the marketplace. Observers today, while noting that engineers still win a fair share of their battles, agree that the company has undergone a radical transformation.

Developing top management consensus in favor of such a major shift can be a delicate and time-consuming business. Bringing along one crucial member of a triumvirate (or at least effectively neutralizing his opposition) can take years. During such a process, even a decision about when to send up the next trial balloon may be politically loaded. As Peter Drucker wisely noted, "Priorities are easy; posteriorities—what jobs *not* to tackle—are tough." His point is consistent with a wide body of psychological research on building commitment and overcoming resistance to change: keeping a dissident actor from quick-triggering with a negative response is no easy chore.

The period of muddling about on the way to major change is not purely a matter of political maneuvering. At least as important is the "marinating time" it provides. In one company I know, the top 12 executives met weekly for several hours, over an 18-month period, in order to draft a modified change of charter for the company. They have used the resulting document, which they call their "Magna Carta," as the jumping-off point for a decade of substantial positive change. It is only two pages long. But it took this management group nearly two years to work through the critical issues involved and to come to terms with the new departures involved, although they had had a fairly good idea from the beginning what the shape of the outcome would be.

Revamping Management's Role

Each of the four seemingly discouraging facts of executive life can, as we have seen, be recast in positive terms. The results add up to a fresh conception of the top management task, one that fits both the disorderly facts of life and their recurrent silver linings. It rejects the traditional notion of the executive as dedicating large, discrete blocks of time to linear chunks called "planning," "deciding," or "implementing" and replaces it with something closer to a notion of the effective executive as a communicator, a persuader, and, above all, a consummate opportunist. He is adept at grasping and taking advantage of each item in the random succession of time and issue fragments that crowd his day.

This reconception of the top management task requires hard thinking about what is and what is not achievable from the top. The CEO does not drive forklifts or install phones; management theory has long acknowledged that limitation. Research is beginning to suggest a further off-limits area—top managers cannot *solve* problems: their attention is fragmented; issues come to them late; and they are shielded from bad news. What they can do is: (1) generally shape business values, and (2) educate by example.

Shaping Business Values

In his landmark study of top management activity, Philip Selznick concludes that the effective institutional leader "is primarily an expert in the promotion and protection of values."[7] Another recent study of leadership, by James McGregor Burns, contrasts lesser forms of management behavior with "transforming leadership," which, in the midst of the disorderly press of events, unleashes organizational energies through the promotion of new, overarching values.[8]

The same theme is echoed by Roy Ash, who created new institutional forms at Litton Industries and the U.S. Office of Management and Budget

---

[7] Philip Selznick, *Leadership in Administration* (Evanston, Ill.: Row, Peterson, 1957), p. 28.
[8] James McGregor Burns, *Leadership* (New York: Harper & Row, 1978).

and is now in the process of reviving Addressograph-Multigraph. As he sees it, the really important change in a company lies in a process of "psychological transformation." One of Ash's recent notes to himself, as quoted in *Fortune*, clarifies his meaning. It reads, "Develop a much greater attachment of everybody to the bottom line—more agony and ecstasy."[9]

As descriptions of the top management task, these terms—institutional leadership, value promotion, transforming leadership—are surprisingly congenial to the disorderly, nonrational realities of most real-life management activity. In an untidy world, where goal setting, option selection, and policy implementation hopelessly fuzz together, the shaping of robust institutional values through a principle of ad hoc opportunism becomes preeminently the mission of the chief executive and his most senior colleagues.

The nature of this value-shaping process is not obvious. Among a group of chief executives (actually mayors) they studied, John Kotter and Paul Lawrence found that the more successful typically spent over a year carefully taking the pulse of key stakeholders, seeding ideas, and nursing along a consensus in favor of a few new directions. The less effective executives were those who plunged into major commitments before they had built adequate support.[10]

My own observations are wholly consistent with those of Kotter and Lawrence. The process of easing a larger organization into a major shift of values seems to require anywhere from three to eight years. A good example is the experience of Walter Spencer of Sherwin-Williams, who spent his first five years as CEO working to introduce a marketing orientation into a previously manufacturing-dominated institution. "When you take a 100-year-old company and change the culture of the organization, and try to do that in Cleveland's traditional business setting—well, it takes time; you just have to keep hammering away at everybody," Spencer told an interviewer from *Forbes*. "The changeover to marketing is probably irreversible now. It's not complete, but we've brought along a lot of young managers with that philosophy, and once you've taken a company this far, you can't go back."[11]

The literature of top management generally ignores the intricacies of effective value management, especially the aspect of timing. Yet almost any chief executive of a large enterprise knows how much time he must spend on patiently building support for his initiatives. Only when crisis is imminent can the process be condensed, and even then some form of consensus-building is needed.

The art of value management, then, blends strategic foresight with a shrewd sense of timing and the political acumen necessary to build stable,

[9] Louis Kraar, "Roy Ash is Having Fun at Addressogrief-Multigrief," *Fortune*, February 27, 1978, p. 47.

[10] John P. Kotter and Paul R. Lawrence, *Mayors in Action* (New York: John Wiley and Sons, 1974).

[11] Harold Seneker, "Why Some CEOs Pop Pills (And Sometimes Quit)," *Forbes*, July 12, 1978, p. 70.

workable coalitions. Fortunately, the practical exercise of these skills—as opposed to the textbook fantasies of rational problem solving—is actually enhanced by the untidiness of typical executive choice processes.

CEO as Exemplar

Top management's actions, over time, constitute the guiding, directing, and signaling process that shapes values in the near chaos of day-to-day operations. As Eli Ginzberg and Ewing Reilley have noted: "Those a few echelons from the top are always alert to the chief executive. Although they attach much importance to what he says, they will be truly impressed only by what he does." [12] Top management is at the apex of the symbolic signaling system, not the hard product delivery system. Because senior managers cannot act directly or promptly to resolve issues, their daily efforts must focus on the sending of effective and appropriate signals. Recounts one chief executive:

"The board's question at my first meeting was trivial: Could I get them speedier information about the installation of new machines? I used it as a simple teaching opportunity. I responded with the data requested but recast it in market share terms. My intent was to wean them away from thinking that the gross number was still an adequate measure of health. That little incident was my first easy opportunity to expose them to share issues."

The executive who sees his role in these terms is aware that symbol management is a source of both unparalleled opportunity and, for the unwary, of unparalleled risk. Knowing that subordinates will eventually make detailed interpretations of his every activity ("With the investment bankers, was he? Maybe it's my division he wants to unload"), he will be scrupulously careful to avoid distracting signals. "People keep searching for clues," notes linguist Julius Roth. "The poorer and fewer the clues, the more desperate the search." [13]

Several business scholars and political scientists have suggested the image of the "leader as educator." Such a leader, in Selznick's words, must be able to "interpret the role of the enterprise, to perceive and develop models of thought and behavior, and to find general, rather than merely partial, perspectives." [14]

Beyond that, he needs to be able to articulate his vision in a compelling way. Warren Bennis underscores the point: "If I were to give off-the-cuff advice to anyone trying to institute change, I would say, 'How clear is the metaphor? How is that understood? How much energy are you devoting to it?' It's the imagery that creates the understanding, the compelling moral necessity that the new way is right. It was the beautiful writing of Darwin

---

[12] Eli Ginzberg and Ewing W. Reilley, *Effecting Change in Large Organizations* (New York: Columbia University Press, 1957), p. 42.

[13] Julius A. Roth, *Timetables* (Indianapolis, Ind.: Bobbs-Merrill, 1963), p. 7.

[14] Philip Selznick, p. 150.

about his travels on the *Beagle*, rather than the content of his writing, that made the difference. The evolutionary idea had really been in the air for quite a while."[15]

If it is in shaping values that the senior executive can most efficiently use his time, it is symbols that are his primary value-shaping tools. As an educator, he has quite an arsenal of pedagogical tricks of the trade at his disposal: manipulation of settings, varied repetition of signals, a range of sensitive responses to subtle feedback cues. Consider:

Careful use of language, including insistently asked questions and attention to the minutiae of written proposals.

Manipulation of settings, including the creation of forums and rules of debate designed to focus on critical concerns.

Shifts of agenda and time allocation to signal, subtly but pervasively, a change in priorities.

Consistent and frequent feedback and reinforcement, including the careful and selective interpretation of past results to stress a chosen theme.

Selective seeding of ideas among various internal power groups, and cultivation of those that win support.

Collectively, these enable the CEO to intervene purposefully and effectively in what one philosopher called "the brute flow of random detail that adds up to everyday experience."

Concluding Note

Senior managers are used to hearing and reading advice about how they can combat sloppiness and introduce rationality or neatness into decision making. I have argued that "sloppiness" is normal, probably inevitable, and usually sensible. Organizations in the process of making important choices almost always look disorderly. But that apparent disorder can provide the latitude and the time required for the development of consensus; and without consensus, efforts at implementation will be doomed from the start.

The task of the senior executive, then, is not to impose an abstract order on an inherently disorderly process, but to become adept at the sorts of intervention by which he can nudge it in the desired direction and to some degree control its course.

The optimist proclaims that we live in the best of all possible worlds; and the pessimist fears this is true.

From James' Branch Cabell, The Silver Stallion, chapter 26.

[15]Warren Bennis, *The Unconscious Conspiracy: Why Leaders Can't Lead* (New York: AMACOM, 1976), p. 93.

Issues

1. How does the concept of leadership as discussed in this article differ from the operant approach discussed earlier?
2. How does this article compare with Mintzberg's ("The manager's job")?
3. Develop a short description of your idea of what a manager really does. Contrast this with other material that specifies what a manager ought to do. Why is there a need for both descriptive (accounts of actual behavior) and normative (recommendations concerning how one ought to behave) theory?

Modification and Integration Processes

31

Annual Salary Evaluation

You have to make salary increase recommendations for eight managers that you supervise. They have just completed their first year with the company and are now to be considered for their first annual raise. Keep in mind that you may be setting precedents and that you need to keep salary costs down. Each worker is currently earning $15,000 per year and you must determine a percent salary increase. Assume a 9% inflation rate in the past and coming year.

Amarito Alvarez

Amarito is not, as far as you can tell, a good performer. You have checked with his peers and they do not feel that he is effective either. He appears to try very hard but you feel that he does not have the skills to do the job.

Ben Berger

Ben is single and seems to live the life of a carefree bachelor. In general, you feel that his job performance is not up to par, and some of his "goofs" are well known to his fellow managers. And you attribute this to his tendency to goof off occasionally. The bothersome part is that Ben seems to have the ability.

Clyde Smith

You consider Clyde to be one of your best subordinates. However, it is apparent that his fellow managers do not consider him to be effective. Clyde has married a rich wife, and as far as you know he does not need additional money. Regardless, he is conscientious and seems to have a knack for the job.

David Thompson

You know that "Doodles" badly needs more money because of certain personal problems he is having. As far as you are concerned, he also happens to

---

Adapted with permission from Edward E. Lawler III, "Pay Raise Dilemma."

be one of the best of your subordinates. For some reason your enthusiasm for him is not shared by the other subordinates and you have heard them make joking remarks about his performance. Doodles has limited managerial talents and appears to be lazy at times, but his performance is generally very good.

Ellen Stevens

Ellen has been very successful so far in the tasks she has undertaken. You are particularly impressed by this, since she has little managerial training. She needs money more than many of the other people, and you are sure that they also respect her because of her good performance. But she is often late or absent; you think this is due to some problems off the job.

Fred Foster

Fred has done an execellent job and it is generally accepted among the others that he is one of the best people. This surprises you because he is generally frivolous and does not seem to care very much about money and promotion. He is not very bright but he pushes himself at his job.

Greta Young

Your opinion is that Greta just is not cutting the mustard. But when you check with others to see how they feel about her, you discover that her work is very highly regarded. You also know that she badly needs a raise. She was recently widowed and is finding it extremely difficult to support her young family of four. But, despite scoring well on a management aptitude test and trying her best, her performance is just not up to par.

Harvey Hammond

Harvey seems to squander his money continually. For his job your view is that he does not do it particularly well. You are quite surprised to find that several of the other new managers think that he is the best of the new group. A check of the records shows that he was rated "high" on managerial potential. His effort to date has not been very high.

Directions

1. First, as an *individual*, indicate the size of the raise that you would give each manager by writing a *percentage* next to his name. Write your reasons in the space provided.
2. Next (after each individual has completed the individual decision), as a *group*, discuss the decisions and arrive at a group consensus regarding how much of a raise to give. (Turn the page.)

<table>
<tr><th>Individual Decisions</th><th></th><th>Group Decisions</th></tr>
<tr><td>__________ %</td><td>Amarito Alvarez
Reasons</td><td>__________ %</td></tr>
<tr><td>__________ %</td><td>Ben Berger
Reasons</td><td>__________ %</td></tr>
<tr><td>__________ %</td><td>Clyde Smith
Reasons</td><td>__________ %</td></tr>
<tr><td>__________ %</td><td>David Thompson
Reasons</td><td>__________ %</td></tr>
<tr><td>__________ %</td><td>Ellen Stevens
Reasons</td><td>__________ %</td></tr>
<tr><td>__________ %</td><td>Fred Foster
Reasons</td><td>__________ %</td></tr>
<tr><td>__________ %</td><td>Greta Young
Reasons</td><td>__________ %</td></tr>
<tr><td>__________ %</td><td>Harvey Hammond
Reasons</td><td>__________ %</td></tr>
</table>

1. Is money a motivator? Does money motivate different people in different ways?
2. What do people use as a comparison in considering the fairness of their pay/raise?
3. Other than salary increases, what are alternative financially based incentive systems? Describe the strengths and weaknesses of each proposed system.
4. Should salary information be kept secret? What are the alternatives? What are the advantages and disadvantages of each?
5. How did your individual decision(s) differ from your group's decision(s)? Why do you think they differed?
6. Consider the process used by your group to decide upon the raises. Propose alternatives of improvements to the process used by your group. In retrospect, what process would you recommend?

**Fremont E. Kast and
James E. Rosenzweig**

Influence Systems in Organizations: Leadership Styles

An adage says, "Leaders are born, not made." This fatalistic view suggests certain inherent abilities and/or personality traits. Also, greatness has been considered a function of being in the right place at the right time. Apparently these views have not been widely accepted, because leadership has been one of the most extensively researched subjects in behavioral science during the twentieth century. It may well be the most written about and discussed aspect of organization and management.

We have emphasized the managerial role of planning, coordinating, and controlling organizational activities in the interest of objective accomplishment. The role includes attention to organization-environment relationships, task-technology considerations, structural arrangements, goals and values, and the psychosocial system. Managers are charged with maintaining and, if possible, improving overall organizational effectiveness, efficiency, and participant satisfaction. Management involves the coordination of both human and material resources toward objective accomplishment; it is more than leadership.

Leadership is an essential part of management with particular emphasis on the human aspects, the psychosocial system. The concept of leadership implies followership; hence, it involves relationships among people. More specifically, leadership suggests differential influence among people in social, particularly organizational, relationships. Leadership is "interpersonal influence, exercised in situations and directed, through the communication process, toward the attainment of a specified goal or goals. Leadership always involves attempts on the part of a leader (influencer) to affect (influence) the behavior of a follower (influencee) or followers in situations."[1] Differential influence is a process that is apparent in informal social relationships and in formal organizations. Typically, designated leaders, such as supervisors,

From Fremont E. Kast and James E. Rosenzweig, *Experiential Exercises and Cases In Management.* © 1976, McGraw-Hill. Reprinted by permission.

[1] Robert Tannenbaum and Fred Massarik, "Leadership: A Frame of Reference," *Management Science*, October 1957, p. 3.

chairpersons, or directors, do have a positive balance of official power in the influence system. However, this power may not always result in effective leadership. The positional authority of a so-called leader may not be enough to persuade subordinates to engage in appropriate activities; influence attempts fail, and leadership is ineffective. Informal patterns of influence often develop because of personal expertise, knowledge, or persuasiveness. Thus, the phenomenon of leadership-followership is always present in groups, but the specific patterns depend greatly on the particular situation.

Much of the effort in leadership research has been devoted to understanding the traits and behaviors of good leaders—with "good" being related to the performance of the group. One goal of such endeavors is to be able to predict who would be good leaders so that they can be selected for positions of responsibility. So far, the results are not clear enough to provide easy answers. A number of forces are involved in every situation, including environmental constraints, organizational climate, group dynamics, follower characteristics, and leadership behavior. "In view of the complexity of the factors that determine the relationships between leader behavior and goup performance, it is apparent that no simple recipe for leader effectiveness will be applicable in more than a small proportion of situations encountered."[2] This conclusion suggests that there is no "one set of ideal leader traits" nor "one best way" to lead.

On the other hand, the situation is far from hopeless. We do have a body of knowledge evolving from behavioral science research on the leadership process. It suggests a contingency view with guidelines for leader behavior depending on the interaction of a number of situational variables. We will consider some of these factors in more detail as we proceed through this exercise. Before continuing, however, it will be important for you to identify your own leadership approach more explicitly. Then you will have an opportunity to compare your style with others in the class and with prescriptions for effective leader behavior.

Procedure

Step 1

Fill out the following Leadership Questionnaire.

Leadership Questionnaire

The following items describe aspects of leadership behavior. Respond to each item in terms of actual past experience; your past experience is the best estimate of the way you would be most likely to act if you were the leader of

---

[2] Ralph M. Stogdill, "Historical Trends in Leadership Theory and Research," *Journal of Contemporary Business*, Autumn 1974, p. 10.

---

a work group. Circle the letter symbolizing the way in which you would be likely to behave:

<table>
<tr><td>(A) Almost Always</td><td>(F) Frequently</td><td>(S) Sometimes</td><td>(I) Infrequently</td><td>(R) Rarely</td></tr>
</table>

If I were the leader of a work group . . .

A	F	S	I	R	1. I would trust the members to exercise good judgment in the interest of the organization.
A	F	S	I	R	2. I would encourage close interpersonal relationships between myself and my subordinates and among group members.
A	F	S	I	R	3. I would stress being ahead of competing groups.
A	F	S	I	R	4. I would provide definite guidelines for work procedure, and expect members to follow them.
A	F	S	I	R	5. I would give members feedback on their performance, both positive and negative.
A	F	S	I	R	6. I would stress the use of group meetings to plan and critique our work.
A	F	S	I	R	7. I would push the group members to work harder.
A	F	S	I	R	8. I would press for acceptance of my expertise and ideas regarding the technical aspects of task performance.
A	F	S	I	R	9. I would seek members' ideas and opinions, including criticism.
A	F	S	I	R	10. I would encourage members to interact in goal setting and planning without my direct involvement.
A	F	S	I	R	11. I would establish definite standards of performance and stress meeting them.
A	F	S	I	R	12. I would assign members to particular tasks based on my perception of their special knowledge and/or skills.
A	F	S	I	R	13. I would be concerned about the personal problems of group members.
A	F	S	I	R	14. I would consider improving "the way we work together" to be as important as improving task accomplishment.
A	F	S	I	R	15. I would urge the group to beat its previous record.
A	F	S	I	R	16. I would assume prime responsibility for coordinating the work of group members.
A	F	S	I	R	17. I would value differences of opinion and try to achieve consensus in problem solving.
A	F	S	I	R	18. I would consider it my responsibility to facilitate resolution of interpersonal conflicts.
A	F	S	I	R	19. I would modify subordinates' objectives in light of organization goals.
A	F	S	I	R	20. I would develop overall plans and schedules and use them to control the group's activities.

Step 2

Score the questionnaire as follows and write the score in the blank space provided in front of each question:

_5_	(A)	Almost Always
_4_	(F)	Frequently
_3_	(S)	Sometimes
_2_	(I)	Infrequently
_1_	(R)	Rarely

Add up the scores for the following groups of questions and write the total in the space provided.

1, 5, 9, 13, 17	__________________	Support
2, 6, 10, 14, 18	__________________	Interaction Facilitation
3, 7, 11, 15, 19	__________________	Goal Emphasis
4, 8, 12, 16, 20	__________________	Work Facilitation

Step 3

Place an X on each of the corresponding lines below (and connect the X's) in order to get a profile of your degree of emphasis on four key dimensions of leadership behavior.[3]

Support: Behavior that enhances someone else's feeling of personal worth and importance.

5	15	25

Interaction Facilitation: Behavior that encourages members of the group to develop close, mutually satisfying relationships.

5	15	25

Goal Emphasis: Behavior that stimulates an enthusiasm for meeting the group's goal or achieving excellent performance.

5	15	25

[3] David G. Bowers and Stanley E. Seashore, "Predicting Organizational Effectiveness with a Four-Factor Theory of Leadership," *Administrative Science Quarterly,* September 1966, p. 247.

<u>Work Facilitation</u>: Behavior
that helps achieve goal attainment by such activities as
scheduling, coordinating, planning,
and by providing resources such
as tools, materials, and technical
knowledge.

| 5 | 15 | 25 |

Based on your general self-insight, does the profile reflect your behavior on these dimensions reasonably accurately? Specifically, is there an element of "how I wish I would behave" and/or "how leaders
are supposed to behave" mixed in with "how I actually behave"?

Step 4

Meet in groups of 4 to 6 to compare profiles and responses to individual
questions.

a. Compare similarities and differences. Where differences occur, explore
the correlation between responses and past experience.

b. Invite feedback from peers in regard to their perception, based on experience in class to date, of your leadership behavior.

Summary and Conceptualization

You have had an opportunity to obtain feedback concerning your leadership
style via a questionnaire and from peers based on experience in class to date.
Additional feedback could be obtained by checking with others outside of
class concerning their perception of your behavior in task-oriented situations. This could be based on experience in a variety of organizations—work,
recreation, living group, or clubs. For example, if you have assumed a leadership role in any of the above activities, you might ask people whose opinion you respect for their perception of your behavior. This could be done in
terms of overall impressions or related to the individual items on the Leadership Questionnaire.

In reviewing the research and writing on leadership, Bowers and Seashore
concluded that in spite of the variety of terms used, there is a great deal of
common conceptual content. They distilled the four dimensions of effectiveness in this exercise:

1. *Support.* Behavior that enhances someone else's feeling of personal
worth and importance.
2. *Interaction Facilitation.* Behavior that encourages members of a group to
develop close, mutually satisfying relationships.
3. *Goal Emphasis.* Behavior that stimulates an enthusiasm for meeting the
group's goal or achieving excellent performance.

4. *Work Facilitation.* Behavior that helps achieve goal attainment by such
   activities as scheduling, coordinating, planning, and by providing resources such as tools, materials, and technical knowledge.[4]

Support and interaction facilitation are obviously "people" concerns.
Emphasizing these dimensions recognizes the need to encourage continued
support of individuals in organizational endeavor and the need to maintain
and improve interpersonal relationships and group processes such as teamwork. Goal emphasis and work facilitation relate to task concerns and to the
path-goal theory of leadership.[5] Good leaders are typically seen as helpful in
both setting goals and in structuring or designing means of achieving them.
This approach builds on the concept of achievement motivation, and if goals
are achieved there is an increase in satisfaction. Performance leads to satisfaction and increased motivation in the future.

In using the above model for prescribing leader behavior we suggest that
all four factors are important and should be emphasized *as much as possible
depending on the constraints of the situation.* But it is unrealistic to expect
simultaneous attention to all the dimensions of leadership effectiveness.
Some tradeoffs are necessary and bound to occur. Goal emphasis may be
paramount in initiating a program of management by objectives. Interaction
facilitation may actually need to be decreased in an organization that seems
to spend nearly all its time in meetings (leaving little time to work on the
task). An appropriate balance should be maintained according to the particular situation.

A key to effective leadership is clarification of expectations between leaders and followers in order to reach a mutual understanding which sets the
tone for the entire relationship. This situational approach to leadership effectiveness certainly involves contingency views. If the leader is a good diagnostician, he/she can ascertain the most appropriate leadership style to employ according to the circumstances. An autocratic style might be most
appropriate if organizational participants expect it; for example, in times of
crisis. In a military combat situation, subordinates typically rely on the decision making of their group leader. The crew of a ship hit by a torpedo would
not be inclined to discuss the alternatives and then vote. If the captain an-
nounces, "Abandon ship," the order would be carried out immediately.

On the other hand, in situations where time permits, a democratic approach which includes subordinates in the decision-making process may be
extremely useful. In still other situations, a bureaucratic approach may be
most effective and efficient. For relatively routine decisions, standard operating procedures might be entirely appropriate. But referring to the rules
when in fact there is an extraordinary set of circumstances might be dysfunctional for the organization. The manager should be as flexible as possible,

[4]Ibid.

[5]Robert J. House and Terence R. Mitchell, "Path-Goal Theory of Leadership," *Journal of
Contemporary Business,* Autumn 1974, pp. 81–97.

gearing his/her style to the specific situation and the individuals involved.

Leaders can influence the behavior of others in a number of ways—suggesting, persuading, or forcing compliance. According to the Chinese philosopher Lao Tse, "When the best leaders' work is done, the people say, 'We did it ourselves.'" This suggests that the more subordinates are involved in the process, the more likely they will be committed to decisions and will implement them. However, there are tradeoffs in terms of time and cost. Autocratic, coercive approaches have appeal in terms of tidiness and speed of response.

Figure 1 illustrates a contingency approach to leadership; appropriate behavior is suggested for polar situations on several key variables—external and internal environment plus subordinates' personality predispositions. Prescriptions for "how to succeed as a leader" are rather straightforward in the extreme cases. Directive, boss-centered, task-oriented behavior is appropriate when the external environment is certain, the internal environment is tightly controlled, and people don't expect to participate (low need for independence and/or little knowledge about the work, e.g.). Participative, subordinate-centered, task-oriented behavior is appropriate when the external environment is uncertain, the internal environment is loosely structured and autonomous, and people expect to participate (high need for independence and/or much knowledge about the work, e.g.). Effective leaders and organizations, by and large, tend to have good matches of styles and situations.

But the issue is not absolutely clear; the middle area or mixed situation can be confounding for the leader. How should we behave when the environment is semiprogrammable, procedures are moderately tight, and subordinates have some knowledge and/or sometimes expect to participate in decision making? Moreover, the three dimensions don't necessarily vary in unison. What if people expect to participate (having just completed an in-company training program) and yet the internal environment is tightly controlled? In essence, leaders need a contingency view that requires situational diagnosis as a foundation, followed by astute matching of behavior and situation. Note that adjustments may take place in leaders and/or followers and/or situations.

As indicated above, the issue of degree of participation in decision making has been discussed at length in the organization and management literature. In most cases a participative style is advocated. Such an approach may or may not be possible; moreover, it may not even be appropriate. Based on research with a number of practicing managers responding to case situations, Vroom and Yetton concluded that most managers would be more effective if they were *both* more autocratic and more participative.[6] They developed a normative model or prescription for leadership and decision making based

---

[6]Victor H. Vroom and Philip W. Yetton, *Leadership and Decision-Making*, Pittsburgh, Penna., University of Pittsburgh Press, 1973.

　　　　　　　　　　　　　　Experiential Organizational Behavior

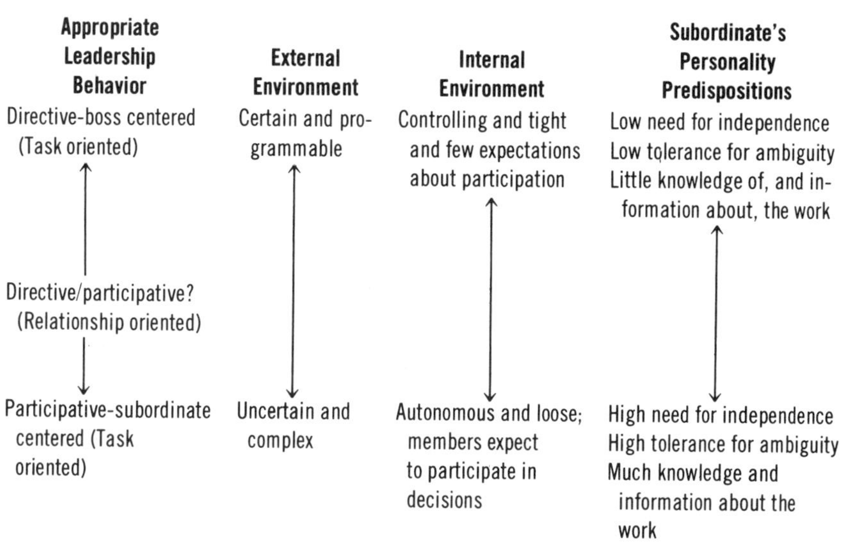

FIGURE 1.   **A contingency approach to leadership.** Source: Jay Lorsch and John J. Morse, <u>Organizations and Their Members: A Contingency Approach</u>, Harper & Row, Publishers, New York, 1974, p. 131.

on situational diagnosis. They found that managers tended to shy away from an autocratic approach even when it was most appropriate according to the model. And, they tended to be less participative than called for by the model in other situations. This suggests that to be more effective, managers need increased flexibility. A leader must be a good diagnostician and match the situation with an appropriate style—sometimes relatively autocratic and sometimes quite participative.

On balance, it is important for leaders to recognize the complexity of human motivation, group dynamics, and organizational climate. The best leaders seem to have a tolerance for ambiguity and the conceptual ability to cope with multidimensional situations. They emphasize both people and production rather than one or the other; they emphasize support and inter-action facilitation as well as goal emphasis and work facilitation; and they are both autocratic and democratic-participative depending on the situation.

**Fremont E. Kast and
James E. Rosenzweig**

Organizational Change:
Municipal Light

Overview

> They would often change who would become constant in happiness or wisdom.
>
> Confucius

In modern society, it seems that the only thing constant is change. Change has become a way of life and the most obvious changes are technological. This is dramatized by equating human history to a 1-hour period.

If man's time on earth is taken as 240 thousand years, he spent 55 minutes of that time in paleolithic (old stone) culture. Five minutes ago, he embarked on neolithic culture—the cultivation of plants, the domestication of animals, the making of pottery, weaving, and the use of the bow and arrow; 3½ minutes ago he began the working of copper; 2½ minutes ago he began to mold bronze; 2 minutes ago he learned to smelt iron; ¼ of a minute ago he learned printing; 5 seconds ago the industrial revolution began; 3⅓ seconds ago he learned to apply electricity; and the time he has had the automobile is less than the interval between the ticks of a watch, i.e., less than one second.[1]

And the automobile has been with us for over 75 years. Think of the technological changes that have occurred in the twentieth century. Thus, it is fairly obvious that we are involved in an accelerating pace of change and that people have, by and large, come to accept such changes. On the other hand, there is evidence of human desires to slow or stop technological changes that are deemed detrimental to the quality of life—pollution of air and water, atomic testing, atomic generating plants, supersonic airplanes, etc. Even simple technological changes are resisted by some. For example, credit cards have resulted in individual behavior changes for most of us—allowing us to carry less cash and to approach buying with a different psychological

From Fremont E. Kast and James E. Rosenzweig, *Experiential Exercises and Cases In Management.* © 1976, McGraw-Hill. Reprinted by permission.

[1] Wilson D. Wallis, as cited in Charles R. Walker, *Modern Technology and Civilization*, New York, McGraw-Hill, 1962, p. 10.

point of view. However, some people have declined to use credit cards at all.

Although technological change is obviously the most dramatic in our society, we have become particularly concerned with sociological change—individual, group, and organization. While recognizing the desirability of adaptation and innovation, it is also important to recognize the need for stability and continuity. For both individuals and organizations, stability *and* adaptation are essential to survival and growth. Change may occur slowly or rapidly, but, in either case, the individual or organization must be able to function on a day-to-day basis.

Changes may occur in either goals or the means of attaining them. In organizations, management is charged with the responsibility for maintaining a dynamic equilibrium by diagnosing situations and designing adjustments that are most appropriate for coping with current conditions. A dynamic equilibrium for an organization would include the following dimensions.

1. Enough stability to facilitate achievement of current goals
2. Enough continuity to ensure orderly change in either ends or means
3. Enough adaptability to react appropriately to external opportunities and demands as well as changing internal conditions
4. Enough innovativeness to allow the organization to be proactive (initiate changes) when conditions warrant

This process is obviously a delicate balancing act which gets more difficult with the accelerating nature of change.

The impetus for change comes from many sources, both internal and external to the organization. For example, the actions of one firm in an industry usually lead to changes in other firms in the industry. They scramble to meet a product innovation; raise or lower prices to remain competitive; and adjust advertising campaigns accordingly. When CBS develops a successful television program, both NBC and ABC are quick to follow with similar offerings. When one airline provides movies on transcontinental flights, others soon follow suit.

The government—local, state, and federal—is another obvious impetus for change. Pollution control and affirmative action in hiring and staffing are good examples.

Internal sources of change include new technological advances, structural realignments, improved managerial techniques for planning and controlling activities, better information systems, and feedback from employees who suggest, request, or demand that something be done differently.

The focus of change efforts can be the products or services delivered as well as the human and technical processes used. A change effort may be directed toward an individual with the desire to get that person to behave differently—to do more or less of something, to quit or start doing something. Similarly, the focus could be a group of people—a committee, task force, work team, or department. Larger-scale change efforts might focus on the relationships between two or more departments or on the organization as a whole. Changes in goals, policies, or procedures typically affect everyone in the organization.

Although many people seem to welcome variety and change in their lives, there is often considerable resistance to change in organizations. A certain amount of resistance is healthy because it preserves enough stability and continuity to get the job done. However, in many cases it hinders organizational progress which may be needed for satisfactory performance or even survival. Why do people resist changes that (according to management) are in their own best interests? One obvious reason is vested interests. When people put much time and effort into learning certain skills and performances, they feel threatened when such skills or procedures become obsolete. In 1974, when the National Football League moved the goalposts from the goal line to the back of the end zone, the place kickers were not enthusiastic. Arguments to the effect that it would improve the overall game by decreasing the number of field goals fell on deaf ears. If a sales representative has built up considerable rapport with customers, a shuffling of sales territories which requires the agent essentially to start over will not be particularly palatable.

Lack of information, particularly if it leads to misunderstanding, is another powerful source of resistance to change. People need to be aware of possible changes in the early stages. It is natural to resist the unknown; therefore, it is important to know exactly what the change proposal is, why it is being proposed, and what the possible consequences are likely to be.

A change in power structure is also likely to foster resistance—particularly if someone's sphere of influence is to be decreased. Diversity of values is also a common source of resistance to change. Widely diverse views of a particular matter make it extremely difficult to get enough consensus to move in the direction of a proposed change.

While there are no panaceas in overcoming resistance to change, there are several guidelines which might be kept in mind.

1. Define the problem explicitly (including current and desired conditions).
2. Provide information in detail (including reasons for, mechanics of, and likely effects).
3. Encourage participation at all stages.
4. Anticipate the feelings of participants.
5. Work with acknowledged informal leaders.
6. Positively reinforce changes.

A number of the issues discussed earlier are illustrated in the case described in this unit—Municipal Light. It involves an organization with a long history and much tradition. It has been quite successful as measured by a number of dimensions. However, the mayor and the city council believed that some changes were necessary and their decision was communicated to a new superintendent. An outside consulting firm wrote a report which served as additional impetus for change. Management's approach was resisted and the issue resulted in accusations, counteraccusations, much bitterness, and, eventually, an unauthorized strike. The purpose of the exercise is to diagnose the case, understand as much as possible, and develop an approach for management to cope with the situation as it currently exists.

The lessons to be learned in this unit revolve around designing workable processes of planned change. Recognizing the need for stability and continuity, how can organizations build into their day-to-day managerial processes the means by which they can adapt and innovate when necessary? The goal is for problem sensing, problem solving, and action planning to be an integral part of the managerial task rather than an ad hoc response to crisis.

Municipal Light

In 1902 the citizens of Hamilton passed a proposal to develop a source of hydroelectric power for street lights and other public purposes. Up until that time all power had been supplied by private companies. During the first half of the twentieth century, a number of dams and steam-generating plants were developed in order to supply a large portion of Hamilton's power needs. The existence of Municipal Light also served as a rate regulator for electric power purchased from private companies. Since its beginning in 1902, Municipal Light has developed into one of America's most efficient electric utilities, powered almost entirely by nonpolluting hydroelectric generating facilities. This self-supporting, tax-paying utility maintains rates that are among the nation's lowest (less than half the national average), with but two rate increases in 66 years. In addition to low rates, Municipal Light provides a spectrum of consumer services: electric range, electric water heater, and electric heating system repair service at no charge—except for parts; advice on heating and air conditioning; free estimates on electric heating costs; advice on use and care of electric appliances; recipes and other household hints; advice on adquate wiring; 24-hour emergency light trouble service; and water-heater rental as low as $1.25 monthly. As a consequence, Municipal Light has built up a good image in the minds of consumers for low rates and free services.

Municipal Light employs approximately 1,800 women and men for the Hamilton service area and the hydroelectric projects. Employees have considerable pride in their organization and enjoy the company's good image with customers. Many jobs have been passed from father to son, and in a number of instances three generations are represented on the Municipal Light payroll. In many cases, several members of the same family are currently working in the organization. Obviously, many traditions and norms have evolved over time with respect to employee relations—among peers as well as among superiors and subordinates. Approximately 700 of the 1,800 employees are represented by the International Brotherhood of Electrical Workers.

In 1972 Charles Newman was appointed superintendent of Municipal Light. He was a retired Air Force brigadier general with a distinguished military career and experience in managing large-scale weapon procurement programs. The appointment was controversial because many Municipal Light workers, as well as some members of the city council, contended that the superintendent should have had experience in an electrical utility. The mayor and a majority of the council, however, felt that managerial skills were transferable and that Mr. Newman was the right person for the job at that particular time. They were concerned that Municipal Light was entering a new era in which the emphasis would have to be placed on cost savings in order that rates could be held down to the current very attractive levels. In this context, the new superintendent accepted a mandate which emphasized public responsiveness and implemented programs designed to develop a greater sensitivity to the needs of Municipal Light's customers and owners, and to provide them with more effective, efficient service.

An outside consulting firm—Donner, Blitzen, and Associates—was hired to conduct a comprehensive study of the organization—the first in its 70-year history. A year later, the study conclusions pointed the way toward an annual saving of over $2 million for the utility's rate payers, plus substantial increases in the speed and efficiency of customer service. An automated customer information system (CIS) was designed to provide near-instantaneous customer data from a control computer. By eliminating duplicate filing systems and reducing incidents of error, CIS would save an estimated $1 million annually. A proposed management reporting system involved a broad range of coordinated reports to assist Municipal Light managers in evaluating performance and analyzing work procedures on a regular systematized basis. Another recommendation involved a work management system to establish a project priority and scheduling procedure together with more precise work control and documentation in the engineering and operations area of the utility. A proposed organization and systems planning and coordination report would provide the necessary research capability and control to coordinate the new and ongoing utility programs. It was anticipated that implementation of all the recommendations should take approximately 3 years.

Municipal Light receives over 18,000 telephone calls a day for service and information, plus several hundred of an administrative nature. In April 1974, an automated centrex telephone system replaced equipment that had been installed in 1935. The new electronic switching means faster, more efficient service for Municipal Light customers.

Automation, plus implementation of the Donner, Blitzen, and Associates study, has resulted in certain personnel changes, reductions in some areas, and additional hiring in others. When the automation program was first started in 1970, the utility made a firm commitment to all personnel that there would be no layoffs or reductions in salary—a commitment that Municipal Light has stood by during the past years. To retain personnel for certain jobs in the utility, a skill redistribution program was created as an ongoing effort. To complement the skill redistribution program as well as to provide opportunities for all personnel to upgrade performance in various disciplines, Municipal Light established a training division in June 1973. The newly formed section was authorized to ascertain training needs in the utility and to develop appropriate courses to augment the already established tuition reimbursement and other education programs. Courses have been conducted in office and technical skills as well as in the management area.

Municipal Light has a firm commitment to Hamilton's Affirmative Action Program. The target for reaching minority parity within the service area in 1975, while 1978 is the goal set for equal representation of women. In 1974, women were admitted to training programs in the electrical trades, an area from which they had been historically excluded. This program was coordinated with the International Brotherhood of Electrical Workers, the Civil Service Commission, and the Hamilton personnel department.

In 1972, Superintendent Newman established a Citizens Policy Advisory Committee, consisting of 14 members who represented a wide spectrum of the community. Their recommendations have been included in policy deliberations on matters such as rates, generation and research, street lighting, underground policy, energy marketing, finances, and environmental impact.

On Wednesday, November 22, 1972, the following story appeared in the Hamilton *Harbinger*.

Newman Suspends 16 at Municipal Light

PRIVATE DETECTIVES TURN UP "ABUSES"

City Light Superintendent Charles Newman disclosed yesterday he has suspended 16 field employees and reprimanded 2 for abusing coffee break periods.

Newman said he hired a private detective firm to shadow Municipal Light crews for one week after getting complaints from citizens that some men were taking extended coffee breaks at their Hamilton cafés.

The investigation also turned up possible abuses of coffee break times by "15 to 18" employees of the Hamilton Engineering Department, according to George Everest, principal assistant city engineer for operations.

However, Everest said he cannot say if there are any actual violations in his department until he has had each reported case checked out. This is being done now.

The three cafés involved, Everest said, are near 2d Avenue and Barstow Street, 7th Avenue N.E. and Interlake Way, and N. 34th Street and Stevens Way N.

Newman said two Municipal Light employees were suspended for 10 days without pay, five were suspended for 2 days and nine for one day. Two others received letters of reprimand.

The superintendent said at least one of the disciplined employees also was disciplined in a similar investigation three years ago, for the same thing.

Everest said his department also has to discipline employees from time to time for coffee break time abuses.

The private detective agency placed the three locations under surveillance during the work week of October 30 through November 3 and made its reports according to vehicle license numbers.

The private eyes timed the length of time crews spent in the cafés. Normal time allowed for coffee breaks is 15 minutes in the forenoon and afternoon, Everest said.

Newman said: "We talked to our people involved and they admitted the abuses. The severity and frequency of the violations varied."

Newman stressed that the infractions involved only a small minority of Municipal Light workers and "I continue to be amazed at the dedication of 99 percent of our employees."

He said those abusing lunch or coffee break periods not only are gypping the city "they also are cheating on their fellow employees."

"I will not stand for this."

He said most of the violators "had been around for a while." He said that if any "extenuating circumstances" turn up later, the disciplinary actions will be rectified.

"We're not against coffee breaks—just the abuse of them," Newman declared.

The president of the security agency involved maintained that his agents did not spy upon employees of the utility. Their job was to check only on vehicles and that this task fell within their overall contract of protecting Municipal Light facilities and equipment. Citizen reaction was quick and varied. Some supported management in its efforts to "shape-up" employees. Others felt that this goal, however meritorious, was overshadowed by the sneaky tactics used. They emphasized that control and discipline should be handled within the organization via normal managerial procedures.

This episode touched off a series of disputes within the organization, some of which were given publicity in the press. Two of the four city council members who voted against the superintendent at his confirmation hearing in 1972 said publicly that Newman hadn't done badly. One stated, "On balance, I would have to say he's done a good job." Another observed: "I like a number of things he's done, changes that I favored such as reducing personnel and opening up the utilities operations. I also hear about morale problems among the rank-and-file workers. There are pluses and minuses. . . ." The majority of the council who supported Newman in the beginning reaffirmed their position by stating, "Yes, we think he is doing a good job, making the kinds of changes we wanted to see." In December 1973, supervisory personnel—not Newman—suspended six more utility workers for coffee break abuses. This time, supervisory personnel did the surveillance rather than the security firm. Newman stated, "Those who were abusing their privileges were being unfair to their fellow workers. I felt that the previous management had failed to stop such abuses and that I must. Letters from the public supported the disciplinary actions 50 to 1."

During this period, a new discipline code was written, at the request of employees, to make penalties more equitable. According to Newman, union leadership failed to attend drafting sessions. The code was put into effect on March 21, 1974. In early April, two foremen were suspended for 3 days for alleged coffee break abuses. One of the foremen, Arnold Knutson, claimed that his crew had to move its truck out of a customer's driveway at 4 PM. Because it was too late to set up again and get anything accomplished by quitting time, he decided to take the crew back to a substation for a coffee break before quitting at 4:30. He maintained that they had not taken a normal 15-minute break during the afternoon. The new rules specified that crews would return to the main dispatching area rather than stop at substations en route. Jack Simmons, the other foreman, did not comment on the specifics of his case, but did say that he wasn't even aware of any new rules covering suspensions, discharges, and other disciplinary measures. Other workers suggested that the new rules were adopted unilaterally by Municipal Light Superintendent Charles Newman without approval of the Civil Service Commission. Newman's comment was, "Municipal Light insists on being able to discipline employees when they fail to put in 8 hours work for 8 hours pay. There are standing work orders, dating back to 1970, explicitly requiring crews to return to headquarters at the close of their last job for the day. Loafing away from headquarters to round out the work day is not acceptable work procedure." He stated that citizens had complained that the two work crews involved were parking their trucks and loafing for 30 minutes or longer at the end of their work day.

The next day, about 700 members of the electrical workers' union walked off the job, refusing to return until the suspensions were rescinded. By the second day, the strike had spread to over 1,000 of the 1,800 employees. An ad hoc committee representing the workers presented the following demands in the form of a memo to Superintendent Newman, the mayor of Hamilton, and the city council. The demands included:

1. Rescinding the suspensions of the two foremen
2. Resignation of Superintendent Newman
3. Suspension of the new work rules until they are approved by the employees, the union, and the Civil Service Commission
4. The development of an employees' bill of rights
5. The suspension of implementation of new programs which appeared to have exceeded the ability of the organization to absorb changes

/signed/

The superintendent responded by saying that he was willing to hold the suspensions in abeyance and meet with the ad hoc committee.

Procedure

Step 1

The class is divided into subgroups of five or six. Groups are randomly assigned to the roles of (a) dissident employees, and (b) managers. There should be at least three manager groups.

Step 2

Meet in groups for 20 minutes to discuss and refine the assigned role. Empathize with the people in the case and try to internalize their points of view. Manager groups should designate three of their members to attend a meeting of employees and managers.

Step 3

Select one of the employee groups (all members) to meet with one of the manager groups (three members). Those not involved in the meeting should be silent observers. (15 minutes)

Step 4

Change the manager group and have the new group (three members) meet with the same employee group. (15 minutes)

Step 5

Change the manager group again and have the new group (three members) meet with the same employee group. (15 minutes)

Step 6

a. The employee group should describe its reactions to each of the three manager groups.
b. Each manager group should explain the rationale underlying its approach to the situation.

Step 7

The entire class discusses the problem, including

a. General observations.
b. Advantages and disadvantages of the various approaches.

Summary and Conceptualization

You have experienced a particular role in a real organization—Municipal Light. Did you have trouble empathizing with the role assigned, i.e., with employees or managers? Typically, some students ask to be reassigned because they just cannot "live the part." In reading the case, they have sided quite definitely with either management or employees, depending on their particular background, experience, and values. Nevertheless, it is good experience to force ourselves to view situations from perspectives other than our own. Although we may not change our minds, we should be able to increase our understanding of different points of view.

Municipal Light is an old, tradition-bound organization with established norms. The superintendent was not an engineer and had had no previous experience in a utility. This was a major departure from past practice and undoubtedly shocked the system. The use of outside consultants was also a first. This approach resulted in a number of proposed changes that promised to have widespread repercussions. While many benefits, including cost reductions, were expected, none had materialized during the period of the case. Expectations of benefits are typically overstated; therefore, they should be scrutinized in order that any cost/benefit analysis will be realistic.

The numerous changes had a definite impact on the general organizational climate. There was a good deal of resistance to change in general and the suspensions over coffee break abuses seemed to be the straw that broke the camel's back.

The several manager groups approached resolution of the current management-employee conflict in different ways. Did you accept a particular approach as most appropriate? Or were there elements in all three approaches that might be useful? Is there one best way?

A broader issue is that of coping with change in general. If you were advising Mr. Newman, what would you suggest for getting commitment to implement "appropriate" changes as of the end of the case?

34

The Moving Dilemma: A Matter of Gravity

A recent television documentary/exposé revealed problems experienced by major national long-haul moving companies in their truck shipping operation.

The primary problem evolved around the weighing process: after pick ups are made, loads are weighed at roadside scales, where "weight tickets" were being altered or simply overstated. In some cases, blank tickets were obtained from private printers and weights were recorded with hand-made tools which were readily available to drivers. These counterfeit weight tickets were then substituted for authentic tickets. In other instances, unscrupulous weight-station attendants dispensed fraudulent tickets to drivers. Drivers, who are paid according to the weight of the load and the distance the load is carried, found all the information needed to falsify their documents by simple inquiries over their citizens band radio. Other drivers were eager to recommend likely accomplices.

In response to this exposé, the president of a major hauler has called you in to help them reduce the negative consequences of these practices. What recommendation would you make?

Issues

1. Identify the key issue(s) and their relationships in this case.
2. Describe your first steps or initial approach to the situation.
3. If the president had told you that she would accept and implement any recommendation you make, what would you do?

Steven Kerr

35

On the Folly of Rewarding A, While Hoping for B

Whether dealing with monkeys, rats, or human beings, it is hardly controversial to state that most organisms seek information concerning what activities are rewarded, and then seek to do (or at least pretend to do) those things, often to the virtual exclusion of activities not rewarded. The extent to which this occurs of course will depend on the perceived attractiveness of the rewards offered, but neither operant nor expectancy theorists would quarrel with the essence of this notion.

Nevertheless, numerous examples exist of reward systems that are fouled up in that behaviors which are rewarded are those which the rewarder is trying to *discourage*, while the behavior he desires is not being rewarded at all.

In an effort to understand and explain this phenomenon, this paper presents examples from society, from organizations in general, and from profit-making firms in particular. Data from a manufacturing company and information from an insurance firm are examined to demonstrate the consequences of such reward systems for the organizations involved, and possible reasons why such reward systems continue to exist are considered.

Societal Examples

Politics

Official goals are "purposely vague and general and do not indicate . . . the host of decisions that must be made among alternative ways of achieving official goals and the priority of multiple goals . . ." (8, p. 66). They usually may be relied on to offend absolutely no one, and in this sense can be considered high-acceptance, low-quality goals. An example might be "build better schools." Operative goals are higher in quality but lower in accept-

Reprinted from *Academy of Management Journal*, 1975, *18*, 769–783.

ance, since they specify where the money will come from, what alternative goals will be ignored, etc.

The American citizenry supposedly wants its candidates for public office to set forth operative goals, making their proposed programs "perfectly clear," specifying sources and uses of funds, etc. However, since operative goals are lower in acceptance, and since aspirants to public office need acceptance (from at least 50.1 percent of the people), most politicians prefer to speak only of official goals, at least until after the election. They of course would agree to speak at the operative level if "punished" for not doing so. The electorate could do this by refusing to support candidates who do not speak at the operative level.

Instead, however, the American voter typically punishes (withholds support from) candidates who frankly discuss where the money will come from, rewards politicians who speak only of official goals, but hopes that candidates (despite the reward system) will discuss the issues operatively. It is academic whether it was moral for Nixon, for example, to refuse to discuss his 1968 "secret plan" to end the Vietnam war, his 1972 operative goals concerning the lifting of price controls, the reshuffling of his cabinet, etc. The point is that the reward system made such refusal rational.

It seems worth mentioning that no manuscript can adequately define what is "moral" and what is not. However, examination of costs and benefits, combined with knowledge of what motivates a particular individual, often will suffice to determine what for him is "rational."[1] If the reward system is so designed that it is irrational to be moral, this does not necessarily mean that immorality will result. But is this not asking for trouble?

War

If some oversimplification may be permitted, let it be assumed that the primary goal of the organization (Pentagon, Luftwaffe, or whatever) is to win. Let it be assumed further that the primary goal of most individuals on the front lines is to get home alive. Then there appears to be an important conflict in goals—personally rational behavior by those at the bottom will endanger goal attainment by those at the top.

But not necessarily! It depends on how the reward system is set up. The Vietnam war was indeed a study of disobedience and rebellion, with terms such as "fragging" (killing one's own commanding officer) and "search and evade" becoming part of the military vocabulary. The difference in subordinates' acceptance of authority between World War II and Vietnam is reported to be considerable, and veterans of the Second World War often have been quoted as being outraged at the mutinous actions of many American soldiers in Vietnam.

[1]In Simon's (10, pp. 76–77) terms, a decision is "subjectively rational" if it maximizes an individual's valued outcomes so far as his knowledge permits. A decision is "personally rational" if it is oriented toward the individual's goals.

Consider, however, some critical differences in the reward system in use during the two conflicts. What did the GI in World War II want? To go home. And when did he get to go home? When the war was won! If he disobeyed the orders to clean out the trenches and take the hills, the war would not be won and he would not go home. Furthermore, what were his chances of attaining his goal (getting home alive) if he obeyed the orders compared to his chances if he did not? What is being suggested is that the rational soldier in World War II, *whether patriotic or not*, probably found it expedient to obey.

Consider the reward system in use in Vietnam. What did the man at the bottom want? To go home. And when did he get to go home? When his tour of duty was over! This was the case *whether or not* the war was won. Furthermore, concerning the relative chance of getting home alive by obeying orders compared to the chance if they were disobeyed, it is worth noting that a mutineer in Vietnam was far more likely to be assigned rest and rehabilitation (on the assumption that fatigue was the cause) than he was to suffer any negative consequence.

In his description of the "zone of indifference," Barnard stated that "a person can and will accept a communication as authoritative only when . . . at the time of his decision, he believes it to be compatible with his personal interests as a whole" (1, p. 165). In light of the reward system used in Vietnam, would it not have been personally irrational for some orders to have been obeyed? Was not the military implementing a system which *rewarded* disobedience, while *hoping* that soldiers (despite the reward system) would obey orders?

Medicine

Theoretically, a physician can make either of two types of error, and intuitively one seems as bad as the other. A doctor can pronounce a patient sick when he is actually well, thus causing him needless anxiety and expense, curtailment of enjoyable foods and activities, and even physical danger by subjecting him to needless medication and surgery. Alternately, a doctor can label a sick person well, and thus avoid treating what may be a serious, even fatal ailment. It might be natural to conclude that physicians seek to minimize both types of error.

Such a conclusion would be wrong.[2] It is estimated that numerous Americans are presently afflicted with iatrogenic (physician *caused*) illnesses (9). This occurs when the doctor is approached by someone complaining of a few stray symptoms. The doctor classifies and organizes these symptoms, gives them a name, and obligingly tells the patient what further symptoms may be

[2] In one study (4) of 14,867 films for signs of tuberculosis, 1,216 positive readings turned out to be clinically negative; only 24 negative readings proved clinically active, a ratio of 50 to 1.

expected. This information often acts as a self-fulfilling prophecy, with the result that from that day on the patient for all practical purposes is sick.

Why does this happen? Why are physicians so reluctant to sustain a type 2 error (pronouncing a sick person well) that they will tolerate many type 1 errors? Again, a look at the reward system is needed. The punishments for a type 2 error are real: guilt, embarrassment, and the threat of lawsuit and scandal. On the other hand, a type 1 error (labeling a well person sick) "is sometimes seen as sound clinical practice, indicating a healthy conservative approach to medicine" (9, p. 69). Type 1 errors also are likely to generate increased income and a stream of steady customers who, being well in a limited physiological sense, will not embarrass the doctor by dying abruptly.

Fellow physicians and the general public therefore are really *rewarding* type 1 errors and at the same time *hoping* fervently that doctors will try not to make them.

General Organizational Examples

Rehabilitation Centers and Orphanages

In terms of the prime beneficiary classification (2, p. 42) organizations such as these are supposed to exist for the "public-in-contact," that is, clients. The orphanage therefore theoretically is interested in placing as many children as possible in good homes. However, often orphanages surround themselves with so many rules concerning adoption that it is nearly impossible to pry a child out of the place. Orphanages may deny adoption unless the applicants are a married couple, both of the same religion as the child, without history of emotional or vocational instability, with a specified minimum income and a private room for the child, etc.

If the primary goal is to place children in good homes, then the rules ought to constitute means toward that goal. Goal displacement results when these "means become ends-in-themselves that displace the original goals" (2, p. 229).

To some extent these rules are required by law. But the influence of the reward system on the orphanage's management should not be ignored. Consider, for example, that the:

1. Number of children enrolled often is the most important determinant of the size of the allocated budget.
2. Number of children under the director's care also will affect the size of his staff.
3. Total organizational size will determine largely the director's prestige at the annual conventions, in the community, etc.

Therefore, to the extent that staff size, total budget, and personal prestige are valued by the orphanage's executive personnel, it becomes rational for them to make it difficult for children to be adopted. After all, who wants to be the director of the smallest orphanage in the state?

If the reward system errs in the opposite direction, paying off only for placements, extensive goal displacement again is likely to result. A common example of vocational rehabilitation in many states, for example, consists of placing someone in a job for which he has little interest and few qualifications, for two months or so, and then "rehabilitating" him again in another position. Such behavior is quite consistent with the prevailing reward system, which pays off for the number of individuals placed in any position for 60 days or more. Rehabilitation counselors also confess to competing with one another to place relatively skilled clients, sometimes ignoring persons with few skills who would be harder to place. Extensively disabled clients find that counselors often prefer to work with those whose disabilities are less severe.[3]

Universities

Society *hopes* that teachers will not neglect their teaching responsibilities but *rewards* them almost entirely for research and publications. This is most true at the large and prestigious universities. Clichés such as "good research and good teaching go together" notwithstanding, professors often find that they must choose between teaching and research-oriented activities when allocating their time. Rewards for good teaching usually are limited to outstanding teacher awards, which are given to only a small percentage of good teachers and which usually bestow little money and fleeting prestige. Punishments for poor teaching also are rare.

Rewards for research and publications, on the other hand, and punishments for failure to accomplish these, are commonly administered by universities at which teachers are employed. Furthermore, publication-oriented resumés usually will be well received at other universities, whereas teaching credentials, harder to document and quantify, are much less transferable. Consequently it is rational for university teachers to concentrate on research, even if to the detriment of teaching and at the expense of their students.

By the same token, it is rational for students to act based upon the goal displacement which has occurred within universities concerning what they are rewarded for. If it is assumed that a primary goal of a university is to transfer knowledge from teacher to student, then grades become identifiable as a means toward that goal, serving as motivational, control, and feedback devices to expedite the knowledge transfer. Instead, however, the grades themselves have become much more important for entrance to graduate school, successful employment, tuition refunds, parental respect, etc., than the knowledge or lack of knowledge they are supposed to signify.

[3]Personal interviews conducted during 1972–73.

It therefore should come as no surprise that information has surfaced in recent years concerning fraternity files for examinations, term-paper writing services, organized cheating at the service academies, and the like. Such activities constitute a personally rational response to a reward system which pays off for grades rather than knowledge.

Business-Related Examples

Ecology

Assume that the president of XYZ Corporation is confronted with the following alternatives:

1. Spend $11 million for antipollution equipment to keep from poisoning fish in the river adjacent to the plant; or
2. Do nothing, in violation of the law, and assume a one in ten chance of being caught, with a resultant $1 million fine plus the necessity of buying the equipment.

Under this not unrealistic set of choices it requires no linear program to determine that XYZ Corporation can maximize its probabilities by flouting the law. Add the fact that XYZ's president is probably being rewarded (by creditors, stockholders, and other salient parts of his task environment) according to criteria totally unrelated to the number of fish poisoned, and his probable course of action becomes clear.

Evaluation of Training

It is axiomatic that those who care about a firm's well-being should insist that the organization get fair value for its expenditures. Yet it is commonly known that firms seldom bother to evaluate a new GRID, MBO, job enrichment program, or whatever, to see if the company is getting its money's worth. Why? Certainly it is not because people have not pointed out that this situation exists; numerous practitioner-oriented articles are written each year to just this point.

The individuals (whether in personnel, manpower planning, or wherever) who normally would be responsible for conducting such evaluations are the same ones often charged with introducing the change effort in the first place. Having convinced top management to spend the money, they usually are quite animated afterwards in collecting arigorous vignettes and anecdotes about how successful the program was. The last thing many desire is a formal, systematic, and revealing evaluation. Although members of top management may actually *hope* for such systematic evaluation, their reward systems continue to *reward* ignorance in this area. And if the personnel department abdicates its responsibility, who is to step into the breach? The change agent himself? Hardly! He is likely to be too busy collecting anecdotal "evidence" of his own, for use with his next client.

Miscellaneous

Many additional examples could be cited of systems which in fact are rewarding behaviors other than those supposedly desired by the rewarder. A few of these are described briefly below.

Most coaches disdain to discuss individual accomplishments, preferring to speak of teamwork, proper attitude, and a one-for-all spirit. Usually, however, rewards are distributed according to individual performance. The college basketball player who feeds his teammates instead of shooting will not compile impressive scoring statistics and is less likely to be drafted by the pros. The ballplayer who hits to right field to advance the runners will win neither the batting nor home run titles, and will be offered smaller raises. It therefore is rational for players to think of themselves first, and the team second.

In business organizations where rewards are dispensed for unit performance or for individual goals achieved, without regard for overall effectiveness, similar attitudes often are observed. Under most Management by Objectives (MBO) systems, goals in areas where quantification is difficult often go unspecified. The organization therefore often is in a position where it *hopes* for employee effort in the areas of team building, interpersonal relations, creativity, etc., but it formally *rewards* none of these. In cases where promotions and raises are formally tied to MBO, the system itself contains a paradox in that it "asks employees to set challenging, risky goals, only to face smaller paychecks and possibly damaged careers if these goals are not accomplished" (5, p. 40).

It is *hoped* that administrators will pay attention to long-run costs and opportunities and will institute programs which will bear fruit later on. However, many organizational reward systems pay off for short-run sales and earnings only. Under such circumstances it is personally rational for officials to sacrifice long-term growth and profit (by selling off equipment and property, or by stifling research and development) for short-term advantages. This probably is most pertinent in the public sector, with the result that many public officials are unwilling to implement programs which will not show benefits by election time.

As a final, clear-cut example of a fouled-up reward system, consider the cost-plus contract or its next of kin, the allocation of next year's budget as a direct function of this year's expenditures. It probably is conceivable that those who award such budgets and contracts really hope for economy and prudence in spending. It is obvious, however, that adopting the proverb "to

---

him who spends shall more be given," rewards not economy, but spending itself.

Two Companies' Experiences

A Manufacturing Organization

A midwest manufacturer of industrial goods had been troubled for some time by aspects of its organizational climate it believed dysfunctional. For research purposes, interviews were conducted with many employees and a questionnaire was administered on a company-wide basis, including plants and offices in several American and Canadian locations. The company strongly encouraged employee participation in the survey, and made available time and space during the workday for completion of the instrument. All employees in attendance during the day of the survey completed the questionnaire. All instruments were collected directly by the researcher, who personally administered each session. Since no one employed by the firm handled the questionnaires, and since respondent names were not asked for, it seems likely that the pledge of anonymity given was believed.

A modified version of the Expect Approval scale (7) was included as part of the questionnaire. The instrument asked respondents to indicate the degree of approval or disapproval they could expect if they performed each of the described actions. A seven-point Likert scale was used, with 1 indicating that the action would probably bring strong disapproval and 7 signifying likely strong approval.

Although normative data for this scale from studies of other organizations are unavailable, it is possible to examine fruitfully the data obtained from this survey in several ways. First, it may be worth noting that the questionnaire data corresponded closely to information gathered through interviews. Furthermore, as can be seen from the results summarized in Table 1, sizable differences between various work units, and between employees at different job levels within the same work unit, were obtained. This suggests that response bias effects (social desirability in particular loomed as a potential concern) are not likely to be severe.

Most importantly, comparisons between scores obtained on the Expect Approval scale and a statement of problems which were the reason for the survey revealed that the same behaviors which managers in each division thought dysfunctional were those which lower level employees claimed were rewarded. As compared to job levels 1 to 8 in Division B (see Table 1), those in Division A claimed a much higher acceptance by management of "conforming" activities. Between 31 and 37 percent of Division A employees at levels 1–8 stated that going along with the majority, agreeing with the boss, and staying on everyone's good side brought approval; only once (level 5–8 responses to one of the three items) did a majority suggest that such actions would generate disapproval.

Furthermore, responses from Division A workers at levels 1–4 indicate that behaviors geared toward risk avoidance were as likely to be rewarded as to be punished. Only at job levels 9 and above was it apparent that the reward system was positively reinforcing behaviors desired by top management. Overall, the same "tendencies toward conservatism and apple-polishing at the lower levels" which divisional management had complained about during the interviews were those claimed by subordinates to be the most rational course of action in light of the existing reward system. Management apparently was not getting the behaviors it was *hoping* for, but it certainly was getting the behaviors it was perceived by subordinates to be *rewarding*.

An Insurance Firm

The Group Health Claims Division of a large eastern insurance company provides another rich illustration of a reward system which reinforces behaviors not desired by top management.

Attempting to measure and reward accuracy in paying surgical claims, the firm systematically keeps track of the number of returned checks and letters of complaint received from policyholders. However, underpayments are likely to provoke cries of outrage from the insured, while overpayments often are accepted in courteous silence. Since it often is impossible to tell from the physician's statement which of two surgical procedures, with different allowable benefits, was performed, and since writing for clarifications will interfere with other standards used by the firm concerning "percentage of claims paid within two days of receipt," the new hire in more than one claims section is soon acquainted with the informal norm: "When in doubt, pay it out!"

The situation would be even worse were it not for the fact that other features of the firm's reward system tend to neutralize those described. For example, annual "merit" increases are given to all employees, in one of the following three amounts:

1. If the worker is "outstanding" (a select category, into which no more than two employees per section may be placed): 5 percent
2. If the worker is "above average" (normally all workers not "outstanding" are so rated): 4 percent
3. If the worker commits gross acts of negligence and irresponsibility for which he might be discharged in many other companies: 3 percent.

Now, since (*a*) the difference between the 5 percent theoretically attainable through hard work and the 4 percent attainable merely by living until the review data is small and (*b*) since insurance firms seldom dispense much of a

TABLE 1

Summary of Two Divisions' Data Relevant to Conforming and Risk-Avoidance Behaviors (extent to which subjects expect approval)

Dimension	Item	Division and Sample	Total Responses	1, 2, or 3 (Disapproval)	4	5, 6, or 7 (Approval)
				Percentage of Workers Responding		
Risk avoidance	Making a risky decision based on the best information available at the time but which turns out wrong.	A, levels 1–4 (lowest)	127	61	25	14
		A, levels 5–8	172	46	31	23
		A, levels 9 and above	17	41	30	30
		B, levels 1–4 (lowest)	31	58	26	16
		B, levels 5–8	19	42	42	16
		B, levels 9 and above	10	50	20	30
Risk	Setting extremely high and challenging standards and goals, and then narrowly failing to make them.	A, levels 1–4	122	47	28	25
		A, levels 5–8	168	33	26	41
		A, levels 9+	17	24	6	70
		B, levels 1–4	31	48	23	29
		B, levels 5–8	18	17	33	50
		B, levels 9+	10	30	0	70
	Setting goals which are extremely easy to make and then making them.	A, levels 1–4	124	35	30	35
		A, levels 5–8	171	47	27	26
		A, levels 9+	17	70	24	6
		B, levels 1–4	31	58	26	16
		B, levels 5–8	19	63	16	21

Dimension	Item	Division and Sample	Total Responses	Percentage of Workers Responding		
				1, 2, or 3 (Disapproval)	4	5, 6, or 7 (Approval)
		B, levels 9+	10	80	0	20
	Being a "yes man" and always agreeing with the boss.	A, levels 1–4	126	46	17	37
		A, levels 5–8	180	54	14	31
		A, levels 9+	17	88	12	0
		B, levels 1–4	32	53	28	19
		B, levels 5–8	19	68	21	11
		B, levels 9+	10	80	10	10
	Always going along with the majority.	A, levels 1–4	125	40	25	35
		A, levels 5–8	173	47	21	32
		A, levels 9+	17	70	12	18
		B, levels 1–4	31	61	23	16
		B, levels 5–8	19	68	11	21
		B, levels 9+	10	80	10	10
	Being careful to stay on the good side everyone so that everyone agrees that you are a great guy.	A, levels 1–4	124	45	18	37
		A, levels 5–8	173	45	22	33
		A, levels, 9+	17	64	6	30
		B, levels 1–4	31	54	23	23
		B, levels 5–8	19	73	11	16
		B, levels, 9+	10	80	10	10

salary increase in cash (rather, the worker's insurance benefits increase, causing him to be further overinsured), many employees are rather indifferent to the possibility of obtaining the extra one percent reward and therefore tend to ignore the norm concerning indiscriminant payments.

However, most employees are not indifferent to the rule which states that, should absences or latenesses total three or more in any six-month period, the entire 4 or 5 percent due at the next "merit" review must be forfeited. In this sense the firm may be described as *hoping* for performance, while *rewarding* attendance. What it gets, of course, is attendance. (If the absence-lateness rule appears to the reader to be stringent, it really is not. The company counts "times" rather than "days" absent, and a ten-day absence therefore counts the same as one lasting two days. A worker in danger of accumulating a third absence within six months merely has to remain ill (away from work) during his second absence until his first absence is more than six months old. The limiting factor is that at some point his salary ceases, and his sickness benefits take over. This usually is sufficient to get the younger workers to return, but for those with 20 or more years' service, the company provides sickness benefits of 90 percent of normal salary, tax-free! Therefore . . . .)

Causes

Extremely diverse instances of systems which reward behavior A although the rewarder apparently hopes for behavior B have been given. These are useful to illustrate the breadth and magnitude of the phenomenon, but the diversity increases the difficulty of determining commonalities and establishing causes. However, four general factors may be pertinent to an explanation of why fouled-up reward systems seem to be so prevelant.

Fascination with an "Objective" Criterion

It has been mentioned elsewhere that:

Most "objective" measures of productivity are objective only in that their subjective elements are *(a)* determined in advance, rather than coming into play at the time of the formal evaluation, and *(b)* well concealed on the rating instrument itself. Thus industrial firms seeking to devise objective rating systems first decide, in an arbitrary manner, what dimensions are to be rated, . . . usually including some items having little to do with organizational effectiveness while excluding others that do. Only then does Personnel Division churn out official-looking documents on which all dimensions chosen to be rated are assigned point values, categories, or whatever (6, p. 92).

Nonetheless, many individuals seek to establish simple, quantifiable standards against which to measure and reward performance. Such efforts may be successful in highly predictable areas within an organization, but are likely to cause goal displacement when applied anywhere else. Overconcern with attendance and lateness in the insurance firm and with number of people placed in the vocational rehabilitation division may have been largely responsible for the problems described in those organizations.

Overemphasis on Highly Visible Behaviors

Difficulties often stem from the fact that some parts of the task are highly visible while other parts are not. For example, publications are easier to demonstrate than teaching, and scoring baskets and hitting home runs are more readily observable than feeding teammates and advancing base runners. Similarly, the adverse consequences of pronouncing a sick person well are more visible than those sustained by labeling a well person sick. Team-building and creativity are other examples of behaviors which may not be rewarded simply because they are hard to observe.

Hypocrisy

In some of the instances described the rewarder may have been getting the desired behavior, notwithstanding claims that the behavior was not desired. This may be true, for example, of management's attitude toward apple-polishing in the manufacturing firm (a behavior which subordinates felt was rewarded, despite management's avowed dislike of the practice). This also may explain politicians' unwillingness to revise the penalties for disobedience of ecology laws, and the failure of top management to devise reward systems which would cause systematic evaluation of training and development programs.

Emphasis on Morality or Equity Rather than Efficiency

Some consideration of other factors prevents the establishment of a system which rewards behaviors desired by the rewarder. The felt obligation of many Americans to vote for one candidate or another, for example, may impair their ability to withhold support from politicians who refuse to discuss the issues. Similarly, the concern for spreading the risks and costs of wartime military service may outweigh the advantage to be obtained by commiting personnel to combat until the war is over.

It should be noted that only with respect to the first two causes are reward systems really paying off for other than desired behaviors. In the case of the third and fourth causes the system *is* rewarding behaviors desired by the rewarder, and the systems are fouled up only from the standpoints of those who believe the rewarder's public statements (cause 3), or those who seek to maximize efficiency rather than other outcomes (cause 4).

Conclusions

Modern organization theory requires a recognition that the members of organizations and society possess divergent goals and motives. It therefore is unlikely that managers and their subordinates will seek the same outcomes. Three possible remedies for this potential problem are suggested.

Selection

It is theoretically possible for organizations to employ only those individuals whose goals and motives are wholly consonant with those of management. In such cases the same behaviors judged by subordinates to be rational would be perceived by management as desirable. State-of-the-art reviews of selection techniques, however, provide scant grounds for hope that such an approach would be successful (for example, see 12).

Training

Another theoretical alternative is for the organization to admit those employees whose goals are not consonant with those of management and then, through training, socialization, or whatever, alter employee goals to make them consonant. However, research on the effectiveness of such training programs, though limited, provides further grounds for pessimism (for example, see 3).

Altering the Reward System

What would have been the result if:

1. Nixon had been assured by his advisors that he could not win reelection except by discussing the issues in detail?
2. Physicians' conduct was subjected to regular examination by review boards for type 1 errors (calling healthy people ill) and to penalties (fines, censure, etc.) for errors of either type?
3. The President of XYZ Corporation had to choose between *(a)* spending $11 million for antipollution equipment, and *(b)* incurring a 50-50 chance of going to jail for five years?

Managers who complain that their workers are not motivated might do well to consider the possibility that they have installed reward systems which are paying off for behaviors other than those they are seeking. This, in part, is what happened in Vietnam, and this is what regularly frustrates societal efforts to bring about honest politicians, civic-minded managers, etc. This certainly is what happened in both the manufacturing and the insurance companies.

A first step for such managers might be to find out what behaviors currently are being rewarded. Perhaps an instrument similar to that used in the manufacturing firm could be useful for this purpose. Chances are excellent that these managers will be surprised by what they find—that their firms are not rewarding what they assume they are. In fact, such undesirable behavior by organizational members as they have observed may be explained largely by the reward systems in use.

This is not to say that all organizational behavior is determined by formal rewards and punishments. Certainly it is true that in the absence of formal reinforcement some soldiers will be patriotic, some presidents will be ecology-minded, and some orphanage directors will care about children. The point, however, is that in such cases the rewarder is not *causing* the behaviors desired but is only a fortunate bystander. For an organization to *act* upon its members, the formal reward system should positively reinforce desired behaviors, not constitute an obstacle to be overcome.

It might be wise to underscore the obvious fact that there is nothing really new in what has been said. In both theory and practice these matters have been mentioned before. Thus in many states Good Samaritan laws have been installed to protect doctors who stop to assist a stricken motorist. In states without such laws it is commonplace for doctors to refuse to stop, for fear of involvement in a subsequent lawsuit. In college basketball additional penalties have been instituted against players who foul their opponents deliberately. It has long been argued by Milton Friedman and others that penalties should be altered so as to make it irrational to disobey the ecology laws, and so on.

By altering the reward system the organization escapes the necessity of selecting only desirable people or of trying to alter undesirable ones. In Skinnerian terms (as described in 11, p. 704), "As for responsibility and goodness—as commonly defined—no one . . . would want or need them. They refer to a man's behaving well despite the absence of positive reinforcement that is obviously sufficient to explain it. Where such reinforcement exists, 'no one needs goodness.'"

References

1. Barnard, Chester I. *The functions of the executive.* Cambridge, Mass.: Harvard University Press, 1964.
2. Blau, Peter M., & Scott, W. Richard. *Formal organizations.* San Francisco: Chandler, 1962.
3. Fiedler, Fred E. Predicting the effects of leadership training and experience from the contingency model. *Journal of Applied Psychology,* 1972, 56, 114–119.
4. Garland, L. H. Studies of the accuracy of diagnostic procedures. *American Journal Roentgenological, Radium Therapy Nuclear Medicine,* 1959, 82, 25–38.
5. Kerr, Steven. Some modifications in MBO as an OD strategy. *Academy of Management Proceedings,* 1973, pp. 39–42.

6. Kerr, Steven. What price objectivity? *American Sociologist*, 1973, 8, 92–93.
7. Litwin, G. H., & Stringer, R. A., Jr. *Motivation and organizational climate.* Boston: Harvard University Press, 1968.
8. Perrow, Charles. The analysis of goals in complex organizations. In A. Etzioni (Ed.), *Readings on Modern Organizations.* Englewood Cliffs, N.J.: Prentice-Hall, 1969.
9. Scheff, Thomas J. Decision rules, types of error, and their consequences in medical diagnosis. In F. Massarik & P. Ratoosh (Eds.), *Mathematical Explorations in Behavioral Science.* Homewood, Ill.: Irwin, 1965.
10. Simon, Herbert A. *Administrative behavior.* New York: Free Press, 1957.
11. Swanson, G. E. Review symposium: Beyond freedom and dignity. *American Journal of Sociology*, 1972, 78, 702–705.
12. Webster, E. *Decision making in the employment interview.* Montreal: Industrial Relations Center, McGill University, 1964.

Issues

1. Identify three possible categories or types of rewards that a company can give and give examples of rewards in each category.
2. Who (or what) determines whether a reward is given in an organization?
3. Identify possible performance related criteria for each of the following workers:
   a. a typist in a typing pool
   b. fertilizer salesman
   c. a university professor
   d. the foreman of a machine shop
   e. an employment counselor
   f. the president of an automobile corporation
4. Is it enough that performance criteria are objective in nature? That is, are there additional qualifications for a good performance measure?

36

The Promotion Decision

Background

The Bosch Corporation, a foundry in Olathe, Kansas, needs to select two new supervisors in their mold department. Each supervisor is responsible for one shift of eight work groups. Each work group has a work group leader and five to eight workers; the leader and workers are all union members. Preliminary screening of the work group leaders has narrowed the list to six candidates. The accompanying report was prepared by the Personnel Department staff from information gathered from work records, interviews, tests, and semi-annual performance appraisals.

Bosch has the policy of a firm commitment to equal opportunity for all workers based strictly on relevant work criteria. The plant is unionized and the management ranks have few blacks (less than 5%) and fewer women than the union employees. To promote this policy, a management committee was formed to make all managerial promotion decisions.

The performance records of these six individuals have been carefully scrutinized. Average performance over a two-year period is shown in the Personnel Report. These data are to be used by the committee to make the final choices.

1. Each group is to rank all six employees with the top two employees to be selected for the promotions. A group consensus should be the final step in reaching agreement. The group should also develop a statement supporting their decision.
2. The group decisions should be placed on a board or chart in front of all class members and discussed.

Issues

1. What parts of the Personnel Report did your group emphasize? Why?
2. Rank the eight criteria in terms of their (1) objectivity and (2) usefulness to your decision.

209

Personnel Report

	Work Group Performance			Managerial Ratings				
	Production Rate (%)	Scrap Rate (%)	Unit Cost ($)	Attitude	Grievances Filed Against (Annual)	Depend-ability	Initiative	Managerial Aptitude Test Score
—Gregorio Diaz Chicano male, 32 2 years college 10 years with Bosch	94.6	2.7	1.01	Fair	8	Good	Good	81
—Robert Friedman White male, 29 High School diploma 10 years with Bosch	91.2	3.1	1.05	Good	6	Good	Fair	89
—Susan Rizzo White female, 31 7 years college 7 years with Bosch	94.8	2.4	.99	Good	12	Good	Fair	80
—Elroy Harris Black male, 33 High School diploma 6 years with Bosch	90.9	5.9	1.10	Excellent	7	Very Good	Good	79
—Dave Smith White male, 30 B.S. Philosophy 6 years with Bosch	98.3	5.4	1.01	Good	5	Very Good	Good	92
—George Puckett White male, 35 High School diploma 10 years with Bosch	95.0	4.3	.99	Good	2	Excellent	Fair	85

3. What additional information concerning each employee would you like to have
   seen to assist in making your decision? What information do you believe should
   have been omitted?
4. Should the immediate superior of the supervisors have been allowed (or required)
   to make this decision alone? Why (or why not)?

James L. Gibson, John M. Ivancevich
and James H. Donnelly, Jr.

37

A New Leadership Position

The Dancey Electronics Company is located in a suburb of Dallas. Management forecasts indicated that the company would enjoy moderate growth during the next ten years. This growth rate would require the promotion of a number of individuals to newly created positions of general manager which would, in turn, require them to spend most of their time working with departmental managers, and less time on production, output, and cost issues.

The majority of present candidates for the three new general manager positions had been with the company for at least 15 years. They were all skilled in the production aspects of operations. Don Kelly, the vice president, felt, however, that none of the candidates had the training or overall insight into company problems to move smoothly into the general manager positions. The board of directors had decided that the three new general managers would be recruited from within Dancey despite these anticipated problems.

Dancey, in attempting to find the best candidates for the new position, hired a consulting firm, Management Analysis Corporation (MAC), to perform an internal search for qualified individuals. Through interviews, testing, and a review of company records, the consulting firm generated a list of six candidates.

One of the candidates found by MAC was Joe Morris. The analysis used to assess Joe involved the study of environmental variables and his current style of leadership. Exhibit 1 presents a profile of Joe's leadership style and various environmental factors which have some impact on this style.

Joe's present style, which is reflected as being high in task orientation and low in relationship orientation, is similar to the style of the other five general

James Gibson, John Ivancevich, and James Donnelly, Jr., *Organizations: Behavior, Structure, Processes.* (Dallas, TX.: Business Publications, 1979), pp. 94–96. © 1979 by Business Publications, Inc.

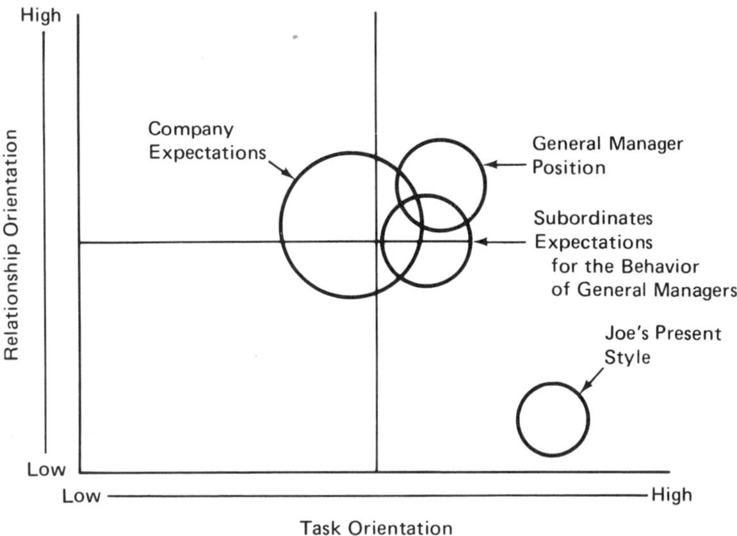

EXHIBIT 1. Morris Profile of Leadership

manager candidates. The expectations of the company, the potential subordinates of the general manager, and the new position of general manager are not consistent with Joe's or any of the other candidates' present leadership styles. The . . . , intersecting area indicates where the expectations of the company, the new position, and subordinates would be consistent. This is assumed by MAC to be the ideal leadership style for candidates to use once they are promoted to the general manager position.

If Joe or any of the other candidates accepted the general manager jobs, they would have to significantly increase their relationships orientation. If they did not change their orientation there would be, according to the consulting firm, a high probability of failure.

Don Kelly was extremely adamant about not going outside of Dancey to find three potentially successful new general managers. He and the entire board of directors wanted to utilize a recruitment-from-within policy to secure the three best general managers. It was Don's belief that a leader could modify the style of leadership he or she has used to meet new situational demands. This belief, and the internal recruitment plan, led Don to call a meeting to discuss a program to improve the compatibility between the three general managers finally selected—Joe Morris, Randy Cooper, and Gregg Shumate—and the environmental factors: the company, the subordinates, and the requirements of the new position.

Issues

1. Do you believe the diagnosis and resulting profile prepared by the Management Analysis Corporation was a necessary step in the process of finding a potentially successful group of general managers? Explain.
2. What alternatives are available to modify the potential effectiveness of Joe Morris in the new general manager position?
3. Why will it be difficult for Joe Morris to modify his style of leadership?

Organizational Behavior: Perspective for Tomorrow

38

The Swing to Practicality in the B-Schools

Not long ago, Harvard Business School found itself the focus of an unwelcome spate of publicity as the press picked up on Harvard University President Derek C. Bok's less-than-complimentary annual report to the Board of Overseers. In it, Bok questioned the B-school's almost single-minded emphasis on the case-history method of teaching. He strongly suggested that the school attempt to make its offerings more relevant to today's business by providing students with a better grounding in ethical standards and in corporate planning amid current social and regulatory upheavals.

While such a public display of academic infighting is both unique and particularly embarrassing for one of the most prestigious business schools, Bok's comments reflect a growing concern inside universities and the business community that B-school instruction should be tailored more to fit the experiences of the real world.

Clearly, this is a tumultuous time for B-schools. An unprecedented number of their deans—65 in all—are resigning or retiring this year, including Stanford University's Arjay Miller and Harvard's Lawrence E. Fouraker. Although many of these departures are normal retirements, the sheer number of resignations this year suggests to some observers that university administrations are scrambling to make their schools more responsive to the real needs of business. As Jack D. Steele, dean of the Graduate School of Business Administration at the University of Southern California, puts it, "[Too] many schools are now coming up with answers to questions that nobody is asking."

Deficiencies

Much of the pressure for change, however, is coming from outside the schools. An increasingly vocal cadre of businessmen is saying that it is about time the schools update their curriculums. "History is important," says

Reprinted from the July 23, 1979 issue of *Business Week* by special permission, © 1979 by McGraw-Hill, Inc., New York, N.Y. 10020. All rights reserved.

Peter C. Krist, senior vice-president at Mobil Oil Corp., "but [the students] spend all their time reading cases instead of *The Wall Street Journal.* American business spends tremendous sums repairing the deficiencies of the education system." A recent editorial in *Consultants News* charges that B-schools have grown far too "scholarly" and that behavioral sciences have replaced line experience as determinants of academic content. But perhaps the most scathing critique comes from Michel C. Bergerac, chairman of Revlon Inc.: "The American educational system has devised the very difficult trick of graduating the most ill-educated people at the highest cost."

To their credit, most B-schools now are taking steps to prepare their graduates better for the practical demands of business. Many have introduced courses on the increased use of computers as management tools, the growing internationalization of American business, and other relatively new trends.

A Fine Line

Some B-schools are trying to spread managerial gospel to the noncorporate world, through courses on public sector management and the like, because businesses deal increasingly with government and the public. Others are narrowing the gap between business and "professional" education through joint programs with law schools, engineering schools, and even medical schools. And recently, a plethora of programs has been developed for seasoned executives who want to update and sharpen their skills.

In essence, the schools are trying to restore the balance between the theoretical and practical by injecting a little more of the latter into their offerings. It means walking a fine line between what USC's Steele calls "esoteric meaninglessness on the one hand and vocationalism on the other." To do that, the Wharton School now relegates most pure research functions to a 45-person staff with only minor classroom responsibility, yet maintains a teaching faculty that may be low on research orientation but high on business experience. "We feel it is O.K. for our [teachers] to get a little cutting oil under their fingernails," notes Wharton Dean Donald C. Carroll.

Other schools increasingly import ideas, as well as guest speakers, from the corporate world. Columbia University's Graduate School of Business, for example, has established a series of advisory committees in such areas as marketing and accounting. The committees comprise corporate executives who meet periodically with faculty members to brainstorm about both current trends and major issues 5 or 10 years down the road. Similarly, at the University of Pittsburgh's Graduate School of Business, professors meet every six weeks with executives from Rockwell International Corp. to discuss such topics as the cancellation of the B-1 bomber and minority business development.

'The Best Mesh'

The participating business themselves often benefit from such exchanges. The University of Chicago, long known as a bastion of theoretical research, is now offering "laboratory" courses in new products and advertising that involve sending second-year students out to work on actual problems at local companies. Last winter the advertising students developed a successful campaign to promote Gator-Ade, a soft drink made by Stokely-Van Camp Inc., while the new-products students ran a simulated test-marketing program for a new product they proposed to Kraft Inc.'s "Mini-Meal" line. Now, Kraft is considering undertaking its own test-marketing of the product.

Meanwhile, the students are gushing in their praise for the program. "The course with Kraft offered the best mesh of education and real-world experience of any course I have taken," says Gary Kash, who has since graduated to become a brand marketing assistant at General Foods Corp.

Although such lab courses still remain rare, numerous schools are trying to get that same balance between the academic and the real world by adopting some new courses. Some, including Wharton, New York University, Amos Tuck, Chicago, and Case Western Reserve, are not only emphasizing courses on computers, basic economics, statistics, and other practical components of management education but are also trying to teach students how to grapple with the new business environment. Carnegie-Mellon University, for one, is offering a new course in "benefit-cost analysis" that shows students how to weigh the impact of new government regulations on business. William R. Dill, dean of NYU's B-school, notes that "the process of business planning is now as open to public scrutiny as the final results," and he has returned to the classroom to teach a course called "Management in a Kibitzer's Society." The course focuses on the demands on business from consumerism, regulatory fervor, and the like, and teaches students to speak the language of environmentalists, religious leaders, and others who shape the context in which their business operates.

Wharton, too, has added several "context" courses, including one on business ethics developed with the American Philosophical Assn. and sponsored by the National Endowment for the Humanities. "The nitty-gritty without the context is dangerous stuff," maintains Wharton's Carroll. "It's hard to find a business problem today without some sort of environmental, regulatory, or social component."

The Public Sector

The schools are also defining the context of business more broadly to include nonbusiness organizations and professions. More than a dozen B-schools, including Harvard, Case Western, and Carnegie-Mellon, now are offering courses, or even joint degrees, in business and law, business and engineering, public sector and fine arts management, and health care. Fully one-sixth of Stanford's business students have signed up for a course in public management, which emphasizes how business can show government ways to improve its performance. "The public sector has got to get more efficient," insists Dean Miller. On the international front, many schools have established programs on international finance and marketing, and a few have even established exchange programs with overseas schools. NYU, for example, currently exchanges about 10 of its best final-year students with schools in France and England. Dill says that plans are in the works for similar student exchanges with Sweden, Spain, Germany, Brazil, Hong Kong, and possibly even the Soviet Union.

Because so much of the course material is new and relevant to today's business problems, many experienced executives, including many who already hold MBA degrees, are returning to B-schools to update their training. Donald P. Jacobs, dean of Northwestern University's B-school, calls education at the executive level "the major frontier for management education," and, in fact, new courses for executives are drawing students in droves. At USC, the number of advanced management and executive education courses has grown since 1975 from 5, with 400 students, to 35, with 2,200 students. And at Stanford, such courses brought in $1.4 million in 1978, a 300% increase from 10 years ago. Indeed, the dramatic rise in popularity of executive retraining programs may be the strongest evidence yet that the B-schools are achieving their goal of dealing with contemporary business issues. Explains Stanford's Miller: "Change is so rapid that businessmen have to come back to campus now to have their batteries recharged."

Issues

1. What does a management student need to learn to prepare for managerial work?
2. What can a student learn in a school of management? What *can't* a student learn?
3. What do employer's look for in a management student? In the first interview— probably in your school's placement office—what does the interviewer want to know? to see? Perhaps you can share job interview experiences with the class.

Recommended Reading

J. Sterling Livingston, "Myth of the well-educated manager," *Harvard Business Review*, January–February 1971, 79–89.

39

Capitalizing on Social Change

When it comes to predicting the future, most managers have long been preoccupied with financial plans and economic forecasts, nearly to the exclusion of any attempts to foresee many long-term social and political changes that can affect their operations dramatically. Yet many have found that such social short-sightedness—particularly in an age of consumer activism and societal protest—can be just as costly as laxity in tracking economic trends.

General Motors Corp. and other auto makers paid dearly for failing to recognize early enough that Ralph Nader's objection to the Corvair model was a forerunner of a broad-based consumer movement for safer products and tougher liability standards. Similarly, by ignoring early warnings from environmentalists, hundreds of manufacturers were forced to retrofit plants with pollution-control gear that could have been incorporated more cheaply in the original plant design. More recently, Nestlé Co. faced a worldwide boycott of its products after it seemingly ignored the public outcry against its marketing of infant formula in underdeveloped countries where it was a far too expensive substitute for mother's milk.

Such costly mistakes, however, may at last be driving home the importance of watching social trends, and recently a number of companies have begun expanding their forecasts well beyond the realm of economics. Some have set up internal departments to predict the future social and political environment in which they will operate, while others are relying on a growing number of consultants who specialize in such crystal-ball gazing. Social predictions even are trickling into strategic plans, and line managers increasingly are called to task for not following them as closely as technical or pricing trends. The ultimate goal is to prevent unexpected social changes from wreaking havoc with profitability. As Robert L. Thaler, a senior vice-president at Security Pacific National Bank, puts it: "If we don't manage social change, change will manage us."

Reprinted from the October 29, 1979 issue of *Business Week* by special permission, © 1979 by McGraw-Hill, Inc., New York, N.Y. 10020. All rights reserved.

Cooperative Effort

While this new interest in assessing the business impact of future social changes often goes no further than informal discussions among managers, some formal forecasting programs do exist, and occasionally, they even transcend traditional corporate rivalries. For example, executives from such companies as AT&T, IBM, and Sperry—all fierce competitors—are sharing their techniques under the auspices of the Diebold Corporate Issues Program (DCIP), sponsored by Diebold Group Inc., New York-based management consultants. For nearly three years, the 20-member corporate group has been meeting periodically to discuss such questions as whether communications breakthroughs will push more employees into working at home, or how companies should change their product development techniques to anticipate any future environmental or consumer concerns.

The executives also explore changing demographics and value systems and, most important, tell each other about structures—new research departments, shifting lines of authority, and the like—they have set up within their organizations to forecast and react to social change. The group's main concern, says Robert F. Kamm, DCIP's director, is that "more and more traditionally non-P&L items are affecting profit and loss."

Corporations within and outside the DCIP are experimenting on their own with ways to keep that effect positive by focusing more closely on social trends. One popular method is "environmental scanning," which involves extensive reading of publications to identify various social and political factors that will help shape the future business environment. For example, PPG Industries Inc. recently hired Cynthia S. Angrist, a Carnegie-Mellon University sociologist, to fill the newly created post of manager of public policy research. She scans the publications of government agencies, public interest groups, research institutes, and other periodicals. She pays particular attention to politically extreme publications or to futurist journals, such as *Alternative Future*, all of which usually run counter to the way corporate America thinks. At management's request, Angrist also researches specific issues, such as a proposed law or an apparent cultural trend, and prepares reports on the issue's long-term ramifications for the company. Although Angrist admits that PPG has not yet managed the formal integration of social, political, and economic trends into its strategic plans, she says her weekly briefings with the company's chairman are evidence that there is "interest at the highest level."

Scanners

Still other coporations are increasingly employing outside research services and consultants specializing in the kind of scanning work that Angrist does. For example, IU International Corp. retains consultant Kurt Lewin, a New York-based economist and specialist on social and political developments

---

abroad, and IU Vice-Chairman Robert F. Calman says Lewin has helped his company ascertain the "mood" of foreign countries, IU also uses Williams Inference Service, a private environmental scanning group, which monitors and analyzes 150 publications each week.

Calman believes that nearly every social trend that will affect business 20 years from now is being "previewed" today somewhere, and he says he employs scanners out of "fear of missing a big opportunity or stepping into a crack." Apparently, Calman's concerns are shared. Although Williams Inference has been around for 15 years, it shuffled along with about six clients for the first 11 years, then signed on nearly 60 more in the last four years alone.

Ironically, even founder James S. Williams admits that scanning reports are often read for entertainment. Nevertheless, some companies are now making organizational changes to make sure that these reports and other social indicators are heeded by managers.

A prime example is Mead Corp.'s Human & Environmental Protection Dept. In just six years, the group has evolved from a run-of-the-mill environmental watchdog staff, sequestered in the research department, to a major part of the company's planning function. Russell E. Kross, the department's director, says it now reviews each of Mead's one- and five-year plans to make sure that they meet regulatory requirements. But in Mead's site-selection process for new plants, the company goes beyond legal issues to include such things as community sentiment. "In the past, we would say 'We've got to build here,'" Kross recalls, noting that the decision to zero in on one site was often based solely on conventional economic factors. Now, he says, Mead routinely selects three or four potential sites for new plants and evaluates each one for impact on local schools, traffic patterns, and the like before committing itself to a single site.

Hiring Its Critics

A few corporations are even eliciting the help of their critics in identifying future trouble spots. Velsicol Chemical Corp., apparently tired of its costly fights with the Environmental Protection Agency and various environmentalists, recently hired two former EPA officials and gave one of them line responsibility—complete with a full budget—to make sure that Velsicol's plants and products meet current safety standards. But a major part of their job is preventing any future problems as well. For example, Velsicol recently trucked fresh water at a cost of $1,200 a week for five months to homes in Tennessee when a preliminary report showed a possible chance that the company's landfill could contaminate wells (BW—May 28).

A handful of companies have become downright formal about factoring social and political concerns into strategic plans. Every Wednesday, for example, 13 top vice-presidents at Security Pacific National Bank check all plans against a rundown of relevant external factors provided regularly by the 16-person in-house staff that handles the company's environmental scanning. When that staff projected that 75% of married women will be working by 1990, the committee decided that the trend calls for more automatic teller machines, pay-by-phone setups, and automatic payroll deposits to speed up banking for busy women. Concurrently, it is looking carefully at its original plan to build more suburban branches.

All of these companies, however, still face a major hurdle in getting operating managers to think beyond the next quarter. "Managers with profit-and-loss responsibility only look at larger issues when they are dragged in kicking and screaming," admits Richard R. Mau, vice-president of corporate and government relations for Sperry Corp. Thus, Sperry, Allied Chemical Corp., and others are tinkering with traditional employee education, appraisal, and incentive plans to spur line managers to grapple with social developments.

Measuring Success

Allied has perhaps the most ambitious program. Since 1974 it has been sending high-level managers through three-day corporate ethics seminars, which deal with situations ranging from questionable gifts and payments to handling employees during a plant closing. Charles J. Bischoff, Allied's director of management resources, says the seminars will eventually include middle managers. Moreover, since 1976, Allied has included a manager's contribution to the community in evaluations for incentive bonuses. "We felt the pocketbook was a good place to attract people's attention," Bischoff says.

Measuring the results of a company's increased awareness to social trends is anything but an exact science. "We measure success by the lack of negative results," concedes DCIP's Kamm.

Still, DCIP members seem to feel they get their money's worth. J. Paul Lyet, Sperry chairman, claims that once a company indicates to its own employees that it is a positive force in the communities in which it operates, the bottom-line payout comes in lowered turnover and improved morale. But Lyet, too, stresses that concentrating on social and political factors is as important as preventive medicine. "It dawned on me," he says, "that it was external factors over which we have no control that influence the stock." As he sums it up, "I realized that many little seeds could flower into bushes of poison ivy."

Issues

1. List and discuss potential sources for information about the future. What sort of information would be useful to: (1) a computer manufacturer, (2) an automobile manufacturer, (3) a national fast-food franchise corporation, or (4) a regional grocery chain?

2. What does "demographics" mean? How do changes in demographics affect business decisions concerning (1) marketing, (2) personnel selection and training, (3) job design, or (4) the traditional 40 hour work week?
3. What is meant by the statement: "if we don't manage social change, change will manage us." Give examples.

Robert Schrank

Sociologist

The Topeka dry dog food plant is run around the clock by 120 employees. It offers an interesting contrast between a continuous process operation and a more traditional manufacturing-type operation in packaging and warehousing. The first employees were recruited specifically for this new experimental plant more than five years ago. About 1,200 people applied for jobs. Sixty-three were hired. In hiring, the emphasis was on a high level of initiative, decision-making ability, and most important, the ability to work as part of a team.

Topeka has a forty-hour, five-day work week and no time clocks. Benefits include nine holidays, two weeks' vacation a year, five days' sick leave (approved by the group team leader), and hospitalization through a major insurance concern.

The management people, who are identifiable from the rest of the work force, emphasized to me repeatedly that it is easier to start up a new plant based on autonomous work teams than it is to introduce these concepts into an existing plant, and that things are made more difficult if there is a union contract. One manager said, "When you have a union situation, you have very different problems. You are limited by the collective-bargaining process."

The number of people in the Topeka plant is small, and employees do express the feeling that they have freedom to communicate with anyone they want, but the size of the plant was not considered a critical factor in developing the autonomous work teams. The Topeka managers felt a critical variable was the size of the work group, not the plant. The number seventeen seemed to be maximum workable group size, affording optimum communication within the team. They then cited a second critical element for a successful work group: The need for a basic trust relationship between the employees and management. One manager said, "If you can win trust, then employees will accept what you are doing; and in order to win trust there

Reprinted from *Ten Thousand Working Days* by Robert Schrank by permission of the MIT Press, Cambridge, Massachusetts. Copyright © 1978 by Massachusetts Institute of Technology.

must be full participation, good communication, and an open atmosphere in the plant."

There is some evidence, however, to suggest that the question of participation and openness is very much related to plant magnitudes. It is one thing to have an open administrative management style in a plant of thirty or forty people per shift. It is yet another thing in a plant of two thousand or ten thousand. It is like comparing a mom-and-pop grocery with A & P. The number of people working in a plant is a critical variable determining the level of openness, for in a large organization there is an inevitable control factor. I believe that to achieve a participative atmosphere, small operating units are required.

Gaines dog food consists of corn, soya, premixed vitamins, and meat meal. The processing section is automated and percentages of the mix are predetermined. The processing group, or team, consists of eight people per shift. They run the entire processing operation, beginning with the receipt of raw materials by freight cars that dump them into floor bins, where they are weighed and then conveyed to storage. The raw materials are then mixed, coated with tallow to make the dogs eat it, and colored red so the dog owners think it is meat. This whole operation is monitored by a computer on the fifth floor with an eight-by-thirty-foot control panel divided into five or six different sections full of red pilot lights. Two or three people might be in the control room at any one time, monitoring the process computer. The objective of the processing group is to produce a minimum of 100 tons of dog food per shift, as well as to assure the packaging room that they never run out of material for packaging.

The processing team has few routine functions. They do a small amount of maintenance, such as periodic lubrication, and monitor the equipment to try and avoid breakdowns. They may attempt to speed up the equipment and try to surpass the 100-ton-a-shift objective. A red light may go on, signaling a malfunction; the men in the control room will decide what to do. They say that sometimes dog food clogs a chute, or is hung up in one of the feeder bins, and it has to be cleared. The processing team is a somewhat typical maintenance crew, where initiative, decision making, and teamwork are essential to the smooth functioning of the process—not that unusual for this type of operation. But there is something else here; this group of workers, like other maintenance people, have a lot of freedom at their workplace, which may contribute to a high level of satisfaction. This is a correlation that may be more universal than is now acknowledged. One of the processors, who had been a machinist on the Santa Fe railroad, said, "I like the Gaines plant 300 percent better because I am not stuck in one place turning railroad wheels on a lathe. Now, as a troubleshooter, I am free to roam around the plant anyplace, anytime. I can stop and talk to people. The day goes like that."

While they kept an eye on that big board, we schmoozed about whether it is better to live in the city or the country, whether girls in Topeka had given up wearing brassieres, and what unions can do for you anyhow. Somebody suggested, "Why don't we speed the mill grinder or the conveyer a bit?" That precipitated the pushing of a button. Then we went back to schmoozing. Schmoozing is common in offices, universities, processing plants, and many service industries. It occurs less in manufacturing plants, and ofttimes workers have figured out the most ingenious ways to do it surreptitiously.

The degree to which employees are permitted to visit, have access to a variety of areas, use the telephone may be a critical element in humanizing a workplace. The scope of schmoozing does not have to do with the work itself, as suggested by Herzberg and others, but is influenced by the nature of the work and how it is organized. Most manufacturing plants, unfortunately, are designed with a maximum amount of employee time at a given place. I consider this an important dissatisfier because it deprives factory workers of freedoms enjoyed by many white-collar and service workers.

One of the first things I would do for blue-collar workers to increase their work satisfaction is to grant them one equal right that the rest of us take for granted, the free use of a telephone at work. Those of us who can reach for a phone any time we wish underestimate its role as a socializer and reliever of daily monotony and boredom. How many times during a working day might a white-collar worker or a professional pick up the phone and dial a friend? The phone conversation may be inconsequential or silly, but it helps relieve tedium and routine and so makes the workday seem easier. The telephone creates a vast network of intimate human contact in an otherwise impersonal world. Some people have thought this notion is quite impractical, yet I know at least two large manufacturing plants that have tried it and found no serious difficulties or abuses. Needless to say, the employees love it.

Like most people in other kinds of workplaces, workers understand the limitations on satisfying their needs and desires in the factory. They are very much aware of both the magic and the curse of mass production technology. It is magical to see raw material start in at one end of a plant and come out as a working thingamajig on the other. It may also be a curse to keep doing the same little task over and over again, but workers know that this is the secret of the magic. They understand this as a group; it is "our secret." They make the best of the life in the plant with humor and camaraderie. When they do participate in decision making, it is mostly through collective bargaining for controls over safety, agreements on productivity levels, and so forth.

While the processing part of the Topeka plant is a modern, automated operation, the warehousing and packaging is in many ways quite traditional. Workers stand all day long at filling stations, holding or feeding boxes or bags under a chute that fills them with a preweighed amount. The containers then go onto a conveyer to a sewing machine that closes the bags, and then to a pallet for warehousing. I would characterize this work as highly repetitive, with little room for autonomy or growth, and no position to rise to but processing. Here there is also a lack of that critical job satisfier, the freedom to walk around and schmooze. (Yet, because workers, like the rest of us, are not of one mold, one worker said, "I like packaging because I do not want to think about the work anyway.") There may be a lesson in this example of two very different types of jobs in the same plant. Given the premise that some jobs like packaging and warehousing are lousy, and some lousy jobs are with us to stay, then maybe we need to rotate the "lousy work."

Much of the literature dealing with workplace problems uses Maslow's concept of a needs hierarchy as the theoretical base. I would argue that a more basic issue at stake is the relationship of the individual to the institution. Can an individual worker achieve autonomy, creativity, or self-actualization in an institution which has as its primary, and in many cases sole, objective increased profit? Some of us have argued that it is in the company's best interest to assure workers their higher order of needs. The trouble with this argument is that we have little evidence to support it. I am fearful that at least some of the definitions of workplace problems have grown out of the behavioral science gardens of people's needs, satisfactions, wishes, and wants. Some of the difficulty may be semantic; concepts such as needs, autonomy, and control are highly relative. I have been amused by how some intellectuals tend to view manual work as a kind of horror. They would be surprised that many manual workers are horrified at the prospect of having to sit at a desk and write all day. Our frame of reference may have more to do with how work is perceived than the claimed objectivity of a test or questionnaire. This raises our old question, "Compared to what?" Terms like needs, satisfaction, autonomy, growth, and, most important, alienation, have become so all-encompassing that I am not sure they have any distinct meaning any longer.

A basic difference between Marx and Maslow is that Marx's assumptions about alienation are based on the conflict between the private ownership of the means and products of production, and the social nature of the factory. Marx uses the term alienation to describe the factory worker's lack of control in his relationship to the raw material, the process or means, and the finished product. This concept is based on an economic and social relationship. Maslow's concept of alienation, on the other hand, is based primarily on the psychological needs of individuals.

It seems odd that many writers dealing with workers and workplace problems seized on the Maslow schema as an explanation of worker dissatisfaction without at least questioning the basis of such concepts as autonomy, participation, creativity, or self-actualization as they apply to mass production workplaces. I have a feeling that behavioral scientists who believe that these concepts can be easily applied to mass production technology are either ignorant of what goes on in manufacturing plants, or vulgarize the meaning of the concepts—which could be interpreted as creating straw men to avoid dealing with real ones, that is, excusing inadequate pay and poor working conditions by concentrating on individual psyches.

Any discussion of workplace problems requires some agreement on the definition of mass production technology. Mass production technology requires an operation that is predesigned, preengineered, and preplanned to the smallest detail in order to guarantee interchangeability of parts. In order to assure cost replication, every step of the production process is costed out and engineered to time. Schedules must be strictly adhered to. No deviation from a specification can be permitted or interchangeability would be threatened. Even the experimental Topeka plant embodied a natural hierarchy of jobs in the difference between packaging and processing. The successful completion of the final product, including costs, depends upon everyone adhering to a master plan. Given this as the basic nature of mass production, where can there be opportunities for autonomy, creativity, and self-actualization? Only by participating in an overall planning process where their inputs can be incorporated can workers really achieve those goals, yet that is the very aspect of work from which they have been excluded. I do not consider worker representation on corporate boards as addressing this problem. It is not an issue of formal representation but of a participatory process. If workers are barred from the planning, they are not represented.

Contemporary difficulty with with Marx's concept of alienation grows out of our doubts about whether what is called socialist, or worker, ownership and control over the means of production has given the workers on the plant floor any greater autonomy or participation than workers in capitalist countries. In so-called socialist countries, factory workers find themselves in a relationship with the means of production that seems to be endemic to factories: highly repetitive work, preplanned and preengineered with little or no participation in decision making. In Yugoslavia things seem to be different to the extent that workers have some say in how plants are run and who manages. The organization of the work and task performance remain similar to all factory production techniques. Marx's concept of alienation failed to note that alienation may be inherent in the nature of mass production technology *regardless of who owns it*. The socialist countries, far from finding a new way to produce things or a new model of work organization have, if anything, emulated the worst features of the capitalist efficiency system to its smallest detail.

The American labor movement has traditionally dealt with "alienation" by seeking more for its members in pay and benefits, while reducing the amount of time they have to spend at the job. Until we have found an alternative to our traditional way of organizing work, history may reveal that this has been the best response to a negative situation.

I believe that at least some of the suggestions for improving the quality of work life reflect a certain nostalgia for the return to craftsmanship. In his 1844 manuscripts, Marx expresses a sadness over the decline of the renaissance craftsman. Such concepts as autonomy, creativity, decision making, and control of one's tools are qualities that are associated with craftsmanship, and, to some extent, hand tools. While being extremely empathetic with that nostalgia, I am also convinced that notions of bringing back craftsmanship are based on either fantasy or ignorance about mass production. So little of the traditional craftsman survives that I hardly think we know anymore what the term means.

As a skilled machinist or toolmaker in the traditional sense, I was not a craftsman. I made no decisions about the raw material, the process, or the product. As distinguished from craftsmanship, my skill was the ability to follow extremely detailed instruction to very fine tolerances. That requires a certain kind of skill, not craftsmanship, and above all, not creativity. I remember an old boss repeating over and over, "Follow the instructions. Follow the prints. Do not deviate from the specifications."

What happened to craftsmanship? How did we evolve from craft to skill, from creativity and inventiveness to a life of following the instructions without deviation? In *Art and Industrial Revolution*, Klingender talks about the end of craftsmanship. The beginning of the end was signaled in 1830 when owners of the Wedgwood Pottery in England hired its first salesman to go out and find out what kind of pottery people were interested in buying. He came back with his report, "Make as many queen-on-a-horse motifs as you can. They'll buy them like hot cakes." Instead of leaving the design to the individual potters, as had traditionally been done, Wedgwood decided to hire a designer to create a series of ceramics with a queen-on-a-horse motif that could then be copied by the potters. That act of engaging a salesman and a designer, both of whom were responding to a market, was the beginning of the end of craftsmanship. Klingender says that because of the designer, the Wedgwood potter became, at best, an "inventor" who could now decide how to do it, but no longer what to do.

As engineers moved into factory production, the "how to do it" became the next victim. Now *companies* decided what was the best way to do it. The best known of these work engineers was Frederick Taylor. He was obsessed with the idea that a man should be a part of the machine. Thus, even the "inventor" trying to decide "how to do it" soon disappeared when equipment and machinery were designed for specific functions, and workers lost control over the method as well as the product.

The final blow came with the notion of interchangeability of parts. The result was Taylor's phenomenally successful effort to fragment all tasks to their smallest element so as to eliminate any possible judgment on the part of the worker—thus assuring no variation in the final product. And it worked. The factory proved to be productive beyond the engineers' wildest dreams. This success is called the industrial revolution; and that it was.

Many behavioral scientists who write on this subject fail to mention the role of the union at the workplace. Union people argue that factors which behavioral scientists refer to as autonomy, participation in decision making, self-esteem, openness, can be achieved only if employees feel they are not subject to the whims and fancies of management, particularly first-line supervisors. This was well illustrated in the Volvo plant. Trade unionists point out that people at the production level are often the victims of new production schemes that ignore their interests. The General Foods planners consulted with the first-level supervisors in the planning for Topeka, but participation of the workers in the planning process was nonexistent. Could the union have been involved in the planning for Topeka? This is a difficult question to answer since the union was not asked, and even if it were, I am not at all certain that it would have been able or willing to do so. Yet it seems clear that it needs to be part of the total planning effort.

On the plant level, a well-functioning union may be an expression of the best humanitarian qualities of the work force. People concerned with quality of work life need to understand more about the role of unions beyond strict contract bargaining. Unfortunately, many consultants on work reorganization are employed by management, and so they tend to be less than fearless on this issue. However, if the unions insist on limiting their role to traditional collective bargaining issues, the question of workplace reorganization may just pass them by. The UAW has begun to recognize this in bargaining with the auto industry. Joint committees have been established to examine issues of workplace organization and operation. This is a step forward for a major union. People concerned with workplace changes need to understand that unions have been dealing with these problems for a long time and therefore are an important arena for participation. Without their involvement, the suspicion that workplace changes are designed to counter union organization will continue to grow.

Even the most recent American experiments that do include union involvement, the autonomous work group at the Rushton Coal Mine in Pennsylvania and the Harmon Industries plant in Bolivar, Tennessee, are experiencing serious difficulties with their work reorganization experiments. The troubles they are encountering lend at least some credence to my fears.

The Rushton experiment took place in a mine of 120 workers. As a result of extensive negotiations between the company, the United Mine Workers, and a group of behavioral scientists at the University of Pennsylvania, an agreement was reached to develop an autonomous work section in the mine. An autonomous work group was formed by seventeen volunteers working on two shifts.

Rushton's troubles have grown out of conflicting motives of the principal groups involved in the experiment. Miners who volunteered to participate in the experiment were hopeful of better salaries and a more satisfying way of going about their daily work. The company's primary interest was the possibility of increased production. The United Mine Workers wanted to find ways to improve the safety conditions in mining work. The behavioral scientists wanted to develop an experimental setting in which they could test some of their ideas regarding autonomous work groups. It is to be expected that each of these participating groups would have their own goals. What they needed was an understanding of their respective motives, and this is a process of negotiation and compromise. What could have emerged from such a procedure were common goals that all groups felt they could work toward. It was when the goals of the "others" were undermined or ignored that trust began to fade and the alliance was in trouble.

At Rushton, an agreement had been made by the company to share the benefits from increased productivity with the workers. When it was time to come through, the company hesitated, insisting that it was unable to detect measurable increases in production. This argument continued for the duration of the experiment, seriously eroding the trust of workers in the entire process. Similarly, the union felt its power eroding when the company decided, without consultation, to expand the experiment to the whole mine. As grievances were increasingly handled through the autonomous group structure rather than through the traditional union procedure, it was perceived as an additional threat to the union's authority to represent the workers.

The insensitivity of the behavioral scientists to the union's position, and to the traditional adversary relationship between company and workers, seemed to weaken their ability to confront the power issues squarely and try to help the concerned parties to achieve a solution. The confrontation might not have worked, but then in the last analysis neither has the experiment.

From the behavioral scientists' point of view, there were further difficulties with the Rushton experiment. How could a small autonomous section of a mine exist within an operation that was thoroughly hierarchical? Similarly, this problem of experiment in isolation was experienced in the Topeka plant, a fragile oasis in the General Foods conglomerate. Perhaps one answer to this problem is that the rest of a work community where an experiment is taking place needs to be informed and, if possible, included in the process. They cannot be treated as outsiders, for eventually their lack of information will lead to resistance and even sabotage, as seems to have occurred at General Foods. Another possible way to address the problem of isolation is to prepare the participants in the experiment for the experience. A question that needs to be asked is, how do we train or help people learn how to be autonomous or how to accept authority for themselves? One of the weaknesses of the Rushton experience was that the experimental group-training sessions of workers and supervisors centered almost exclusively on safety issues. They might have done better had they focused on how to prepare people for autonomy, since this is such an uncommon feature of our social life. How could we expect coal miners or any of us to begin magically to function autonomously? The work experiment had been sold to the union leadership as a way to improve safety practices in the mine. This became the union's public position. Had the union been able to embrace the issue of autonomy, it could have probably been taken more seriously as a training focus. This means that the union itself should be willing to examine its own attachment to authority and hierarchy if it is to contribute to the problem of reorganizing work—not easily achieved in an organization with the tradition of John L. Lewis and Tony Boyle, who are not exactly your participative types.

The Harmon Industries International, Inc., Automotive Division's mirror manufacturing plant in Bolivar, Tennessee, has been the site of another experiment in participation. The leadership of this innovation included the president of Harmon International, a vice president of the United Auto Workers, and a behavioral science consultant. Like all of the experiments I have looked at, this effort did not grow out of any grassroots efforts of the workers themselves. I am doubtful that even after three years of efforts at Bolivar the workers have embraced the experiment as theirs. In the long run, this will be a most serious shortcoming; without broad-based support, there will be little to maintain the experiment's integrity when there is a change of ownership or when the consultant's relationship comes to an end.

The way the program was developed at Bolivar tended to negate grassroots support. The start-up activities included elaborate and intimate questionnaires and tests that in effect said to workers, "Look we think you have problems; maybe we can even give them a psychological label. We want to help you." This sort of initial approach from consultants can only confuse any further efforts toward mutual control. No wonder then that an evaluation report from the Institute of Social Research shows that only 30 percent of the workers interviewed at Bolivar felt that the program was at all participatory.

This situation is further evidenced in one of the more-publicized achievements of the Bolivar project, Earned Idle Time (EIT). Workers here demonstrated their enthusiasm for the opportunity to knock off early when they had filled their daily quotas. The support for EIT lends accuracy to the trade unionist's argument that shorter working hours and increased benefits are the real contributions to the improvement of the quality of working life. On the other hand, earned idle time may be the most attractive alternative to workers who do not feel real inclusion in the change effort. This was the view expressed by the auto workers at Volvo who stopped working when they had assembled their thirty-one trucks.

The Bolivar plant has now been sold to the Beatrice Foods conglomerate. I predict that, like Topeka, the innovations at Bolivar will slowly disintegrate and the plant will go back to its traditional model. This seems to me the inevitable result of the absence of grassroots support. It means that workers involved in such projects need some real commitment to an autonomous workplace if they are to be the ultimate source of ongoing support for such projects. This can be encouraged by the show of genuine good faith and partnership on the part of the company.

The issues of humanizing work and creating participatory structures have not caught on in the United States, though they frequently find support and interest in Europe. In criticizing the Rushton, Bolivar, and Topeka projects, I have tried to treat them as learning opportunities, for that, after all, is what an experiment is about. I do not believe that we should cease experimentation because we have not yet been able to get any broad support for workplace change. On the contrary, experimentation helps us become more aware of the issues, and the pitfalls that should be avoided.

A dialectic of workplace change emerges from this discussion. The polarities that I have discussed are those of power and creativity. Workers who want to move in the direction of participative structures will need to confront the issues of power and control. The process of change needs to be mutually shared by all involved, or the outcome will not be a really participative model. The demand for a structural redistribution of power is not sufficient to address the problem of change toward a humanistic, as against a technological, workplace. If we are to change our institutional arrangements from hierarchy to participation, particularly in our workplaces, we will need to look to transformations in ourselves as well. As long as we are imbued with the legitimacy of hierarchical authority, with the sovereignty of the status quo, we will never be able to generate the new and original participative forms that we seek. This means if we are to be equal to the task of reorganizing our workplaces, we need to think about how we can reeducate ourselves and become aware of our own assumptions about the nature of our social life together. Unless the issue is approached in terms of these complexities, I fear that all the worker participation and quality-of-work-life efforts will fail.

I believe that the journey of my own growth has helped me to perceive at least some of the complexity of these issues. As a labor union organizer, I used to believe that by securing more benefits workers were increasing their power and thus paving the way for a more egalitarian system. I now believe that merely achieving economic security or creating structures that assure a limited amount of worker participation through union representation will not achieve these changes. An egalitarian world through participation means that people must behave together in a new way. Many of the things I fought for as a labor leader have now come to pass, yet we are no closer to nonauthoritarian social life than we were in 1930. Perhaps because of the hierarchical mushrooming of our system, I think at times that we are even further away.

My observations of workplace experiments have convinced me that autonomous and participatory behavior will not result from mere structural manipulation. Yes, we may organize work so as to minimize hierarchy or redistribute decision-making prerogatives, but nothing firm will be achieved unless we somehow help people, and help ourselves, to become aware of our own behavior and how we must change. I have spent the last twenty years of my life searching for workable alternatives to authoritarianism, only to find that ultimately I must fight the authoritarian within myself. Only when in my routine behavior I can embody the ideals I have been fighting for—only then can I understand what is truly involved in reorganizing work on a participative basis.

One last sociological word about the decline of the Protestant work ethic and the rise of schmoozing: Manufacturing and farming jobs are decreasing in the labor market. Service jobs in the private and public sectors are on the increase. Income transfers, such as social security, unemployment insurance, welfare, and food stamps, money people receive for which they do no work, have increased almost geometrically to the point of 200 billion dollars

Experiential Organizational Behavior

a year and steadily rising. All of this is to say that there are increasingly attractive alternatives to hard work and people are learning how to use them. Why work hard if we have a choice? The answer is, we may not, unless somehow work can be made more rewarding.

Issues

1. Identify characteristics of job enrichment described in the Topeka dog food plant, e.g. variety, autonomy.
2. Contrast the views of Marx and Maslow concerning worker alienation. Which view do you identify with most closely?
3. Define and discuss the concepts of participative decision making (PDM) and quality of work life (QWL).
4. How do your views of work, PDM, and QWL differ from those in the article?

41

New Benefits for New Lifestyles

As Americans divorce and remarry with increasing frequency, share homes without marriage, pass up or postpone parenthood, and move out of centuries-old sex roles, companies are beginning to realize that the corporate fringe benefits that employees need are different from those they needed in the past. Many are concluding that they must offer a range of benefit plans to match the changed realities of new lifestyles.

"Benefits traditionally have been designed to fit the needs of a breadwinner-dependent spouse family," says Anna Maria Rappaport, a Chicago vice-president of William M. Mercer Inc., the benefits consulting arm of Marsh & McLennan Cos. "New patterns of benefits are needed to better accommodate the variety of family patterns."

Five important trends have transformed the way of life that traditional benefits were designed to serve:

■ Fewer male employees are now the sole support of their families. Statistically, today's married man is more likely to have a wife in the labor force than to have one whose primary occupation is homemaking.

■ More couples are remaining childless, and those who do become parents have considerably smaller families than did their predecessors. The number of families having a fourth child has been cut in half in a decade.

■ Marriage itself is not the overwhelming norm it once was. At the beginning of the 1970s, 70% of all households were maintained by married couples. Today, with growing numbers of Americans living alone or living together without marriage, the figure is just above 60%. Census Bureau Director Vincent Barabba predicts that the figure will drop to 55% by 1990.

■ Work spans have become more discontinuous, especially among women. Working women are likely to take sabbaticals during their children's younger years.

■ Retirement age is no longer pegged at 65 because of inflation and new

Reprinted from the February 11, 1980 issue of *Business Week* by special permission, © 1980 by McGraw-Hill, Inc., New York, N.Y. 10020. All rights reserved.

236

legislation changing the rules on mandatory retirement. Today it ranges from 60 to 70.

In short, the work force is characterized by a greater variety of family and behavior patterns than before. As a result, a personnel chief planning a benefits package must consider, for instance, an employee's obligations not only to a spouse and at-home children but possibly to a former spouse, children living elsewhere, or a live-in partner who is not a marriage partner.

"We're going to be confronted with real major issues of people's relations one to another," says George B. Swick, chairman of Buck Consultants Inc., a benefits-plan designer in New York City. "I think employers have got to become aware of these things."

Such awareness will lead to more choices for individual employees, predicts Rappaport. Employees who do not need health insurance, perhaps because they are covered by more generous plans offered by their spouses' employers, may get the chance to put the coverage money into another benefit—a thrift plan, additional time off, or even cash, Rappaport speculates. Life insurance coverage, now often two or three times salary, may be cut to no more than a year's salary, reflecting the fact that many workers have no one depending on their earning power. Workers who need more life insurance would be permitted to buy additional coverage through payroll deductions while the company could shift the money it previously spent for extra life insurance into other benefits.

Robert D. Paul, vice-chairman of Martin E. Segal Co., New York City-based actuaries, envisages five different mixes of benefits, each keyed to a different place in the life cycle or a different life-style. They would provide plans suitable for single workers, those married without children, employees with young dependents, parents facing the heavy expenses of college years, and emptynesters interested in accumulating savings for retirement.

Federal Activism

Paul concedes that most companies are not yet ready for such a sweeping change. But he urges them to make their present benefit packages more useful by substituting "defined contribution" plans (which earmark a fixed sum for benefits and then deliver as much of those benefits as the money will buy) for "defined benefit" plans (which specify the benefits to be delivered and then amass the money to pay for them). This will help the women who now make up such a large part of the work force, Paul says. Defined benefit plans are seldom vested before 10 years, which he thinks is too long a waiting period for a woman who may be separating two job periods with an interval for child rearing.

So far, however, the most common corporate response to the new trends has been the rewriting of health insurance policies so that workers covered under both their own and their spouses' plans cannot collect more than 100% of their medical expenses. Theodore P. Picard, an industrial relations official of Safeway Stores Inc., in San Jose, Calif., reports that the savings from such "coordination of benefits" provisions have been high enough in some cases to pay for health and welfare benefits for retirees.

Although family patterns were clearly changing all through the 1970s, many employers are just now considering the need for change, says Rappaport, because the revolution in lifestyles coincided with a period of federal activism on benefit rules. With Washington issuing new rules on pension requirements and then on pregnancy benefits and retirement, few benefit specialists had time to think about "where we're going and what's best for employees," she says. Now member consulting companies have instructed the Employee Benefits Research Institute of Washington to create a computer model showing the effect of demographic changes in the work force 30 or 40 years from now.

Demographic changes will create pressures for new types of benefits long before then, Paul warns. For instance, two-career families—especially those with women in professional jobs—"tend to be more intelligent about wanting to have expenditures tax-sheltered," he says. That means they will want employers to buy services, with before-tax dollars, that formerly came out of the family budget. Paul predicts that company-paid auto and homeowners insurance will head the list if Congress approves them as employee benefits.

Counter to Needs

The more sophisticated employee also realizes that at present many of the benefits he receives "run exactly counter to people's needs," says Jerry S. Rosenbloom, professor of insurance at the University of Pennsylvania's Wharton School. For instance, group life insurance coverage is usually tied to a worker's salary, giving the least coverage to young workers with big mortgages, young children, and spouses of limited earning power, while executives whose major child-rearing and home-buying expenses are behind them get the most dollar protection. Rosenbloom expects more companies to adopt "survivorship" plans, which provide guaranteed income until the youngest surviving child reaches adulthood and then steeply reduce benefits.

The courts will have to resolve such prickly issues as whether pension survivor benefits obligate companies to make payments to longtime partners of unmarried employees. But most of the questions about what kind of benefit plan is best for an increasingly varied work force will be answered by the companies and employees themselves. The ultimate do-it-yourself answer is the so-called cafeteria plan, in which workers receive credits based on their seniority and wage levels and "spend" them on a variety of benefits. But only a handful of companies have such plans, notably American Can Co. and TRW Inc. (BW—Nov. 13, 1978), and experts believe that the administrative problems of running programs with such broad choices will discourage many others from trying them.

1. Describe the general expectations or needs of each of the five groups mentioned
   in the article in terms of what they want from (1) the actual content of their job and
   (2) the benefits available to satisfy off-the-job needs, e.g. health insurance, vacation plans.

	Job Content	**Job Benefits**
Single employees		
Married employees without children		
Employees with dependents		
Employees with college-age dependents		
Empty-nesters		

Compare your responses with your responses to Job Design Preferences (#10).

42

Rules of Thumb

The study of organizational behavior and managerial work has been characterized by the balance of the art of management with the science of human behavior, of descriptive and normative theories and approaches to organizations, individuals, and jobs. While managers and supervisors tend to avoid fancy, classroom theories, and models and the like, there is room for contributions by students of organizational behavior. Management training is based on a combination of history, cliches, experience, science, and speculation.

Given your exposure to the material as well as the philosophy of this book, consider the following assignment:

You have been asked to address a group of managers. Given their needs and your knowledge, you have been asked to provide three rules of thumb—three summary ideas, concepts, or recommendations—that you believe can assist them in doing a better job. They must be short (25 words or less *each*) and to the point, but also consistent with the "science of organizational behavior." Carefully prepare your three "rules" for presentation to the managers.

43

1995: The Year in Review

Beyond the "here and now" aspects of management—supervising employees, scheduling production, dealing with customers—there remains a strong need for vision, creativity, and proaction concerning the future and the environment of business. As one moves up the organizational hierarchy, this time perspective shifts from tomorrow or next week to one, five, ten, or twenty years into the future. Given this perspective, consider the following assignment:

The year is 1995. You are the editor of the business section of an internationally recognized daily newspaper. At year's end, your job is to prepare a list of the five major stories in the business world for the preceeding year. Write the headline and draft (or be prepared to elaborate) the first sentences of each of the five major business stories that you would expect for that year.

Issues

1. What are the implications for business of each of the stories you identified?
2. Research or speculate on predictions made in the *past* concerning how futurists predicted the way life would be *today*. Were the predictions fulfilled? What events were not anticipated?